Be Not Content

A Subterranean Journal

William J. Craddock

Transreal Books
Los Gatos, California
June 26, 2012

This book is for Carole and Peredur.

With special thanks to Teresa Craddock

The first edition appeared in print, Doubleday & Company, Inc., Garden City , New York. The new ebook and print editions appeared in 2012, Transreal Books, Los Gatos, California, by arrangement with Teresa Craddock. Cover photo by Teresa Craddock, cover design by Rudy Rucker.

ISBN: 978-0-9847585-5-5

www.rudyrucker.com/transrealbooks

Contents

Introduction, by Rudy Rucker

Be Not Content is a coming-of-age novel set in San Jose, California, in the mid 1960s—describing William Craddock's experiences as a young acidhead.

This is a deep and well-written book, a unique chronicle of the earliest days of the great psychedelic upheaval. It's filled with warmth and empathy, tragic at times, and very funny in spots—reminding me of William Burroughs's Yage Letters and Phillip K. Dick's A Scanner Darkly, two other wastrel masterpieces where laughter plays counterpoint against the sad oboes of doom.

Billy Craddock was born July 16, 1946, and grew up in Los Gatos, California, the son of William and Camille Craddock. The family was well-off, with William Sr. an executive. As a teenager, Billy said he expected to die at twenty-two, but that he wanted to be a Hells Angel and a published author by the time he was twenty-one.

At nineteen he was in fact a prospect for the Hell's Angels, and he rode his chopper up to Oakland for a party in a bar. A vicious fight broke out, with knives and chains. Billy escaped out the bathroom window and decided not to be in the Angels after all. Instead he joined the equally outlaw Night Riders motorcycle club of San Jose for a few years.

During his biker and acidhead times, Craddock was also an on-and-off student at San Jose State, an English major. Early on, he managed to sell an article about motorcycle gangs to the magazine *Easyriders*—under the pen-name William James. And he wrote some columns for a local paper, the *Los Gatos Times Observer*.

But that was just a warm-up. Billy finished writing his classic psychedelic novel three months after turning twenty-one. *Be Not Content* reads as if written by a mature professional.

It's as if all those trips aged Craddock by dozens of years, and he mentions this possibility:

> So much "lived-time" used up in so little "clock-time" and the world still pretty much the same and us still pretty much the same except for having grown even farther away from the straight-world and its children, having grown hairier on the outside and older-younger on the inside because of the passage of so much lived-time...
>
> "Decrepit, old, tired minds," said [the narrator's friend] Baxtor, "being carried around in twenty-year-old bodies. A ludicrous spectacle. People have been conditioned to expect some sort of body-mind correlation. How will they react to the sight of a drooling, senile twenty-five-year-old being wheeled into the park by attendants? What excuse would you give? You couldn't say, 'Well, there's nothing really *wrong* with him. He's just old.'"
>
> While we waited for senility we made treks back and forth, from San Jose to Sur, to San Francisco, to Berkeley, to L.A. and into Mexico ... back to San Jose where we sometimes went to school or got jobs and then quit or got fired.
>
> We talked for whole nights far into the next day, about experiences and religion, Zen, Tibet and the Tao, prison and our friends in it, philosophy and the stars, insanity and music, new drugs and ancient drugs rediscovered, love and cops, bullshit and its universal appeal, poets and dictators, power and the cosmos, and it was all so real and new.

Be Not Content appeared in a Doubleday Projections edition in 1970. What would Craddock write next?

In a note written for *Gale Contemporary Authors*, he reported, "Doubleday tentatively accepted *Be Not Content* in 1968. While waiting for the anticipated wild joy of actual publication I wrote a second and much longer novel (intended as a sequel and wrap-up of *Be Not Content*) entitled *Backtrack*, which followed the first book's main characters through the disillusioning reentry years immediately after the winter of 1967 and the death of hippie-hope. This grand opus was rejected after due consideration."

In 1972, Doubleday instead published Craddock's downbeat *Twilight Candelabra*, a novel involving Satanism and a murder. Craddock may have been trying to write a novel more in tune with what his editors imagined the commercial market to be. His next novel was *The Fall of Because,* "a satire overlaying a serious allegorical treatment of 'modern magick.'" This one was rejected by Doubleday.

Craddock finished the first draft of *Be Not Content* in September, 1967, and two months later he married Carole Anne Bronzich for a year and a half. In 1975 he married for the second time, to Teresa Lynne Thorne, a native of San Jose. Thorne's father was a lawyer who'd represented George Jackson, the Soledad brothers, and the Hell's Angels. Her parents took Billy's hippie/biker looks in stride.

Billy had dated Teresa for awhile, checking out if she'd be someone he could live with. Teresa tells a story of Billy accompanying her to shopping mall. "He told me he wanted to wait in the parking lot," says Teresa. "So I left him there in the car with a glass of water and the window open—and when I got back from my shopping, he told me he was on acid. You could never tell when Billy was high. He didn't show it."

Craddock found a novel way to get engaged. He gave Teresa a copy of *Be Not Content*, and when she asked for an autograph, he wrote his marriage proposal on the fly-leaf.

In 1975 the newlyweds spent some time as the caretakers of an empty mansion above Los Gatos. Billy wrote a somewhat autobiographical California novel, *The Fading Grass*. For whatever reason it too was deemed unpublishable. Finally, in 1976, aged thirty, Billy wrote one more novel, *A Passage of Shadows*, and that one also failed to sell.

At this point he abandoned his career as a novelist. He drifted away from psychedelics. He made a little money writing for the Santa Cruz *Good Times*, a column a week.

"It's not the publishing that matters," Billy would gamely tell Teresa. "It's the writing."

I got my first copy of *Be Not Content* in 1972, shortly after taking a job as an assistant professor of mathematics at a small college in upstate New York. I think I may have found the novel in a hip bookshop at Dupont Circle, Washington, DC. I quickly began to idolize Craddock. I had my own memories of the psychedelic revolution, and when reading *Be Not Content* I felt—"*Yes*. This is the way it was. This guy got it right."

I wrote Craddock a fan letter, enclosing what was at that time my sole publication, a technical math paper on higher infinities. As if. Billy wrote a friendly note back, saying that he'd only passed his high-school geometry class by cheating wildly off the girl in front of him, but that he was happy to know someone was reading him "over on the other side of the island."

The years went by. In 1986, my wife, three kids and I moved to Los Gatos, California. I had a job as a professor of math and computer science at San Jose State. Soon after arriving I saw one of Craddock's columns in the *Good Times* free weekly paper.

I learned that Craddock had grown up in my new town, had attended the same high school where my children were going, that he'd gone to the very same San Jose State college were I now worked, and that we'd been born within a few months of each other. My mystic double! I thought of seeking him out, but I wasn't sure how to start—and I had the feeling that, as writers, we'd inevitably meet without having to plan it.

More years went by. I'd lent out my original copy of *Be Not Content* without getting it back, and in 2003 I decided I couldn't live without it any longer. I bought a used copy online for the exorbitant price of $140.

The fee hurt, but it was pure joy to reread this rewarding volume. I recognized numerous teachings that by now I'd totally integrated into my worldview, and multiple headtricks that I'd used in the transreal science-fiction novels I myself had published.

And still I had some hope of meeting Billy Craddock. But then it was too late. Here's a note I made in my journals on September 25, 2005.

A fan who'd bought Craddock's old motorcycle emailed that Billy had died over a year ago, on March 16, 2004. Today I went to the all-new San Jose State library to look up his obit. It's on microfilm, from the *San Jose Mercury News*. It's eerie searching out the microfilm, in a graphically uncluttered basement room that vaguely resembles a mausoleum — I feel like a reporter in *Citizen Kane*.

I pull open a huge flat metal drawer with ranks and ranks of microfilm boxes, my hand reaches in, plucks out the box with Billy's obit. I go to the microfilm reader, the same big clunky kind of machine as ever, and grind forward past March 16, 2004. I'm looking for a big article, but it's just a little tiny thing on March 20, with a picture of Billy looking tired and sad, his eyes hidden in dark sockets, the obit written by, I think, his widow Teresa. How little recognition my hero received.

And how bum, how alien, how weird it would have been for Billy to see this microfilm room in a flash-forward vision while walking careless and high around this San Jose campus forty years ago—what if he'd suddenly seen, whoah, a hand pulling out this very box of microfilm with its image of his weary, suffering future-shocked face.

I leave the library, and the bell on SJSU's Tower Hall is ringing to mark an hour, tolling deep and reverberant, the sounds overlapping and forming beats.

We really die, nobody escapes, all of us on the one big trip.

The fan who'd bought Billy's bike gave me Teresa Craddock's phone number, and I talked to her about me trying to find a publisher for *Be Not Content*. She encouraged me to try. Nothing came of it—the publishers I talked to weren't interested in Sixties acid books, they seemed to think the story had already been told. I lost track of Teresa, posted some thoughts about Craddock and *Be Not Content* on my blog, and early in 2012, a reader of my blog put me in touch with Teresa again.

By this point, I'd started up my own small publishing venture, Transreal Books. I went ahead and made an agreement with Teresa Craddock that I'd republish *Be Not Content* myself. I feel it's a very important book that needs to be remembered. Nobody ever wrote about the psychedelic revolution as well as William Craddock.

A key point that he makes is that taking psychedelic trips was never, or at least not for very long, *fun*, in the usual sense of the word. There were three problematic areas: freak-outs, seeing God, and coming down.

In the harrowing final chapters of *Be Not Content*, our hero Abel Egregore becomes obsessed with the seeing-God and the coming-down issues. He goes further and further on his peak trip experiences, and he does in fact talk to God, but it's not enough. Coming down becomes insufferable, and he begins going on nightmarish trips that last for days and days.

Acid, Abel imagines, has changed the rules to the extent that he should be able to obtain complete enlightenment and a fundamental understanding of the nature of reality. But he's not getting there. In a turning-point scene, Abel's sage friend Baxter describes his own end of the road.

> We're going to grow old and die. That's all. That's all there is. The enlightenment-game is just that . . . another game. It's a variation manufactured to occupy the minds of those mortals foolish enough to overindulge in mental exercises directed toward seeing through the illusion. Beyond the illusion there's nothing. Now, I know that you maintain that the nothing behind the illusion is the 'Void' and a perfect state of wise Buddha-being; but Abel, that's only a more sophisticated variation on the old bullshit heaven concept. You've simply eliminated all the things that you can't accept, can't believe in—the harps and streets of gold and winged angels and benevolent old daddy God and all the rest—after which you had nothing, which is uncomfortable, so you ripped off some validation from the Tibetans and called

> your nothing 'The Perfect, Empty Void.' But it's nothing, Abel. When you get right down to it, it's nothing.

Yet our hero isn't willing to view the Void or the One or the Absolute as an *empty* nothing. The ultimate nothing is, if you will, filled with light and with a hum. Craddock puts it thus:

> It's the sound of the miraculous space between eternity—between paradise. You only have to *listen* to hear it. And beyond the music of the earth is the music of deep within you. It's the magic you once *knew* existed. It *does* exist. Everything is perfect—OM—endlessly—OM—infinity is ours—peace, my friends. I love you. I am you. We are simply IT. There's nothing else to know.

And, knowing this, ordinary life is enough. A classic mystic illumination. And all of this was written by a man of twenty-one. Incredible.

Nobody I've talked to seems able to locate *Backtrack*—Craddock's sequel to *Be Not Content*. One hypothesis is that the single typed manuscript was lost in a fire that destroyed the house where Craddock was living with his first wife Carole around 1969. Or conceivably someone in Billy's circle still has possession of the manuscript. Or, who knows, Mindless Eddie ate it, just like in the final chapter of *Be Not Content.*

In any case three other unpublished novels by Craddock survive—*The Fall of Because*, *The Fading Grass*, and *A Passage of Shadows*. These are still in the hands of his widow Teresa—I've seen one of them—and they may yet appear in print someday, if not from Transreal Books, then from some other publisher.

My guess is that *Be Not Content* will remain Craddock's lucky strike, the outstanding early success that overshadows the rest of a writer's career. My friendNick Herbert of Boulder Creek, an aging hippie writer himself, puts it like this:

> *Be Not Content* is a little-appreciated masterpiece. Craddock

> truly captures the idealistic intensity of those days when we all felt that enlightenment, wisdom, telepathy, alien contact and/or Childhood's End was so close you could almost smell it. Where anything seemed possible and every encounter felt like it could be the door to another world. Where did all that wildness go?

Ah, Nick, the wildness is still here, if only we look.

Let's close with my favorite teaching from the good book of *Be Not Content*:

> "But don't you feel like you're wasting *time*?"
> "How can you waste *time*? Man, that's ridiculous."

Relax and enjoy this wonderful work. Read it slowly. You have time. Oh—and don't worry, the book really does start with Chapter Thirty Two.

Rudy Rucker
Los Gatos, California
May 11, 2012

Author's Pitch

BE NOT CONTENT
EXCERPTS FROM THE LIFE OF ABEL EGREGORE
by William J. Craddock

Being a skeletal history and chronicle of the experiences of a single, minor freak connected to a single, minor tribe of acid freaks in California, beginning in the early days of the Psychedelic Revolution, including a brief sampling of an insignificant number of individuals involved, their ideas and their ideals, and a flickering glimpse of but a scant few of the problems, obstacles, superstitions, fears, misunderstandings, joys, insights, loves and frustrations that they faced, manufactured and struggled with in their once pure quest for the elusive path to even more elusive enlightenment in a set constructed exclusively of intricate but obvious illusions of which they occasionally (with infinite sadness, regretting the revelation) realized that they were undeniably a micro-part.

"Be not content with this system of things . . ."

—Jesus Christ

"And in all the bitterness which by Thy mercy followed our worldly affairs, as we looked towards the end, why we should suffer all this, darkness met us; and we turned away groaning and saying, *How long shall these things be?* This too we often said; and so saying forsook them not, for as yet there dawned nothing certain, which, these forsaken, we might embrace."

—*St. Augustine*

"Escape from this! Bestir yourself! Move into the wider realm."

—*Dr. Faust*

"Turn on, tune in, drop out."

—*Dr. Leary*

CHAPTER THIRTY TWO – contains a pattern

Abel pulled himself up out of sleep into the stifling heat of his dark apartment. *Down,* said his mind, and Abel repeated, "Down." Trucks, busses, cars and planes racketed outside, while babies howled and mothers shouted, banging cans and faucets in the apartments below and to the left. The apartment on the right was empty. Abel kicked the sweat-wet sheet off his body and placed his ear against the wall, listening to the buzzing quiet. It was hot. Not just hot, but summer-city-hot. Sticky, motionless, heavy air hung like oil smoke. Abel pushed through it and stood up.

In the closet-kitchen, a fly, who had breakfasted on toothpaste and urine, lit on the stale remains of a powdered-sugar doughnut and signaled for a circling companion to join him. With micro-vibration conversation concerning the merits of sugar over urine, the flies ate, watching the multi-image shadow move in the other room.

Abel threw open the faded burlap curtain and let the hot cement and asphalt sun hit him full in the face. A crimson headache ripped across his temples and he took a full breath . . . holding it . . . trying to get behind the pain-throb . . . trying to dig it. When he felt faint he exhaled and let the curtain fall into place. His eyes adjusted quickly to the familiar murk. The brown plastic timepiece, stamped "made in USA," said a quarter after twelve.

The flies' cut-emerald vision filled with scattered prism-images as Abel entered the kitchen. Fly-chanted danger vibrations bounced back and forth, but the heavy scream of the city drowned out the tiny signals, as Abel filled a convenient and only slightly dirty glass from the sink without even noticing the feeding flies. A cigarette had burned another hole in the small Goodwill table and Abel swept the ashes onto the floor. The flies, ever wary of a brutal, unjustified attack, hummed a shrill "Beware" and shot into space, executing evasive maneuvers. Abel stood very still, watching their flight. He counted slowly to himself. At seventy-two, the bravest of the flies relit on the doughnut and cautiously began to feed once more.

Abel moved quickly and set the empty glass over the fly. Too late, the fly zuzzed to escape, banging again and again into the transparent walls of its prison. Abel kneeled on the floor to watch. Sweat ran from his armpits, down over his ribs, across his naked hips and onto the linoleum.

Inside the inverted glass, the fly made a quick inspection tour of the world it was now limited to. A last angry rush at the invisible barrier, then it crawled to the doughnut and continued to feed. Abel watched and sweated, sweated and watched. The captured fly's companion lit on Abel's back to drink sweat, nuzzing a favorable comparison between sweat and sugar, sugar and urine, toothpaste and bullshit. On a whim, it decided to taste blood. Abel slapped at the fly and rose to his feet.

In the other room, the clock said a quarter past twelve, and Abel momentarily feared a time warp. Then he realized that the clock had stopped . . . possibly days ago. He spun the little radioactive hands until they pointed to high noon, rewound the clock and replaced it on the shelf beneath the quotation by Meher Baba. He searched absently for underwear, found none and pulled on a pair of pants without them. He searched carefully for a cigarette, found none, and rolled a joint instead.

Across town in a gray room on the second story of an old, soon to be condemned house, Curt opened his eyes to greet the nearly spent day with a simple but eloquent, "Fuck." The sun was in such a position that it shone directly into his red-rimmed eyes. Curt considered rising, thought better of it, and turned over to fall back into the realm of Somnus. He defeated the sun by the simple act of closing his eyes.

Directly across the hall, Carla hummed softly to herself as she finished stitching a forest green shift. The unmistakable odor of hashish drifted up from the living room where Ted, Christy and David were passing a pipe, waiting for a pot of brown rice to heat.

Outside, colorless citizens hurried past on their way home from various places of employment, unaware that they were under close scrutiny from the old house's tower, where Mindless Eddie followed their every move with comfortably fogged and lost eyes, reciting rhyming words to himself when they applied and humming perfect oms when nothing or everything applied.

The tower door opened to admit Christy, softened by hash and smiling at her one-time lover. "Hi, Eddie. Want some rice? Rice is nice."

Eddie ommed softly, smiled, suddenly frightened himself and fell instantly into a peaceful om once more.

Christy set the rice down and glanced out the tower window. It was nearly six, but the summer sun still clung to mid-day heat. Christy sat on Eddie's unmade bed—the bed she'd loved Eddie in for over a year before he finally broke his mind. In those days, Eddie was wild and strange and funny and . . . and then one night, with everyone high on acid, the stereo going full blast downstairs, Eddie and Christy in bed upstairs exploring cosmic love, Carla and Abel across the hall laughing at the patterned ceiling. . . TENSION . . . tension that suddenly everyone in the house felt. Silence . . . a last nervous laugh, the thought, "What's happening? What's bumming out?" hanging in the atmosphere. Carla had asked, "What's wrong?" in a fearful whisper, afraid that voicing the anxiety would somehow shove it into existence. The words echoed and rang and draped themselves over chairs and spelled themselves out in poster-lettering on the walls and ran on the floor and hissed in the impossible wind and suddenly everything was WRONG and Eddie leaped to his feet, ran into a wall, stumbled into the kitchen and swallowed five caps of very good acid and a leering tab of STP.

Nobody knew what to do about it, so they simply kept nervous eyes on him and wished the voyager well. They watched while Eddie began to breathe hard and then harder. Power crackled and blasted all around him. It wasn't a screamer. It was a quiet wilt. After about an hour and a half, Eddie rolled to his left side, twitched, gurgled, and wild-strange-funny-Eddie split for elsewhere, leaving Mindless Eddie to hold down the robot in his absence. That was five months ago. Now Christy no longer really tried to get through to Eddie.

She watched him eat his rice, and remembered last year's love. The love that was going to last forever. The love that lasted thirteen months. A long time. Now Christy slept with Ted and, she reflected, Ted was just as good, just as satisfying, just as easy to love. As a matter of fact, everyone she'd tried so far had been easy and good to love. Except, of course, for Dorsey, but then . . . he had a problem. That "one true love forever and ever" thing must be bullshit. Unless it's yet to come, in which case . . . but it's probably bullshit. So much bullshit. How do you pick out the reallies?

"A world full of bullshit," sighed Christy as she rose from Eddie's bed. "How can there be so much bullshit, Eddie?"

"Ommmm," said Eddie, and three grains of rice slid down his chin. The door clicked shut and Eddie was alone.

Downstairs, the pipe was relit and making the rounds. "How's Eddie?" asked Ted.

"Farout," replied Christy, taking a hit of hash. "He's far out."

The sun was going out for the night and things were getting pleasantly muted as Abel crawled out of the bathtub and lit another joint. Feeling pretty good, mind wandering comfortably, he climbed back into his clothes and drank a glass of chocolate milk, leaning on the sink, watching the night take over. He ran a hand through his blond beard and picked his nose. Lights were going on all over the neighborhood, and now it was cool enough to breathe a little.

Mumble-clunk-phizz-think, went Abel's head. He listened to it intently for awhile, then remembered that the refrigerator door was open and then remembered that he was getting dressed to go out and was looking for his boots and he went to find his boots and after two steps re-remembered the refrigerator door and went to shut it and suddenly remembered the fly.

Abel looked at the fly and the fly, sitting on but no longer eating the stale doughnut, looked at Abel. Abel put his nose on the glass so that his eyes were less than an inch from the fly. It was combing its hair. Abel carefully slipped the burning roach of his most recent joint under the glass with the well-groomed bug. The fly vibrated "FIRE" and spun around the glass like a wall-of-death-barrel motorcyclist.

The smoke hit him and he fell on his back, dangerously close to the smoldering roach. Abel removed the glass and picked up the fly by one of its cellophane wings. It kicked its legs feebly. "Stoned," said Abel. He placed the loaded fly on the palm of his left hand, watching closely as the fly revived slightly and began to comb its hair again.

"Soul brother," said Abel, adding, "Everyone's gotta be friends," and wondering why it was so hard to be friends with everyone when it was so obviously the way things should be.

Hmmmmmm-yes-think-mmmmmmm, said Abel's head, and he'd been listening to it for some time when he remembered that he was going out and hadn't found his boots yet. He refocused on the palm of his hand and saw that the fly had disappeared. Vanished in a flash of fly magic. Gone where, fly? Aha! It now clung to the wall, where it was foolishly trying to eat a paint spot. Abel rolled up a comic book and squashed the fly with *Doctor Strange*. Boots on the chair next to the electric fan, and undeniably nighttime when they were found. A pile of typing paper lay on the writing desk. Abel grabbed the pile and stuck it under his arm as he made for the door.

Stars stars stars, his eyes told him as he walked shuffle-weave across the fifteen streets that separated him from his friends. The sun was down and the day had started.

Fifteen, now fourteen, now thirteen streets away, Curt was up, awake and arguing with Ted. "Love . . . sure, love. I've said it and heard it said and so've you and so's everybody who's been with the scene, but for shitsake what good's it doing us? I mean, you love a cop and he busts your ass anyhow. You love the citizens and they kick you out of their parks, cities and forests just the same. All right . . . I love everybody . . . but it's about time something got *done*! We can't just sit around and *love*. The fuckin middle-class majority is gonna wipe us out! Things are bad, man! And they aren't getting *better* . . . they're getting *worse*. They're getting worse!"

Ted waved his hands in small circles in front of his chest. "It takes time, man. It all takes time. If you lose sight of the love thing, then you're the same as them. You're just another minority fighting for the right to live in fat-city. Fighting, man. No more fighting."

"Aw, bullshit."

"Of course . . . bullshit . . . heavy games and bullshit. But it's what *this* life is all about. We have to make the best of it while we're here. If you want out of the bullshit and out of game existence, go talk to Eddie. He's out of it . . . really out of it. He found the way. You could find it too, if you really want out." Christy floated past like a phantom, depositing a joint in Curt's hand, placing a kiss on Ted's mouth. "Mmmmmhmmmmm," she hummed in total agreement with everything everything everything, and then floated out of the room, into the kitchen, where she began to wash the cooking pot.

Curt filled his lungs with smoke and handed the joint to Ted. Without exhaling, in the familiar weed-smoker's voice, he said, "Bull shit." Two words . . . and then he went upstairs to listen to the radio.

"Babble babble has accused the United States of aggression in the babble babble sparg although the spokesman for the bargle babble denies all quensler franles and stated that babble fargle while chief babble announced today to the ravnet of babble graggle narcotics consumption has risen to prelets wenren in a serious babble babble and steps must be herlendaz for any bargle babble yew ess forces in babble and gabble gaggle captured the morlog gangy minor casualties were reported while the enemy's losses were estimated as massive by genless maxor war has broken out once again on the peninsula of garble the spokesman for the united garble babble said this morning at a conference in rengen that such open defiance of the treaty of wancon could and would not go unpunished bargle numkren stood firm in his orifax that the troops now rushing to the molly semp border had god on their side in this matter of utmost importance to the free people of the oberhav shutmore belaral rioting broke out for the third consecutive day in the babble trenton of salber police armed with tear gas and dogs rushed to the babble babble babble garble . . . and friends," said the radio, "are pimples putting the skids on *your* romance?"

"It can't be. It can't be actually happening. It can not be!" said Curt, taking a tiny purple tablet from a bottle on his dresser and putting it under his tongue.

Only two streets away now, Abel smiled at a squad car as it crept past, and instantly regretted it when the black-and-white hell-mobile spun around in the middle of the street and pulled alongside him. Without being told, Abel walked over to the car and stuck his head in the window. "Hi," he said.

The cop looked him in the eye and said nothing. Abel withdrew his head and started to walk away. "Hold it," said the cop, as he stepped out of the car, adjusting his gunbelt and placing his helmet at a jaunty angle on his cop head. "You just hold it right there pal."

"Hey, Curt," Christy shouted up the stairs, "You wanna go to the beach tonight with me an Ted?"

"No," said Curt, "I just took some acid and I wanna see where it takes me."

"You want us to stay around for a while?"

"No. It's okay. I'll prob'ly be here when you get back." Downstairs, a door slammed. Seconds passed, then Ted's Volkswagen bus started and drove off. In the room across the hall, Carla was listening to Dylan while she sewed the hem on her shift. An occasional om could be heard from Eddie's tower.

The cop had frisked Abel, had found nothing, had eye-balled the stack of papers, and had racked his rudimentary brain for something to arrest this obvious felon for, all to no avail. The cop wrote in his notebook, radioed the station to let them know that he hadn't been beaten or robbed or raped or otherwise molested, removed his helmet, got back into his shoulder harness, shifted gears and roared off. Abel walked the remaining two streets and knocked on Curt-Christy-Carla-Ted-Eddie's door.

"Someone at the door," said Carla. Then louder, "Hey! Someone's at the door!"

"Bullshit," said Curt. He'd already decided on a bum trip and was bracing himself for the onslaught. It wouldn't be long now, and he didn't want to be bothered.

Carla stomped to the front door and opened it to admit Abel.

"Hi, Carla, is Curt around?"

"Upstairs and in a shitty mood."

Abel climbed the stairs and stepped into Curt's room.

"What're you up to, Curt?"

"Bullshit."

"You and everyone else, man," said Abel, throwing himself into a cluttered chair. "I brought you something to read."

"Bullshit."

"Well . . . yeah, but remember last month you asked what I had to show for the past four years?"

"Nope."

"Yeah, well you did. And it started me thinking. I mean, when people ask you what you've been up to, you always say, 'nothing' or, 'not much' or something like that, you know? And it's usually pretty true, but that's a hell of a thing to admit, cuz even if it's true you have to pretend it isn't or else you have to fess up to the fact that the show's over and all the rest is just cleaning up popcorn and gum wrappers. Excuse this rap, man. I'm into this tail-end crink come-down and I got the mouth runs. But anyhow, I mean, what would you say if someone asked you what you had to show for the past four years?"

"Bullshit."

"Uh-huh, but see, if they didn't happen to be into the scene themselves all along, then they might not really be hip to that. I mean, they might not pick up on all the running around and finding it and then losing it and running around some more and all the other action and reaction that's behind your final answer, you know?"

Curt rolled over, faced the wall and showed Abel his back. "Bullshit."

Abel considered this, and then said, "Have you noticed that you hear that expression more and more these days? Not that it doesn't sum things up pretty well, but I wonder if the language isn't in danger of degenerating to the point where it'll consist of one word?"

"Bullshit," said Curt.

"Exactly," said Abel and lit a cigarette. "Anyhow," he continued, "I started thinking, and after doing that for awhile, I got this," Abel held up the manuscript, "and pulled it all together and finished it. It ends six months ago—otherwise it'd never end."

Curt said nothing.

Abel nodded and went on. "I've been up for like days, man, pounding the typewriter, putting down all the things that came to mind about the last couple of years. I stuck in all the little things I wrote during the time that I wasn't writing anything. Tales of Punon, man. I finished it . . . anyway, I'm finished with it. I thought you might like to read it. You're in it . . . a little. I didn't know you too well back then."

Curt rolled to his back, squeezed his eyes shut tight and sighed. "Look, man," he said, "I just took some acid and I don't wanna read anything."

"Oh . . . wow . . . sorry, man. I didn't know."

Curt waved his hand to say it was all right and also to signify that the conversation was over.

Abel got up and moved to Curt's dresser. "I'll leave it here anyway, in case you change your mind or like . . ."

"Yeah, yeah."

Abel turned to go. "Have a good trip."

"Yeah, yeah. See you tomorrow."

Carla was eating an orange downstairs. The orange was grown in Florida. It was picked while still green, shipped to an orange doctor who injected artificial orange-color under its lumpy skin, and then stamped it with a symbol that said it was a smiling orange. The orange had nothing to do with anything in particular; Carla just happened to be eating it when Abel reached the bottom of the stairs. Abel looked right past the orange from Florida and said, "You wanna go over to my place?"

"You think Curt'll be okay?" asked Carla from behind the green, but orange-colored orange.

Abel yelled up the stairs, "Hey, Curt! Is it okay if me an Carla go over to my place?"

Curt slammed his door.

"It's okay," said Abel. "Say . . . how's Eddie?"

Carla spit an orange seed. "Far out," and they left the house. Curt was trembling slightly, his eyes closed, his teeth set. The acid was coming on slow and making him nervous—tight. He got up from the bed and listened at his door. The house was silent. He opened the door and stepped into the hallway, where the walls were flashing faintly and seemed to glow with a pale blue light. Curt opened

Eddie's door and peered in. Eddie's eyes locked with a click on Curt's and, for a micro-second eternity, Curt contacted the spinning insanity. He jerked his eyes away quickly. "What're you doing, Eddie?"

Eddie pointed to a crayon that he'd been eating.

Curt nodded and back-stepped out of the room, shutting the door behind him. The door went click, and Eddie imitated the sound perfectly, then said, "Om."

Curt was high—ragged high. Not the very high of beyond words, but the high of too many. He lit another cigarette and went back to his room. Slow. Purposely slow. Walking the getting thin line. Abel's manuscript lay on the dresser and it alone was out of place in the familiar room. A scene shift. A repeat. Back to walking the getting thin line. And Abel's manuscript lay on the dresser. It alone was out of place in the familiar room. This could be repeated again . . . and again . . . indefinitely, or it could be completely ignored. Completely is hard to do, but completely ignored is the best of all available short-term, stop-gap easy outs. "Bullshit," said Curt, and picked the manuscript up. The typewritten words danced like gassed insects across the dead, white pages. Curt thumbed through the pile, took it to his bed, sat down and, without thinking, began to read . . .

CHAPTER ONE – THE DESERT OF PARAN

I didn't feel much like riding all the way back from Oakland to San Jose on wet streets just to beat on some punk and maybe get myself shot at or busted. But Indian was not only a brother, he was my president, and I was wearing the one-percenter patch, which meant I was tight-bound to the rules, and a Night Rider bike had been burned by a citizen, and Indian'd said go, so I stomped out of the party, following The Prez, Philco, Bob and Quack Jack, started my hog and swung onto the freeway, hauling ass to keep up.

Cold, hard rain in San Jose. The water thrown by my front tire was hitting me square between the eyes as we wheeled off the freeway into East Jose, pulled onto a back street and shut our machines down.

"Third house up," said Indian. His long brown hair and beard all wet and wind-snarled—dark eyes tight and bright for action. Indian Maker—twenty-four-years old, absolute commander of the thirteen brothers who made up the San Jose Chapter of the Night Riders MC. "Awright. Bob an me'll go up to the front door. Quack an Abel round back while Philo getsiz bike outta the garage. When the punk comes to the door, you guys kick the back one in. Got it?"

"Got it, man."

"Do it."

An old, beat-out sort of greenish house with a backyard full of garbage. Quack and I went around and waited until we heard Indian knock and the door open. Then Quack kicked the back door twice, it broke, and we ran into a kitchen with an open door that showed us the living room, where Indian and Bob were booting a fat guy in the stomach, while he swore at them and yelled and cried.

A Mexican ran out of the bedroom with a baseball bat—fast—like a speeded up movie. He swung the bat and hit Bob on the arm, Quack kicked the Mexican in the balls, the Mexican hollered and threw the bat, which crashed into a TV set, and I kicked him in the back of the head as he went down. Done. The fat guy and the Mexican lay there like dead meat—defeated. Our triumph. Me and my brothers.

Indian broke a chair against a wall, and the others messed the place up, while I went out to see if Philco had the bike.

"You got it, Phil?" I yelled from the driveway.

He shouted back, "Yeah, an I stomped a Beezer he had! An I do mean *had*!"

I ran back into the house. Everything was wiped out. Quack and Bob were pissing on the two ruined bike thieves. Adrenalin buzzing all through me. Tight jaws and blood-fat head. It was good. I felt tall and strong and wild and unbeatable and good good *good.* Before all gods and God, I repent it these some years later, (and was actually to repent it very soon) but the feeling was *good.*

"He's got the bike. Let's go!" I said.

Indian threw a lamp against the wall. "Let's go!" and our boots clattered down cement steps, into the yard.

We heard Philco's bike start as we ran down the wet street. It was raining for real now. A woman peered out of a door at us, and Bob yelled, "Get back in the fuckin house!" The woman disappeared with a door slam.

Rain in Quack's open carburetor and he couldn't get the machine started. Philco pulled up beside us and said, "Hurry up, man!" Quack kicked, but the engine wouldn't even cough.

"Leave it, man!" said Philco, "It's a wreck anyhow! There's no registration on it. Hop on behind an I'll pack you. We'll bag you another bike."

Quack booted the old hog to its side and jumped on behind Philco. We blasted down the street, swerving onto sidewalks and through yards, missing the squad car that skidded around the corner with its siren wailing for order.

Indian and I cut down an alley and shot across town, while Philco, Quack and Bob split in the other direction. I followed Indian's taillight through a vacant lot and into a garage in back of Laura's house, (Laura being a good little pill-head who Indian lived with from time to time) closed the garage door and went inside to wait for word from the others. We drank coffee and told Laura all about the last few hours, exaggerating only the slightest bit, digging the suspense of peeking out windows for the never-to-come cops. Bob rolled in about 10:30, and said that he'd lost the cop, as well as Philco and Quack, by jack-rabbiting down side roads. We waited for Philco's machine to pull in.

Early morning. Bob and Laura asleep. "You think they got em, Indian?"

"Philco can't be got, man."

The afternoon paper told us that Philco, packing the extra weight of Quack Jack, had foolishly made for the freeway where the high-speed cop cars had the advantage. He tried to pull off on a clover-leaf, and lost it on the rain-slick pavement. Quack died and Philco broke his hip and went to jail.

That weekend, we went to an all-club party in Oakland and raised money to buy Quack a funeral. Everybody gave at least a buck and said it was too bad about ole Quack, but he died an outlaw's death, the best any of us could ask for, and it showed a lot of class. It surely did show a lot of class.

Quack Jack, who claimed to have been "a fuckin good Pharmacist's Mate" while he was in the Navy, and, on that recommendation, became the club's doctor and actually set and splinted a broken arm that Indian'd got from falling off a roof roaring drunk at a great party in Redwood City. Quack Jack, with his Fu Manchu mustache and little paintbrush goatee, and snakes and knives and hearts and nudes and names tattooed all over his arms, dead at twenty-three. But he went out in style—class on all sides, right up to the finish.

Quack's funeral never came off because a stepfather showed up and carted the body off to Oregon for burial. The Night Riders held a special meeting and we decided to spend the funeral money on wine for an all-club in honor of dead Quack. The party was held in Oakland and everybody got fucked out of their heads and had a fine time, except for Oily Al who rode his bike into an empty swimming pool, broke his shoulder and his wrist, and had to sell his only slightly twisted machine to pay doctor bills.

CHAPTER TWO – ALLEN AND KADDISH

On our backs in sleeping bags, a half dead bottle of wine, many snubbed out cig butts and four roaches in the leaves between us, our bikes dripping oil with their engines cooling beside us, Indian and I watching the stars through swaying black-silhouette trees. Two weeks into September and winter on its way.

A tight feeling in my stomach, a tight feeling in my head. Tight body—tight mind. Not just the wine and the weed. Something more. But no words for it. Afraid to search for the words. Say instead, "Quack Jack's dead. Just like that, man. Ole Quack's dead."

"Deader'n dead," agrees Indian, eyes closed and hands behind his head.

"He was a *brother.*"

"I'm hip, man. He still is. Now he's a *dead* brother."

The weed's got me mellow, the wine's got me tight, the wine's got me muddled, the weed's got me thoughty. It's just thinking aloud when I say, "I wonder what the movie was like for ole Quack. Seems like he sure as hell had a small part in the big picture. I mean, it was the whole movie for him, but it wasn't nuthin really."

Indian with his eyes still closed, "What?"

"Nuthin. Just thinkin."

"Hah," tossing a pinecone at my head. "That's what college is doin to ya."

And the blues set in for real. "Indian, why'd you have to remind me of college? I gotta go back in a week an I been tryin to forget. I don't wanna do that scene anymore." Balancing himself on an elbow, looking me dead in the eye, "Yeah you do. A *college* man." Big smile. "That's just what the ole club needs. Just stay on top of it, man. Don't let em get to your head where it counts. Maybe you can take up law.

We could use a lawyer."

Strange to hear Indian pulling for college. It made me wonder if maybe there was actually a good, solid, meaningful, eventual point to it. But, "I don't wanna be a *lawyer,* man. You go to college. I'm not goin back."

The Night Riders MC and college. Roles and scenes I'd been juggling for nearly two years. It's hard to say how it happened—how, at eighteen, I became an outlaw motorcyclist majoring in English at San Jose State College. Since it's not even completely clear to me, I'm gonna have one hell of a time making it sound reasonable to anyone else. But I've been told that it needs an explanation, so I'll do my best to explain . . . or at least record the variables that lined themselves up to get me there.

In junior high school I was already reading every book that looked interesting to me—even books that didn't look particularly interesting but were impressively bound or extra dusty. Edgar Rice Burroughs, Marcus Aurelius, Thome Smith, Jack Kerouac, Ray Bradbury, Mary Baker Eddy, Epictetus, Sax Rohmer, Montaigne, Douglas Hunt—a random selection—anything that happened to be laying around the house or the local bookstore. The other kids on the block went out for baseball or football or whatever was in season. I read books. I didn't always understand them, was even willing to *admit* that I didn't always understand them, but I read them. The words were there, kicking around inside my head. All those conflicting ideas and projections. One author's definitive answer canceled by the very next author's definitive answer which was canceled in turn by the next's. I used to sit on my bed in my comfortably dark room with summer going on behind the blue drapes, my mother throwing open the door periodically to demand, "Why aren't you outside *doing something?*" while I pondered word-concepts and wondered if there really was a Jesus Christ, a Judas Iscariot, a Gautama Buddha, a Shiva, a Yellow Peril, a President of the United States.

At thirteen, I wrote morbid poetry from the depths of my soul, and it sounded exactly like morbid poetry written from the relatively shallow depths of a thirteen-year-old's soul.

I read more books.

"You're too young," my mother insisted, forcing me outdoors to run around in the sun. "You're trying to think too deeply. All that reading will ruin your eyes and all that thinking will warp your mind."

She was probably right.

Sax Rohmer, Aldous Huxley, and a kid from San Francisco named Joey Grant were responsible for my smoking marijuana at age fourteen. It didn't do much for me. A cruel blow. I almost felt cheated. I *did* feel that I'd been lied to, and that the lawmakers and law-enforcers of the land were off their collective asses in forbidding, upon pain of imprisonment, the use of such an innocent little weed. Especially when they endorsed the consumption of alcohol. A single beer, which I'd downed earlier that same summer, had made me dizzy, fogged and finally sicker than a sick dog. Two joints of marijuana, on the other hand, made me sleepy. High was to come later.

Fourteen years old, quiet, neat, a good student from a good home, never-been-in-trouble, and, I often reminded myself with a sly grin to cover the sometimes-creepy twinge, an undetected felon. It put my mental image of myself in a strange light.

I entered high school and took all college-prep courses. Everyone expected me to go to college. I expected to go to college. That's where people who read and think a lot go—to college. High school and then college. The next eight to ten years of my life were already mapped-out, the script written. And, when you're fourteen, ten years is most of a lifetime. I knew that I'd be going to school for life. As a freshman, it didn't really bother me. I'd always been good at doing school. It was an easy game to play, and the alternatives were presented as utterly bleak and ugly. I enjoyed reading, had no trouble memorizing facts and rules, and I sincerely wanted to learn as much as possible about as many things as I possibly could. My future was secure.

The expectations I brought with me to high school survived less than a year. I'll admit that I was unfair—didn't really give it a full chance—but I'd anticipated something on the order of a coeducational monastery devoted to holy knowledge. At least some sort of classic institution of higher learning. I got, instead, high school. Rote memorization of long pages of uninspired textbooks dealing with uninspiring subjects, dull lectures read by tired teachers anxious to get home and have a drink and watch teevee, rallies designed to instill school spirit in students anxious to get home and have a taboo cigarette and some fun, classroom rules and hall rules and campus rules and school rules and afterschool rules and parking-lot rules and dress codes and behavior regulations, heavily supervised school dances with music provided by the school orchestra which refused to play rock'n'roll for fear the students would become excited and riot or fornicate—and younger teachers reprimanded or dismissed for discussing Communism or sex education or religion or the Negro problem or any other real problem. High school was, I decided, a high school in name only, controlled by people who'd never been able to pull their minds out of high school. They geared everything down to that level, stunting new generations like feral children.

After a too-short summer vacation of friends with driver's licenses and cars, unimaginable freedom and mobility, beach parties and drive-ins and sweet young girl-women and agonized love into hot new flesh-fumbling, and fewer books and less thinking, I returned to school feeling incredibly wise, feeling so far above it all that a sneer became one of my most comfortable facial expressions. There was nothing I couldn't handle with a blast of quick wit bordering on sarcasm. The small-town high school cliques and upper circles were laughably superficial and self-important. I scoffed at the so-called teachers and their pitiful, limited power. School was too easy to be taken seriously, so I quit taking it seriously. My grades dropped slightly when I stopped studying or doing homework, but I found that with only a minimum of effort I could keep them at the college entrance level—no sweat. I saw myself as a kind of super-being—homo superior—observing lesser creatures from a lofty height, dabbling in their affairs when the mood hit me, when it was to my advantage. No gods to bow down to. Just me and an unbelievably simple game. Some of the books I'd read became suddenly clear. So wise that I became a wise-guy. I could impress naive instructors with my weight-of-the-world expression, or with my sad-deep-thinker look, or with a series of memorized quotations from unassigned great literature. At other times, a calculating glint in my eyes informed people that I'd seen through the structure, had figured it out, and couldn't be touched. And the sad thing was, I received validation. It worked. Easy. Too easy.

By the end of my sophomore year I was dissatisfied, somewhat disgusted and, I realized now, lonely.

My sixteenth summer I got my driver's license and my first motorcycle, a little Harley-Davidson two-stroke. Four months later, it was the down-payment on the most beautiful bike in the world, a huge, hulking, oil leaking, smoke-belching, tank-, fender- and seat-rattling 1951 Harley 74 that leaned on a bent kickstand in a pool of black oil at the very back of Sam Arena's old cycle shop in San Jose. I must've spray-painted that old hog fifty times and fifty different colors the first month I had it. I used to clean the engine with a toothbrush after every ride. I saved my money and re-chromed parts, bought a Bates seat and a small tank to replace the massive four-gallon factory job, a three foot chrome stinger and new rubber, front and back. That hog wasn't just my only real possession, my machine and my transportation, it was my faithful mount, my companion, my freedom. It was my bike. It took me anywhere I wanted to go as fast as I wanted to go. Straddling it, I was fifty-five horses powerful in complete command of the situation. My first teenage carburetor-speed-sparkplug love affair, and I had it bad.

The summer before my senior year at high school, I met three members of the Oakland chapter of the Hell's Angels. My bike had thrown its chain in heavy downtown traffic, and I was fumbling to get it back on the sprocket, sweating, swearing, covered with grease and frustration, while horns screamed in hot anger and businessmen leaned out their car windows, yelling at me, telling me to *move it*! and *get that wreck outta the street*! Suddenly, the horn-honks and shouts began to falter and die.

I heard the distinctive rumble of big 74's behind me. A single horn continued to sound. A voice yelled, "Shut the fuck up!" and there was absolute silence . . . except for the roar of bikes. I turned and saw three choppers worming their way through the jungle of cars. They pulled up beside me and one of the riders dismounted. "You got a lil trouble," he said, stooping to finger the chain. I read the colors on his back—HELL'S ANGELS MC—OAKLAND. Having heard my share of horror stories concerning the outlaw overlords, I waited to be beaten to death. Instead, they repaired my bike, stood by while I started it, then motioned for me to follow across the intersection. I wasn't about to argue.

We stopped at a diner in San Jose and, although still nervous and unsure, I strode in proud behind the supernatural outlaws and sat with them at the counter. All eyes swung to watch us take our seats. Needless to say, I was impressed. I bought them burgers and beers and wished I looked old enough to have a beer myself.

"Where you outta," asked the one who'd fixed my chain. He wore a full beard and a wool watchcap, silver swastika pinned over a pair of redwings, and, of course, the diamond 1%er patch.

"Los Gatos."

"Where'zat? Oh yeah," taking a bite of his burger, "Tha'lil pee-dinkin town over by Campbell. I know a chick in Campbell. Loss Gatus, huh?" He finished his beer in a gulp.

Not much more was said. I couldn't really think of anything to say and I was afraid of saying something wrong. The Angelstalked among themselves—a strange, intriguing language. When they'd finished eating they got up to go and I thanked them all again for helping me out.

The one with the beard said, "Sure, man. Thanks for the food. You're good people," swinging his leg over his bike and lighting a cigarette. "Hey, tell ya whatcha oughta do, man." He nodded at my bike. "Getcher self a new setta bars for your scooter. Them big longhorns look like somethin you ripped off from a fuckin cop-bike. Y'know?"

They thundered off toward the City and I rode home suffering from the first case of hero-worship I'd had in four years.

The very next day I bought a new set of handle bars for my bike.

I was in my final year of high school, had been threatened with expulsion for wearing sideburns, had sworn that, once I graduated, I'd never let another human dictate the length of my hair or the style of my clothing, I was still riding bike and was more disgusted and discontent with structured education and The System than ever, when I met Indian at an all-night drive-in. He was wearing Night Riders colors—a tophatted skeleton on a chopper—the first I'd seen. He walked over to my bike, looked at it, looked at me, took a drink from his bottle of wine and said, "I'm Indian. You with a club?"

I began riding with Indian, following him to parties and on short runs. Through Indian, I met Bob Lee, a good-looking, black-haired, lean, twenty-eight-year-old rider who became the club's Veepee; and Johnny Strater, thirty-seven, who'd come from Oklahoma in '54, sang great old downhome songs and played the guitar, was the best bike mechanic and street fighter I ever met, and was also the truest of honest friends, watching over me like an older brother (which, in fact, he was) until warrants and hassles forced him to split for LA. Indian introduced me to Quack Jack when Quack's name was still "The Cowboy" because he always wore high-heeled cowboy boots, and to Ernie who wore braces on both legs and yet was such a wild strong cat that he went on to become president of a chapter of the Angels. I met Philco, and Jim the Creature, and Redman with his strange, kind, blue eyes and flame hair—and Loopy, and Portegy, and Oily Al and all the others who were to become my brothers.

The outlaws showed me what it meant to have brothers. I'd had friends before, of course. Even good friends and a best friend or two. But never brothers, absolutely loyal no matter what came or went. If you were a brother you could depend on your brothers to feed you, clothe you, fight for you against impossible odds, even go to jail for you if necessary. Brothers.

When I graduated from high school and moved into an apartment of my own in San Jose, I spent more and more time with Indian and the outlaw bike riders. I made the run to Monterey with the Angels and started making it to their parties in Oakland. Indian stayed at my apartment for a week when the cops were after him for setting a car on fire, and I stayed at Indian's countless houses and apartments from time to time. Living with the outlaws, I learned to talk like them, act like them and even think like them on the surface, which was where most of their thinking took place. I liked them. Simple as that. Regardless of what's been said or will be said about the outlaws, they were good to me. I liked them and I liked the scene.

It was basic and out-front and wild and better than joining a circus. *All the world's a stage.* It sounded likely to me, and I figured I'd at least play an exciting part.

Indian asked me to join the Night Riders three weeks before I was to enter San Jose State College. I accepted, went through initiation, and stitched the colors and 1%er patch to my jacket. I was one of them. An outlaw. I was eighteen and the whole concept was truly appalling.

College wasn't a difficult scene to maintain. I already knew the language and the rules. They allowed you to bend the role a little and get away with it. The other students thought I was a trifle weird, a curiosity, but I liked the arrangement. I made friends, but never really close friends. There was always a distance. They were college students, while I was an outlaw going to college.

Two years later, with Quack dead, another summer dead, and a new semester of college about to happen, I was seeing myself once again as an observer rather than an actual participant. Not really a college student and, I'd begun to realize, not really an outlaw no matter how hard I tried, no matter how well I'd learned to play the part. Just Abel Egregore . . . alone . . . playing a tired game of solitaire.

I didn't want to go back to college but, in October, I found myself under classrooms, memorizing lists, taking exams, trying to ignore the restless whispers and the smell of bullshit, wondering whether I should get behind it or make a move and get out from under it.

In this state of mind, on a gray dreary Monday morning, I sat in the college cafeteria listening with an eighth of an ear to Andre LaMer, an ex-Marine Paratrooper who'd gone AWOL to become San Jose State's resident madman poet. He'd let his hair and beard grow long—an incredible, black, shaggy mane—and he wandered around college campuses hollering his loud, crazy poems *to* anyone who'd listen and *at* those who wouldn't. I'd met him earlier in the year at one such poem-holler. I'd never seen him before in my life, but he walked right up to me and started rapping a thousand miles an hour about Kerouac and our destiny as Saints and the rebirth of Truth and his holy mission that had to do with opening eyes.

Now he was telling me how and why he'd gone AWOL from the service, saying, "A screamin eagle. That's what we used to call ourselves—screamin eagles. They tole us we was worth six regular guys, an I believed it. I was really into it, man. I used to go down to this dance place, y'know, an just beat guys up for the fun of it. Wap! Man, for no reason—just WAP! An then on my first leave I was sittin aroun this friend's house smokin weed cuz there wasn't any beer, an the record-player was doin Buddy Holly, an I started to sing along, an my body started to move an I went right with it, an I started to laugh, y'know, just for the kick of laughin, an pretty soon I got to dancin aroun. Whoooo! Great! An my buddies was all puttin me down and I didn't give a shit—just dancin and singin an yellin. An all of a sudden I realized I was *high*! Wow! I was yellin, 'I'm high! I'm happy an I'm high! Yowie!' An my buddies're shakin their heads an tryin to think where they can get a sixpack, while I'm sayin, 'I'm *high*! I'm alive an it's *great* to be alive, an I'm happy an it's *great* to be happy, an I'm high an it's *great* to be high, an it's *so* great to be alive an happy an high!' "

I said, "Yeah. Keep it down, okay?" As usual, Andre was speaking at the top of his lungs. Halfway across the cafeteria people were turning to watch his performance.

"Yeah!" bellowed Andre, smiling and hunching his shoulders like he always did when he got excited—which was most of the time. "Then on my next leave I took acid on the beach an cried for three hours an went home an wrote my first poem. A great poem! I still got it, man. A *great* poem! I read it to my buddies back at camp an they all said I was outta my mind, an I thought it over an said, 'Hell yeah! I *am,* an that's *great*!' An I went an tole my Sarge that I was crazy an didn't wanna be a Marine no more, an he said, 'Tough shit, LaMer.' So I got this chick to bring me some acid an I took it right on the base an went an tole the Sarge that I *wasn't* a Marine no more, an they *still* wouldn't let me out. So I ate a dirt san'witch durin inspection an tole everybody in my platoon to take acid an throw down their rifles an tune in to love, an the Sarge made me do pushups in the sun an after every one I was spose to yell, 'KILL!' but I'd just smile an yell, 'LOVE!' An so the Sarge got pissed off an tole me I was in for bad trouble an would probly get shot an my name'd be synonymous with traitorous dog, an I jumped up an kissed him right on the nose, an he kicked me in the balls—yeah! He did!—an confined me to quarters till they could get a firing squad together or whatever they was gonna do. So that night I went over the hill, an it was easy cuz there wasn't no hill to go over . . . just a big cyclone fence, an I climbed over it an walked away an never went back! An they ain't got me yet an they ain't *gonna* get me, cuz the Truth shall make you *free*!"

"Mmhm. Right," I said, watching a guy with a small goatee walk toward us. He stopped in front of me and nodded hello.

"Are you Abel Egregore?" He asked.

No harm in answering. He didn't look like a cop. I said that I was the man he was looking for.

He stuck out his hand. "I'm Lee Steiner of *The Student Voice.* Can I talk to you for a minute?"

I recognized him then. *The Student Voice* was the college's radical newspaper. At this time it was banned from the campus. Steiner was a leftist, had been called a subversive, and was antiwar in general and anti-Vietnam war in particular. For this reason I felt it my duty to look down on him. The one-percenters were pro-Vietnam war and anti anti-war demonstrators. No real good reason for it. We hated the establishment, and yet we were suddenly on the establishment's side. It started as an accident really. A well respected Hell's Angel from the powerful Oakland chapter had been watching a peace demonstration. The demonstrators were being held at bay by a handful of cops. More than a thousand demonstrators. A little band of cops. The demonstrators allowed themselves to be herded, pushed and abused. It blew the big *Angel's* mind. He saw a sea of cowards and that is what he acted against. One lone *Angel,* right through the cop's lines and no stopping him. "I'm one man! I'm one fuckin man! You're cowards! You're yellow-pussy-snotnosed cowards!" Grabbing a picket-sign from a cringing demonstrator and beating the shit out of anyone within reach, until he went down under a nightstick storm.

The next day, the Hell's Angels were suddenly the darlings of the Rightists and the unexpected champions of the establishment.

All the clubs under the one-percenter patch automatically followed the Angels. I was a one-percenter, so I was now pro-Vietnam war and anti-peace demonstrator.

Steiner said, "I understand that you're a Hell's Angel."

"I'm a Night Rider."

"You're in contact with the Hell's Angels, aren't you?"

"Sure."

"Well, we were wondering if you could get the Angels to appear on campus Friday to debate the Vietnam Day Committee."

I thought about it and decided that it might be good for a laugh. Indian would dig the publicity.

"I'll try," I said. Why not? Saying it's easy. Besides, the more I thought about it, the better it sounded. That night I talked to Indian and he talked to the Angels. They weren't too enthusiastic about the idea. They had their own problems, and the role of Defenders of The American Way was starting to itch.

On Friday, I cut class and put on my colors and rode out to the bar on First Street, where Night Riders and Gypsy Jokers and a lone Angel from Sacramento were getting high for the debate. It was raining, and most of them had been forced to leave their bikes at home. It was disappointing, because we wanted to ride in in force to make a good showing. A good showing's important. Instead, we pulled onto the campus in a station wagon, jumped out in front of a big crowd and swaggered down Seventh Street in a loose pack, digging the attention, walking tall, feeling good.

The college'd set up a platform in front of the cafeteria and we climbed on, shoulder to shoulder with the VDC. God, what a circus. If I hadn't been part of it, I would've howled at the whole insane show. Of all the outlaws, only Here, a sandy-haired, broad-shouldered Night Rider, really had anything to say. He came on with a great blast of homespun humor and common-man patriotism that won an enthusiastic round of applause and cheers from the students. The rest of my brothers, drunk and loaded, mumbled or shouted fragmented catch-phrases about American Freedom and how anybody who didn't wanna fight was a gutless queer. The college people cheered even louder. I had strange Nazi visions when the VDC, using well prepared, intelligent arguments, pointed out the flaws in our thinking, and were booed off the stage.

As the "debate" bumbled on, I went through some uncool feelings. I was listening too much and it was a mistake. I kept telling myself that I should be laughing at the sea of fools, but the more I listened, the sadder I got. Can you hear what I'm saying? I was starting to feel that I didn't necessarily *want* to laugh at fools—didn't want to *see* fools. Confusion.

Then there was a rumble in the crowd, and someone yelled, "It's Ginsberg! Allen Ginsberg's here!" and coming through the wall of bodies was a small, furry man with glasses. My mind went zzzzt, and crumbled and I looked again and it was, indeed, my long-time literary hero, Allen Ginsberg.

"He's so small!" I thought, "So small but so holy. Those eyes are the holy of his poems. How can we stand against Ginsberg?"

"Don't you people *want* to be happy?" he cried.

"No!" was the crowd's reply. A giggle swept the assembly when the people realized what they had said. "No." And the sheer downheadedness of this answer stopped me frozen cold. I *did* want to be happy . . . didn't I?

Allen Ginsberg, benevolently overlooking the sad reply to his question, read a poem to the Angels, saying that it was the cops who were the heat, not the pacifists.

"We want to goof, and smoke pot, and ball our lovers, just like *you,*" he cried sincerely. Embarrassing sincerity. No one prepared for such naked feeling. He chanted and prayed for peace, ringing finger-cymbals.

Nobody seemed to be listening. The crowd jeered him and I felt ashamed. I watched the scene and saw all my structures falling to ruin. This man was saying truths. He *knew* something.

"Dumb-ass faggot," sneered a Gypsy Jay, and I sneered right along without thinking. It was the expected response.

Quick-takes and bright flashes. Everything moving too fast—too fast. I couldn't catch it all, and I *wanted* to catch it all. I knew it was important—big. We moved to an auditorium and "debated" some more. Everybody talking. Nobody listening. Me frantically trying to slow things down enough for an examination—falling in and out of my programmed role—confused. Ginsberg had to be at a reading in The City, so he gave me the poem he'd read, asking me to give it to the president of the Angels. Then he was gone. I looked at the poem, read it four times, read it again, stared at all the college faces and then at my outlaw brothers, and suddenly there was only the word MOVE—a word that'd been growing for over a year. I walked out into the rain, saying goodbye to no one, sloshed home making one quick stop at a house belonging to a guy named Zad who I'd met and liked at college, and who'd been trying to get me to take acid for months, because it would, "Save your poor violent soul, Abel, straighten you out and show you the real path." I bought a cap from him, went home, dripped into my apartment and dropped some of that LSD-25 I'd been hearing so much about—just for a change—just to re-shake the dice, re-shuffle the cards—on the spur of the moment, with a dark mind, just because everything was so hollow and fake. And that was really the beginning of the more frantic segment of the search.

I had been told by the reverent few (it sounds funny now, but at one time there actually were only a few) who had taken it that LSD was "weird stuff . . . weirder than you can possibly imagine," and I anticipated a remarkable experience, but was in no way prepared for the mind-staggering voyage into distant dimensions that was my first acid trip.

Hosanna, brothers! So died a street fighter. My tight little shell of hard-guy-game drizzled right out of my poor little pants and puddled on the floor. I saw my world shrink to a micro-speck floating in the eternity of the cosmos, and I smelled enlightenment, and was promised answers to the questions I didn't even know how to ask, and I relearned that hostility and working it out on other beings was utterly wrong, and I refelt the feelings I had learned it was sophisticated and cool to ignore and I said, "God forgive me," and didn't leave the apartment for two days, wondering where I should start. Dazzled, as they say. Drugged, as they say. Insane, as they say. But I knew better.

Narcotics agents must carefully scrub their hands after they've been in a place where LSD-25 has been produced lest they absorb even the smallest, micro-amount through their skin. This is true. Ask them and they will assure you that it's true. For, "If an agent receives a single dose of LSD, he can no longer be trusted to serve in an official capacity." Like everyone who has taken a sufficient dose of acid, unlike the narcotic agent who is afraid to, I *know why.*

CHAPTER THREE – IN THE BEGINNING THERE WAS CHAOS. HAD WE BEEN ABLE TO "ABIDE IN THAT STATE," CONFUSION WOULD NEVER HAVE DAWNED.

Days of reconstruction followed. Piles of discarded concepts littered my room, making it difficult to move about. Up to this time, I thought I had it all figured out. Which is to say . . . I no longer thought about it except in moments of weakness. Nobody else seemed terribly concerned about understanding the reasons behind mind and existence and the point to all this endless movement—only a few strange old philosophers who were quoted from time to time, but for the most part dismissed as quaintly gifted eccentrics. I figured the thing was kicks . . . sensation. What you had to do was pick out a role that looked good (or simply accept the one you were given if you hadn't the will to resist) and then play the part. Rich man, adventurer, accountant, whatever you got. You played it for whatever it was worth, followed the rules that applied and went along with the movie, and that was life. Simple. Not much to it, but then, even very small minds were expected to understand and cope with it. If you did it right and really got behind the role, it kept you from thinking about the absurdity of a blundering lifetime which would stumble to an end with nothing of any lasting value accomplished.

After the Ginsberg meeting and the acid and the days sitting alone remembering everything I'd ever done or read or heard or said or thought, I looked around and re-flashed on all the props, and the movie I thought was going to be life turned out to be merely the cartoon. With the symbol for eternity branded on my brain I dropped back into the world of petty fumbling. "Give me a script!" I pleaded.

"You gotta write your own," was the unvoiced reply.

"I don't know enough. The production's too big! It's too elaborate and intricate and perfect. How can I stoop to defiling it with another hack-written farce? I don't know enough. I'm not wise enough. I don't know what to do."

I decided to search for someone or something to instruct me, even though a god-voice in the back of my skull sneered, "You know what to do. You've seen where it's all at. You know where it's all going and where it all came from. You just won't admit it. You won't accept it. You want to hang on to your games and your role. You want to delay the inevitable by searching for 'the answers.' You already *know* the Answer."

"I don't! If I did, it was too big and I couldn't hold it."

"Sure . . ." whispered the voice. It was fading, so I was soon able to ignore it. Keep the old wheel of life turning just a little longer, please. Just a little while longer. Just a little bit longer.

I re-read all the books I'd liked with new understanding, and read new ones that I'd heard about but never bothered to read when I had the club and my bike and knew everything I needed to know.

"They've *all* seen it," I realized in amazement, "In a world of enlightened sages, I couldn't see what was happening. Why didn't someone tell me?"

Then, I'd read some more, and meditate, and then jump up and say, "They *tried* to tell me! I just couldn't hear it. I wouldn't listen."

Humble for the first time since about age six (at which time I learned that being humble was a sign of a sadly introverted personality and was to be avoided) I saw the universe through new eyes. I understood how comforting religion must be for those who believe.

"It's all love," I said with conviction. Those guys are right. Why couldn't I see? (Love being such a simple, constantly validated, pleasant sounding solution to the world's injustices. The LSD experience cut right through the Zen games and intellectual disillusionment of the once worshiped Beat generation. Acid's first and most powerful message was love).

I watched the sun come up on an unbelievable Friday morning, stepped out under the magic blue sky, started my bike for the first time in a week, then changed my mind and walked through the clean new-day air to the college campus. I stuck my head into a classroom, smiled all around, took a deep breath and was about to announce to the good people that from now on, everything was going to be *all right,* and that it was great to see them and great to have them see me, when the instructor cut my hello short by saying, "Do you *mind?* I am trying to conduct a class." A girl whispered to her friend, "He's drunk." Edges got hard. Faces got ugly. I pulled my head out of the classroom and ran into the cafeteria, where I bought a cup of coffee and sat down for a quiet think. The herds of moving people made me suddenly uneasy.

A guy I'd gone to high school with, who wore white shirts, slacks and blue tennis shoes, and whom I saw from time to time without ever really seeing, appeared in front of me and began to talk.

"Abel!" he said, "How've you been?"

I couldn't remember his name. Chances are, I'd never known his name. "Hey, man!" I said, glad to see him and relatively sure he was a man and wouldn't be offended by the designation.

"What've you been up to?" He pulled up a chair and sat down, warmed by my enthusiastic greeting.

"Wow," I said with a laugh, and shook my head, assuming that he was in on it.

"What's that mean?" he asked, chuckling a bit himself.

"Heh, heh," I countered stupidly, and began to panic. I didn't know what to say. I'd forgotten how to carry on an everyday conversation. Danger, man. Your cool's gone and so's your cover. Insert a simple game. But all games look so transparent today.

During a long silence, the nameless one shifted in his chair and arranged crumbs in a line on the table. He looked at the wall clock and said, "Oops! I got a class," picking up his books, "See you, Abel."

"Okay," I said, also jumping up, which looked, I realized later, rather odd. "Yeah, okay. That'll be great."

Making his mouth smile with a noticeable effort, he said,

"Yeah . . . uh . . . take it easy," and left . . . hurriedly, it seemed to me.

I was standing up and couldn't think of a good reason to be, so I sat down. I had no reason to be sitting down, so I stood up again . . . and freaked. I saw my coffee cup, grabbed this excuse happily, and sat down again. I'd expected everyone to pat me on the back and say, "Well, man, you finally *made* it, eh? Now let's get this cosmos in gear and *do* something." When nothing of the sort happened, a beady-eyed, smirking suspicion began to drip like slime through my head. Maybe I'd failed the test. *The Acid Test.* Maybe I hadn't passed, and the entire cosmos was *still* waiting for me to see the light so things could start happening.

I was considering this frightening possibility, watching it grow into a probability, when Ted Coleman, an artist with thick, curly black hair, thick glasses, and a thick body that I'd smoked weed and stumbled around the city with, came over to my table and kicked the back of my chair, saying, "What's happening, man?"

Since it could have been part of the test, requiring a correct answer, I decided to be honest, in hopes of salvation. I said, "I don't know," sadly.

Ted studied my face and sat down. "*You* are wiped out. What are you on?"

"Nothing. I'm not on anything. Do I look that bad?"

"You look great. You just look loaded."

A few minutes of silence broken only by cafeteria noises. Then, Ted took a sip of my cold coffee, made a wry face, and said, "What've you been doing?"

The cafeteria noises stopped—waiting for my answer. I said immediately, "I took some acid."

"Too much, man! When?"

"Uh . . . last week."

"Still feel it?"

"Does it ever wear off, man?"

"Not completely, but it fades. How'd you like it?"

Nothing to say but, "Wow."

"Yup. That's what everybody says."

It imploded in my stomach, bowels and head at the same time.

I could talk to this person. He understood. It was real! The experience was as big as I thought it was. Others had seen it. The shared wow—the sacred wow.

A cat named Larry, who I'd seen a couple of times, came over to talk to Ted. Ted told him that I'd taken acid, and Larry said, "That's beautiful! Welcome to the Movement for the Rebirth of Fun. Are the bike clubs turning on to acid now?" A hopeful missionary, anxious to turn on the world. Especially the part of the world that made it uncomfortable to live in.

At this time, although every outlaw I knew smoked weed, and had done so long before the flower people picked it up, not many had tried LSD. "Not so much to acid," I replied.

"They gotta be turned on," said Larry. "You gotta tell em all to take it. Everybody's gotta take acid."

We said friendly words and laughed and Ted told me about some of his acid trips in which he had seen visions of the Buddha and visited Hell and Heaven and Purgatory, while I said, "Wow," or "Yes," and felt that I'd found my people at last. It's a great feeling, one of the greatest of the entire psychedelic experience, to look into another being's eyes and see that they've seen the same incredible thing that you have. It validates the vision and makes you think that perhaps there's something happening after all.

Larry pulled his beard and said, "Hey, why don't you come with me an Ted to this party tonight? Meet some people."

"Great!"

"Okay, let's make it over to my place and smoke dope till it's time to go."

Larry, a skinny blond twenty-year-old with pale blue eyes and a three-hair beard, lived in a little shack in back of a big house four blocks from the college. The door was always wide open or at least unlocked, even though he kept huge stashes of weed at all times. He was the most out-front cat I ever met, and was never busted due to a more powerful destiny.

The walls of the shack were covered with posters and prints. Brando, Sophia Loren, Albert Schweitzer, Bob Dylan, all looked down or up at you from their places on the walls, between dance posters, eye-traps and little signs Larry'd made himself, saying things like, "Teach a cop how to fuck" or "Love now and get it over with." Pasted on the ceiling was a giant picture of Oscar Wilde in full drag—make-up, earrings, the works. This picture raised many questions about Larry's sex life. It wasn't until I'd known him for long months that I became completely convinced that he wasn't on the lean toward gay. And it wasn't until much, much later that the full, frightening, pitiful implication of the picture finally hit me.

Larry's picture of Wilde. Such an amazing, mind-rotting statement, and so few of his friends ever really dug it.

On the window-sill, a little marijuana plant struggled for the sun in a chipped Mexican clay pot. The pot was labeled "pot" and the weed plant was labeled "weed plant." On top of a bookcase, a plaster bust of JFK stood like a shrine with a copper incense burner in front of it. To the left of the bookcase, a bulletin board devoted entirely to unflattering photos, cartoons and drawings of LBJ. A beautiful collection, coveted by many. Right in the middle of the floor was a water pipe and a shoe box full of cleaned weed.

"I gotta take a crap," Larry said as we stepped in. "Will you fill the pipe, Ted?"

It was the first weed I'd smoked—dared to smoke—since the acid, and I got higher than I ever hoped to be. By the time Ted and Larry were ready to leave for the party, I was so stoned that I'd given up even trying to talk. I just smiled at everything that was said to me, and nodded my head up and down as the words went by. I felt beautiful and saw nothing but beauty. I was a little child being led and protected by two wise saints. On the perfect path to all-the-way-up now. Awake, finally, and headed for truth.

I followed them into the mystical, multi-colored Ford, hand-painted by Larry himself, with flowers, op-art-patterns, arrows pointing everywhere, PEACE printed on the trunk and LOVE on the doors, and we headed for Boulder Creek and the party.

Larry and Ted in the front seat, happy-talking things that I'm not yet in on, and me in the back seat. A big back seat, a little me. An unbelievably big back seat. Seven miles from one door handle to the other. So much bigger on the inside than it looked from the outside. Everything so much bigger on the inside.

Ted saying, " . . . and the first Monk said, 'Put the woman down. I did, two hours ago.'"

Larry saying, "Yeah, but if he really had, he wouldn't have known what the second Monk was talking about, man."

"No, no. That's going too far."

"Of course, man! You have to!"

"Okay, then how about if there's . . ." over winding mountain roads, through enchanted forests and down a long, dirt deer-path.

CHAPTER FOUR – "WE WILL ATTAIN NEW REALMS"

Larry parked the car in front of a little elf-like hidden mountain cabin surrounded by a small herd of beat-up VW's, panel trucks, dented Fords and Chevies. I climbed out and stood in the yard, hearing unreal drifting music and crowd-sound. The two-room cabin was so full of people that I hesitated at the door, thinking that, if one more person stepped inside, the structure would rip out at the seams, leaving an untidy pile of rubble and many angry strangers pointing accusing fingers in my direction. But Ted said, "Cumon in, Abel," holding the door open for me, so I took a deep breath and crossed the threshold.

The cabin miraculously remained intact, and the door banged shut behind me as I stepped over and around stretched-out bodies, trying to avoid tramping people while I peered through the smoky dark. A single blue lamp lit the room. Dylan's then new album, "*another side*" was filling the heavy air with sound as it turned thirty-three and a third times per minute on an unseen stereo.

It's all just a dream, babe,
a vacuum, a scheme, babe . . .

sang Dylan in his rasping, nasal, thirsty, suffering and perfect voice. Like an idiot I froze and did a big, low, gulping "uuh," hearing what he was saying for the first time. I mean, I'd listened to Dylan before. I owned his albums and sat in front of record players while his words banged against my head. I even told people how much I *liked* Dylan—what a great "folk-singer" he was. But this time, frozen to the floor, mouth hanging open, I *heard* Dylan, and apologized to his genius for never having listened.

A gigantic brass water pipe, containing nearly two lids of smoldering weed, stood on its dragon's paw supports between two fantastic men. One wore a handlebar mustache with the ends waxed sharp—round, rimless glasses on the very tip of his nose like Ben Franklin. He looked to be about twenty-four. The other had long, light brown hair and a huge whiskbroom mustache that drooped almost to his chin. They sat Buddha-like on crossed legs, facing each other, engaged in serious dope smoking and conversation. Blue haze and paisleys everywhere. All signs pointing straight or crooked to very high Up. I felt that the whole thing was being staged for my benefit.

"We will attain new realms," said the whiskbroom Buddha. "We will be the first stumbling mortals to break through on holy hemp. I can feel the ole Void pulling for us." He took an incredible pull on the pipe and passed the mouthpiece with a grand flourish.

"I rejoice at your coming death, Baxtor," said his companion.

Taking the mouthpiece once more, Baxter nodded, saying, "I will miss your doomed, but pleasant, Carlgame, Carl."

Exhaling, Carl said, "Not from the Final All of the Void, you won't."

"True," replied Baxtor, rocking happily with his hands on his knees. His eyes closed and he made a laugh-sound that went, "Hnnnn-hnnnnn-bowaughhhh," way up inside his skull.

My attention was so totally ensnared by these two stoned sages and their (in the state I was in) temptingly meaningful, frustratingly obscure conversation, that Ted was shaking my shoulder and saying, "You all right, man? Hey, you okay?" before I even realized he'd been talking to me.

I smiled and pointed to the pair on either side of the hookah. "Holy wise men. Listen. Wow."

Ted smiled back and said, "Baxtor and Carl. This is Carl's cabin. Carl . . . Baxtor . . . this is Abel."

Carl extended his hand, and I took it. Baxtor extended the hookah's mouthpiece, and I took that. Beyond high now. Into a zone where everything's just about ready to have already happened, making it all cool. Any second now. Dig all you can while you still can.

Curt Webber, a dark-eyed, clean-shaven, sharp-featured, twenty-two-year-old leftist whom I'd met in an English class a year ago at college, came in from the other room with a pretty Negro chick. He raised his eyebrows when he saw me, walked over and said, "Well yes indeed. Abel. Abel Egregore, I do believe. You meet the least likely. Mmmhmmm."

With my eyes all over the lovely black girl, I said, "Hullo . . . uh, Curt, and . . .

"Her name's Jeri," said Curt, putting his arm around her waist. "Yes. Mmmmhmm."

Ted told Curt that I'd taken acid, indicating, I suspected, that I could now be spoken to on a different level. I hoped to prove worthy.

"Ah!" said Curt, extending his left arm as Jeri wandered off silently. He let his arm fall to his side, empty. "Welcome to the Land of the Damned." He showed me his teeth, covered them, and walked away.

The room seemed to go quieter. I thought I heard the sound of uncomfortable body-shifts. Paranoid visions of elaborate deceptions elbowed for center stage. I turned to Ted, suddenly suspicious. He read my eyes and shrugged the message off with, "Curt's spaced behind negative energy tonight. He's decided to play the anti-Christ. Ignore it, man. Forget it." He guided me around the room, introducing me to what seemed to be an endless number of beautiful and strange people all full of smiles and glad hellos.

Somebody, maybe several somebodies were singing, "Row, row, row your boat gently down the stream . . .

"Wow!" I groaned, hearing it heavy. "That's . . . wow."

" . . . merrily, merrily, merrily, merrily. Life is but a dream. Yes life is but a dream. Row, row, row your boat gently down the stream . . ."

"Ted, I never heard that before. I mean, I heard it, but I never *heard* it. You know? Everything's . . .

"Of course, man. It's really all *that* big. Dig?"

"Man! I've sure got a lot of thinkin to do. I feel like . . . I feel like I've just been . . . ah, shit, I wish I wasn't so stoned so I could *talk* to you. Except . . . if I wasn't so stoned, I wouldn't *be* talking to you. I feel like I've been blind. Y'know? I feel like I oughta be thanking everyone. God, this must really sound stupid to you. I don't know what I'm talkin about."

"I think maybe you do. Just let it all go, man."

"I don't wanna make a fool of myself, man. I feel so good, I'm afraid I'll blow it."

"Don't worry about it. We're all fools. If you *know* you're a fool, then you're already one step up. Let's dig some people," and Ted steered me around the cabin again, telling me names that slipped right on through, showing me faces that merged into a smiling montage.

The night was all joyous discoveries, many of which brought me almost to the point of tears, to laughter and astonished wows regularly. Whole new horizons. I felt humble and honored to be in a room with and listening to such enlightened powers. I felt in flash after flash that I'd never been so high before, never so aware and never—at least not since a long, long half-remembered time ago—so hopeful and happy.

One of the few faults I'd found with weed was the fact that it was hard to be violent while you were behind it. In the bike clubs, we called it being yellow-fucked, and you had to counteract the feeling with plenty of wine, or else you didn't want to fight or even bug anybody, which is dangerous when the people around you *do.*

Now, talking (or rather listening—I said very little) to these new-found friends, I came to the realization that this was not the fault of weed, but the fault of fighting. Nobody wanted to fight. The talk was of love—a word I'd been ashamed to say aloud—and of enlightenment, which I'd read about and thought about abstractly, but didn't think "real people" discussed. There was talk of change and of a peaceful, world-wide revolution of all-powerful understanding and love. The talk was of love, all the more exciting and beautiful because it seemed honest. This was shortly before the mass media and the merchants and promo-men leapt on the printed letters of the word and discovered that it could be painted "psychedelic" and sold in brilliantly colored plastics for some money.

The talk was of love, and it ripped my mind time and time again to realize that it had been said by so many prophets from the beginning of consciousness, and no one wanted to listen. *Now* someone was listening, and we swore (I, silently) that we'd never stop listening and never forget. It was all so simple. No obstacles that wouldn't crumble under the bright light of the truth of love.

I watched and listened and thought, "My God . . . it might just happen!" and fell asleep in the first, gray glow of dawn on the crowded floor of the quiet cabin, in between Ted and a heart-pulling little eighteen-year-old chick who told me that the name, Abel, was very important. Her name was Julia Cain and she inspired dreams.

Long dreams of brave, reverent, clear-eyed Neo-American Indians, standing on wind-blown high mountain sides, watching the godless, blind-worm, white, sprawling civilization vomit and cough itself to death in the garbage-pit valleys below. Waiting for the world to begin. It will be beautiful. It will be real this time.

A weathered old medicine man built sand magic and drew the symbols for peace and love with his strong, red fingers. "Listen to Julia," he whispered. "Listen to the daughter of the dove and your eyes will open."

He was a dream-created, wise-medicine-man of my own mind-of-then, or he would have added, "Even the faintest light is painful and hard to look at for newly opened eyes." Like the *Sepher Zohar.* A book so powerful and all-illuminating that it blinds you and you can't understand a single word.

But, "Listen to Julia," the medicine-man said, and I woke twice that morning with those words in my head. Listen to Julia Cain, the girl who knows the importance of your name.

CHAPTER FIVE – CAIN, JULIA

Julia Cain was a woman-child experience that flashed in and then out of my physical life so quickly and with such a brilliant light-show of beauty and innocence and powerful pull that I never had a chance to discover the faults and minor flaws that she must (as we all must) have had. It was Curt Webber who, long after Julia had become only a sometimes memory, ruined my day but showed me an important lesson of the real world by reading me the Dictionary definition of innocent.

"Listen to this, man. 'Innocent.' It means, 'Free from guilt or sin, or from evil action or effect; specif: a). Doing or thinking no evil; unacquainted with evil; pure. b). Free from blame, censure, or guilt.' And also, things like, 'Spotless' and 'Unsullied,' and then, right at the end, 'One who is innocent; a) A young child, b) A simpleton; also, an idiot.' Kind of shows you where everything's at, don't it?"

But, when I first met Julia, and for long months after, I saw her as perfect, flawless; the girl that can never really be. And she isn't any more. But for a sadly short, utopian time, Julia actually was. As was Julia's world. The two are one and the same.

The day after the gathering at Carl's, I opened my eyes, they stayed open this time, connected themselves to my brain, and I was awake. I found myself alone on stranger Carl's strange cabin floor, covered with a blanket. Outside the window, the sun had jumped past noon. I answered my "where-am-I" easily, and dug being alive and conscious. What greater feeling? At this time, there was none.

"Are you awake?" asked a soft voice behind me.

I rolled over and faced Julia, who sat curled up in a big chair, wearing a sunflower-patterned shift.

"Hmmm . . . I guess so. Where is everyone?"

Julia's voice was lovely, and she never moved her wide eyes from my face (or anyone's face) when she spoke. She counted off on her fingers, "Carl went to school. Sherry went to work. Ted is outside walking in the woods with Norman, and the others have gone their separate ways without telling me their destinations. Would you like something to eat?"

"No-thank-you. Do you live here?" I asked, getting to my feet.

"No. I'm just here now. Would you like an apple?" She handed me one, and I took it from her. An apple-gift from my first, genuine, pure, early-honest flower-child, although the category was yet to come, the label yet to be coined.

A bite from the apple, and I wondered how I was going to get back to San Jose. "Did Larry leave?"

"Yes, but he'll be back. He had to go on a *mission* or something," she smiled. And when she did, I suddenly realized that she was as cute in the hard light of full day as she had been the night before. That can't be said about too many chicks. "Would you like to go for a walk?" she asked.

I pushed my hair back and nodded.

She slipped her small hand into mine and led me out of the cabin into the sunshine and mountain air. I began to fall in love with her as my hand warmed to hers. Warm hand, warm mind, warm world, after an Eskimo existence.

We walked through the forest, shafts of sunlight cutting through the trees, birds in and out of the spaces between, chasing bugs or one another or maybe just digging the feel of their wings against the air. Julia sang an Old English ballad in a high, sweet, clear voice, and then hummed softly to herself, no particular melody, dreamy and slow with her head down watching the little sun-lit clouds of silver dust that her bare feet caused as we moved along the path. We found a ring of mushrooms beside a spongy, moss-covered log that had long ago been a proud, tall redwood giant, and she told me very seriously, with no trace of make-believe, that, "The forest's little magic beings, who are now only tiny blue spirits, danced here a few nights ago. Maybe last night. No, probably a few nights ago. That's what makes the mushrooms grow in a ring like this."

More realistic reasons learned from Natural Science classes

came to mind, but they would have sounded cold and hard in the soft, warm forest, so I smiled and said, "Have you seen them dance?"

She stretched out on her stomach in the leaves with her hands under her chin, and sighed, "They're only little blue lights now. You can just barely see them. But I watch them dance whenever I can."

"I'd like to see them."

"I'd like for you to see them, Abel."

I sat with my back against the fallen tree, and Julia recited a poem. A simple children's poem about mushrooms and a girl who lived inside one with a cricket. I can only remember the part that went . . .

> And the cricket's name was Warble
> And he wore a mushroom cap.
> The girl loved Warble dearly,
> And he slept upon her lap.

The poem told how Warble saved the girl from a spider, and was finally eaten by a bird who felt very sorry about it after the girl explained to him what he had done.

"Do you like that poem?" asked Julia, when she'd finished reciting.

"Mmhm. Where'd you learn it?"

"I made it up," she said.

"I like it even more, then. Do you write a lot of them?"

"No. I just make them up. Do you know any poems?"

I recited some lines from *Howl,* but I don't think she was very impressed. "Do you know who wrote that?" I asked.

"Allen Ginsberg," she replied. I was surprised to find that she knew everything he'd published. She knew at least one work of every poet I brought up. The talk turned to music. I think Julia knew all music. Music was alive and everywhere for her.

We started back to the cabin, and I was struck by the thought that since I'd first seen Julia I'd felt that I'd known her for a long time. That sounds trite, but what can I say? How else do you describe that feeling? I simply felt that I'd known her for a long time. I told her so.

"You *have* known me for a long time," she replied. "But it was a long time ago."

"In school?" trying to remember.

She laughed and put her cheek against my arm. "In a kind of school," she said softly.

I thought how strange she was, and beautiful in exactly the way a chick should be. The most beautiful chick I'd ever known. Or maybe . . . maybe it was just me. It didn't matter. It was all the same. It was good. A new kind of good. No, an old kind of good, almost remembered from early inferred promises.

When Larry returned with the car I didn't want to leave, but I had no acceptable excuse for staying. I couldn't very well have moved in with Carl, who I'd only met the night before. So, I left Julia and went home to San Jose, feeling new and clean and awake and far beyond Boy Scout reverent. Even the downtown smog seemed to sparkle.

For the next week or so I hung with Ted and Larry, getting rides up to see Julia when they went to visit Carl, and through this I got to know Carl and his chick, Sherry, and Baxter and Baxter's friends, and, through them, many more. But they were all background people at first. Julia was the kaleidoscope window to this special time between. All joyous color and sound and magic and hope, and maybe just the same old chips of glass, beads and mirrors, but seen in a glorious new way.

Julia lived in a world where everything flowed like a well-organized fairy tale. She saw gods in everything, and only beauty in her gods. In Julia there was the whisper of shadows but, with so much sunlight surrounding her, they went unnoticed.

"Egregores," she said on our second meeting. "Now I know Egregores. Abel Egregores. Your name's really Egregores?"

"No. It's Egregore. No *s* on the end."

She pursed her lips, puzzled. Then her mouth curled up at the corners and she cocked her head to one side. "As you wish," she said, giving me a knowing wink—which went right past and was lost; Egregores being, at the time, an unheard of (by me) Angel, and merely a variation on my last name. Many things to learn.

CHAPTER SIX—IS FOR INDIAN

After my introduction to Julia, after I'd slowly (actually, far too rapidly) filtered through mist levels of joyous contemplation of the peace that was on its way—after I'd come down—I found myself caught once again in the snare of all-day-every-day reality and imagined responsibilities, and I'd already missed three club meetings plus a mandatory Angel-Joker-Rider party in Oakland . . . not to mention many days of school which I dismissed as unimportant.

Down and thinking, feeling stranded, unwilling to admit it and face up to changes, I made a half-hearted attempt at crawling back into my familiar, past-tangled role. It wasn't working anymore. I rattled inside my shell. My old foundation had been eaten away by acid. "Let it crumble," I decided. "Let the winds sweep it away. That Abel's dead. Dead as Quack Jack. Dead as a doorknob."

But it wasn't quite that easy. The old Abel-body looked so much like the new Abel-body that most people couldn't tell the difference. Sometimes, edges overlapped and I couldn't tell the difference myself. Old Abel's games ran up to New Abel, greeted him as their old friend and feeder, and wanted to tag along wherever he went. I knew I was gonna have to kick through and run out naked if I was ever gonna leave the ruins at all.

On a fogged-in Tuesday afternoon, I got out of bed, put my colors on over my leather armor, and glanced at my costumed reflection in the bathroom mirror, thinking, "That was one rough stud. Ohhh yes," as I stuck my hands into gloves and cinched up all around. Into the carport to kick lonely bike until it agreed to start (cold and neglected though it was, poor faithful machine) and I took off for Redwood City where the Night Riders were holding the meeting.

The streets were fairly dry, but the air itself was so damp with fat fog that, when I pulled into Poncho's garage, I had to wipe water from my eyes before I could see Red Man, lying on his back in a puddle of oil, working on his brake linkage, drinking wine from a gallon jug, letting it run into his already soaked red beard and hair so that pink drops spattered on his greasy T-shirt when he sat up to say, "Abel! Where the fuh-h-hk you been? Everbody's pissed off't you for missin all them meetins, man."

"Yeah, I got hungup," I said, feeling at home all of a sudden, picking up smooth on the familiar script. "I'm goin to see Indian right now."

Red Man lay on his back again and banged the linkage with a wrench. "Okay, man. Tell'im I need his vise-grips." Clang, bash, "Shiht," and he took another glug of wine.

I climbed the broken stairs and walked into Poncho's furniture-less house—a house stripped for action. My brothers were standing in a circle around Mama Beverly who lay naked on the wine-bottle strewn floor with her sausage legs spread wide.

Mama Bev had been discovered in Watsonville by Jim the Creature. Jim brought her home with him and offered her to the club. She had short, ratty, greasy black hair, greasy black teeth, chewed on, ragged, greasy black fingernails, and greasy black underwear . . . when she wore underwear. Only about five-foot-one, little Mama Bev weighed maybe one-sixty or seventy. The club had taken her on as its Mama when she announced at a party that she was willing to do anything that wouldn't kill her. And Mama Bev was hard to kill.

Inside the circle, standing over Mama Bev, was Indian, his arm around Little Pete, a prospect awaiting the vote and his initiation. "Mama Beverly," said Indian, "you think ole Pete here'd make a good Night Rider? Whadya think?"

Mama Bev waved her grubby, round-soled, red-toed feet in the air, saying, "Only one way I can tell. Haul out his pecker!" Indian threw back his head and roared, the *Riders* howled and hooted, and Red Man, coming in from the garage, stumble-drunk by this time, yelled, "Lesee howee drings *wine*! Hooo yah!"

A bottle jumped forward and Indian handed it to Little Pete, watched while he chugalugged as much as he could hold, then grabbed the bottle back and drained twice as much—gloop, gloop, kerploosh and "Aughhhh!"—while the outlaws cheered and slapped their president on the back. That bottle all but gone, Indian heaved it at the far wall where it shattered in a pink explosion, just enough wine left to leave a wet octopus, arms reaching for the floor, on the long-since ruined wallpaper. "Yah!" and Indian called for another bottle. "Drink up, Pete!" Little Pete held the bottle with both hands, found his mouth after three tries, and swallowed the wine that didn't burble out around the corners of his numb lips onto his dripping chest and the front of his pants. He swayed and would have fallen but for Indian's arm around his shoulders. "Buh . . . uuh . . . uhgh . . . cn drih numore."

"You can't *drink* no more?" bawled Indian. "We're just warmin up, man! Maybe you'd dig it more if it was seasoned up a liddle!" leaning over to pour wine between Mama Bev's legs. She squirmed like a full piece of laboring intestine and bellowed, "Fuck, thas *cold*, you mutha! How bout pourin a lil in this hole up here!" pointing to her extra-large, snaggle-toothed mouth. Creature poured wine in the general direction of her face, and she kept her mouth wide as the wine splashed over her and ran into a red puddle-halo surrounding her beachball head.

"Drink wine!" said Indian.

"Drink wine!" echoed the Night Riders.

Little Pete fell to his knees under a shove from Indian, and began drinking wine from the deep Mama Bev receptacle. Indian laughed and dug it. The Night Riders laughed and shouted encouragement and dug it. Mama Bev giggled and squeaked and dug it. Little Pete puked on the floor.

Nina came in from the kitchen and looked at Mama Beverly and Little Pete's performance. Her upper lip curled slightly in disgust. None of the riders' chicks thought too much of Mama Beverly.

Nina was Here's old lady. Bleached hair, good brown eyes, a nice little ass, only neglected teeth and the beginning of hard frown-lines barred her way to real beauty. She was twenty-two and had a two-year-old son called Rodger-dodger by an unknown ex-husband in Texas. Rodger-dodger sometimes came to club parties with Nina, and would ride with Here, balanced between Here's legs on the tank. Rodger-dodger could say, "do it to it," "piss on it," and "mutherfukker," which everyone thought was pretty good for a two-year-old kid.

Nina said, "Hey, Abel. Indian's uptight with you," as she walked past.

"I know."

She pulled a pack of cigarettes from a coat on the floor, checked to see what Here was doing, then went back into the kitchen where Linda and Rosa were drinking beer, smoking cigs, waiting for their men to get drunk enough to go home to bed.

Indian was saying, "Now maybe we'll think about an initiation." He saw me standing by the door and said, "Where you been, Abel," in his coldest voice.

I waited until he was standing directly in front of me, hands on his hips, wine-red eyes boring into my head, before I said, "Sorry, man. I been fucked up."

His expression didn't change. His eyes didn't move from my own. Thirty seconds went by. Then he put his hand on my shoulder and nodded. "Let's talk," he said, steering me outside.

We sat on the steps and Indian spit into the yard. "What's buggin you, Abel? You ain't been your ole self for a long time now. What's got you screwed up, man?"

I tried to think of a good way of putting it down—a way of saying it that would conform to the rules—and I couldn't. I kicked my boot against the step and shook my head. "I don't know, man. I don't know. I don't think I can make it with the club any more."

Indian pulled his mustache. "How come?" His voice totally cool, emotionless and flat. He's got it down pat. He's been doing it a long time.

I looked at my boots. No help there. How do you tell your hard friend that you're tired of playing his game? That you've been faking it? How do you tell your old barbarian brother that you want to talk to God? How do you tell him that you want to save your soul and the soul of man?

"I don't know, Indian. I mean . . . it's like . . . well, I mean . . . you're my brothers, the only brothers I've got, and that counts, that's . . . that counts, man . . . but I'm just gettin tired. Y'know? It's not makin any sense anymore. Fuckin around an gettin screwed up all the time an hasslin people an gettin hassled back an goin to jail an all that shit. For what? I just think maybe there's somethin else . . ." left hanging because it's no good—it's not coming across.

Indian lit a cigarette and flipped the match into the dirt next to Fat Richie's bike. "Like what?" Still cool. Still waiting.

"I don't know. I wanna find out."

Indian stood up and blew smoke from his nose. He put his eyes on the rooftops, then rolled them down the street, following a big truck that was rumbling toward the dump. "There's nuthin else, man," serious and soft. "I been a lotta things, but all that time I was just waitin to be an outlaw. Just waitin to get right here. There *ain't* nuthin else. There's just us . . . an everybody else out there wishin they was us an not havin the guts to do it." How do you tell people? How do you tell people that both of their imagined alternatives are actually the same and don't really matter in the first place because there's something much bigger? You don't tell them. You say something that they can understand, like, "I'm just tired of hasslin all the time, Indian."

"Everything's a hassle, man! Here at least you got brothers to help you hassle." A new thought struck him. "You want to be a *citizen*?" He made "citizen" sound like "maggot." Indian spit again and pushed the hair out of his eyes. "You wanna work your ass off behind some fuckin desk, or drivin a rig for some rich shit head, an watch television for kicks an maybe have a beer at night? *Nobody* wants to be no fat-assed, straight fucker citizen! Not even the *citizens . . . especially* not the citizens! They live like cows an die like cows. They get their rocks off by watchin movies about people doin the shit they ain't got the fuckin guts to try. Whatta they got, man? They got *nuthin*! They got bills an ulcers an fat dumb wives that can't fuck for shit an houses that they ain't even allowed to mess up when they feel like it an a whole fuckin lotta *crap*!"

"I know that, man . . ."

"Well then *what*? This is *it*, man. This is the best thing that ever happened to any of us. We're outlaws, man! That means we're the freest fuckin people on the earth! We can do or say anything we damn well wanna, an we got brothers to back us up. Not just *friends*, man. Not just people you bought off. *Brothers*! There ain't a dude in that house there that wouldn't take on fifty fuckers if they was to jump your ass. It don't make no difference if you're right or wrong. Your brothers'll back you. You wanna piece a ass? Any time a the day'r night, you got Mama Bev. You wanna ole lady? Somebody to sleep with? We got all kindsa good-people-chicks followin us around just hot to trot. You wanna *place* to sleep? You got it, man. You wanna bike, or a shirt, or somethin done? You got brothers to help you get it. You hear what I'm saying, man? What else you want?"

Nothing I can tell you about, Indian. You don't have a word for it. You won't be able to hear it. But you don't say this to the President of the Night Riders, even if he's your long-time brother, so I said, "I got some things I wanna learn. I've gotta find out some things."

Indian looked at me hard—singed my eyes with his own—then dropped his gaze to the ground. He nodded his head. "You wanna be a full-time college boy, is that it?"

"No, man . . ."

"I been that route. You know that? You know I been to college?"

"No. I didn't know that."

"No lie, man. I went for a whole fuckin semester. Outta the army an into college on the uncle-sam-loves-all-you-dumb-ass-ex-GI plan. I quit. I quit cuz they was after my brain. I thought you was gonna make it through hip, but I guess they got to your head, man. I thought you tole me you didn't even wanna go."

"I don't. That isn't it."

"Well *what* then?"

"I don't know! I can't explain, Indian! I just wanna find somethin out!"

Indian pinched out his cigarette. Something I'd been trying to put across had reached him or he would have pinched me out as well. "Okay, man. We got no chains on ya."

Silence . . . while I felt bad. The outlaws were, as Indian said, the best and most loyal friends I'd ever had. Like the war-buddies veterans are forever telling you about in bars over nostalgic beers.

Crass, foul-mouthed and dirty, but loyal to their brothers who fought beside them. A loyalty and feeling of brotherhood that doesn't exist in the business world, in the world of respectable society, in the straight world.

"It's not that I don't feel for the club no more, Indian. It's just . . . things aren't the same with me now."

"I'm hip, man. It's okay. I mean it. Don't hang up your colors yet. Think about it for a while." He kicked my leg with the side of his boot and started up the steps. "Now let's start the meetin."

And that was pretty much the end of my outlaw bike rider thing. Of course it wasn't nearly as clean a break as I've summed it up to be, nor did it happen in one night. But for the sake of the narrative, to avoid overlapping, unrelated scenes, let this symbolize the end of a period of my life and thoughts. The end of a role.

I lost the will to raise hell for the fun of raising hell. When that happens, there's nothing to do but quit. When I did, I also gave up my armor and lost the protection of the fear attached to the diamond one-percenter patch. When I took it off and tried to love everybody instead of kicking the crap out of them, I lost the citizens' "respect." They no longer gave me fast service in stores, smiled nice or said "Yessir" when I spoke to them, or dropped their eyes when I looked in their direction. With nothing to fear from me, no chance of my pushing their face in, they began to call me a faggot for wearing my hair long, an idiot for smiling too much, and a coward for not wanting to fight them anymore. I pulled validation and strength from visions of ancient gladiators turned Christian, and understood just how rough it must have been for them to turn the other cheek.

A week later, I quit college. A hard decision, because I'd prepared for college all my life. There'd never been any real question about whether or not I'd go to college or about its importance. Everyone who wanted to make it went to college. But now I saw it as a game I couldn't afford to play any longer. I wanted to start living something real. Tired of preparing for a nebulous future, I wanted to live and learn about Now.

CHAPTER SEVEN – THE EARLY ACID-EATERS. A CATALOGUE OF THE PLAYERS.

With false confidence and hungry curiosity born of time-fade, I took a second acid trip. This one with Baxtor and Brian Kelly, an old friend from Los Gatos who went to college and then went insane about the same time I did. My second trip was as astounding, possibly more ego-wilting, and definitely more frightening than my first because I thought I was prepared for it and was, therefore, totally unprepared for it—armed with a creaky wheelbarrow full of crazy dated charts and preconceptions. In Brian's old rattling clunk, we drove through San Jose, the three of us completely spaced, utterly lost—twisted buildings dancing, windows leering, street buckling, car shrinking, us shrinking, kaleidoscope fractured clear-light street lamps and traffic-control signs—my face pressed against the windshield, seeing cartoon mushrooms and impossible Wonderland scenes. "Whooo! Man, can you *see* to drive?"

"No," admitted Brian, looking like a frantic Troll clutching the huge steering-wheel.

"Whater we searching for?" I asked, really scared, trying to remember how and when it started.

"Mexico!" shouted Baxtor. He said *Mexico* at regular intervals all night. The only word we could get out of him.

"Hold tight," said Brian. "It's gonna take all three of us to guide this ship in."

We did big circles around the town for years, (our time) for hours, (clock time) stopped once at a gas station that siphoned off brain cells, fueled up and drove off to circle some more, going nowhere, just driving because that's what we were doing when the acid came on so that was the last thing any of us could remember ever having done, and we drove all night until the sun started to rise and we recognized the street that led to my apartment.

An amazing experience, most of which had to be forgotten before I could find my way back down. When I did, I was ready to listen. I wanted to listen to everything. The world was bigger than ever and microscopic compared to a square inch of inner space. Julia smiled encouragement. Things were going to be beautiful.

It was a time of swiftly made, sincerely close, serious friendships. The early acid-eaters huddled together apart from the hostile world of the uninitiated; those who'd never trembled and freaked on the swaying tightrope of thin-line sanity, crying for all of mankind and the futility of ridiculously short birth-to-death life; those who'd never crumbled and melted under powerful, ego-killing doses of questionably pure chemicals to lie on cheap apartment floors confessing and repenting personal failures and the misunderstandings and selfishness of all humanity, renouncing, after long painful battles, all games and, therefore, all claim to life as a separate entity, dying at last in a nova-flash of micro-second enlightenment and total love beyond emotional love, to be reborn again instantly, but only after countless Eternities as one with the Void, discovering to your joy, to your amazement, to your flickering sadness, that the world and the I and the talk and the task still remained and you'd been granted or cursed with one more chance—one more time around.

And the beauty! The unfathomable *beauty* and joy that was *right there*, all around, everywhere, just waiting to be seen and appreciated. The acid freaks tried to tell people, and they failed miserably. It had to be seen and felt to be *believed*, to be understood.

And those who saw it believed, and understood or came close to understanding, and it changed them. It changed them noticeably. They became freaks.

Because it was new and incredible and vast, and because there was only a small number of freaks around and no way or reason to weekend fake it in those great early days, we recognized and rejoiced in the discovery of fellow tribesmen almost immediately upon meeting eyes—in LA, in Big Sur, in Berkeley, in San Francisco, in unknown small towns—and we accepted them instantly on the common bond of having shared the acid test.

You'd meet a guy, or a guy and his chick on the road hitch-hiking, or just wandering through Big Sur or Golden Gate Park or Downtown-Anywhere, maybe the guy would have long hair, the chick wearing beads and a big flower, both of them wearing new eyes, maybe they'd be barefoot in the rain, or just walking along smiling—but you'd know. Your eyes would meet and you'd know. The Negroes understand this. In all their sadness and frustration and humiliation, they have this over the lonely white-man. Honkies are sadder and more alone than anything else on the earth. And they don't know it, which is four times sadder.

It was great, truly great to come on to a stranger with, "Hey man, what's happening?"

"Just groovin through. What's the scene like here?"

"Cool. The heat's doin its thing but it's not too tight. Where you from?"

And it could be Sacramento or Nevada or Colorado—somewhere. It didn't matter. We were all part of the same thing. It was a fine flash to hear about tribes springing up all over the country.

"Yeah? What's happening there?"

"We got things goin. It's catchin on. You got a cigarette?"

"Got the makins. Wanna roll one?"

"Great. Hey, I got a joint. Is there someplace we can go?"

Comfortable, easy, you were old friends, although you'd never met. When people started getting busted after turning on with unknown "hippies," and when long-haired, smiling cops began to appear, then we all became more paranoid and suspicious, and grew more clannish and sullen with strangers. But at first, the scene was open and free and friendly. There was a beautiful flash to meeting another acid freak. It reminded you that you were part of something big.

A cyclone, a torrent of divergent but somehow unified ideas, and strange people, and lost people, and ecstatic people, and honestly-trying-to-be-honest people, and beautiful people, and good people, bound together by a glimpse or a promise of "The Peace." Bound by visions of perfect existences. No "psychedelic" music yet. No magazine coverage of "The Terrifying Nightmare Drug, LSD." No pictorials on "A Day in the Life of A Hippie." Bound only by visions passed through personal contact. A glorious soul-secret. The beginning of something big and fine.

Frank Baxtor (called "Frank" only by his chicks, and "Baxtor" by everyone else) became one of my closest friends following my break with the Night Riders. At twenty-three, he was already an ex-gambler, ex-drunk, ex-conman, ex-student-body-President who'd dropped out of Cal at Berkeley twice (as a straight-A philosophy major) to eat acid, smoke weed, wander beaches and sit around quickly-found and soon-left girlfriends' cabins and apartments, trying to unravel the mysteries of the cosmos and himself, while unwinding and hopelessly knotting the ropes of bullshit he'd wrapped and people had wrapped around him.

Months before I met him, when he'd first begun to take acid (because he "liked weed and bennies") as a self-centered, very cool and calculating card-shark-philosophy-student, he'd enjoyed colorful, controlled, ecstasy-sampling, no-worry trips, rambling around the beaches and forests of LA and Big Sur with his college roommate, Bill Preston, laughing at everything and vowing to take acid at least twice a week for the rest of his life.

He gave it a good try, but, after four beautiful months of grace, he stumbled upon the dangerous and uncomfortable path of deep thought and introspection, probably because his immense, well-fortified ego had slowly degenerated to a point where it was still huge and armored and fighting hard for its perpetuation, but no longer invulnerable, and he began to have outwardly catatonic, inwardly shrieking, insane, end-of-the-world, unfathomably intricate and detailed (the fault of his brilliant and lightning-fast, always seven steps ahead of itself mind), science fiction, escape-proof, pathetic experiences, which would leave him flat on his back, refusing to connect with anything for fear of a cosmic burn, staring at the ceiling with his teeth clenched for sometimes three or four days, talking to no one, eating nothing—far away, trying hard to get back.

And he always found his way pretty close to back. He'd crawl out of his room after one of his dark recovery periods, suddenly appear at someone's house, nod his head and smile at the questions, say, "Big egos die hard. That's just the way it is. I'm sorry. Believe me, I'm sorry. If I alone, as I suspect, am holding the collective conscious to the bullshit of routine reality, then I would think that someone would be kind enough to give me at least a hint as to exactly what it is that I'm expected to do. Op-op—I know . . . I know! Against the rules to ask. Yes."

Then he would immediately find and eat more acid, repeating the mind-shattering experience "one more time" and then one more time, convinced (or possibly simply praying) that one more trip would show him the Ultimate Truth and the Exit and free him from the elaborate labyrinth that he'd wound his way into—while his friends shook their heads or laughed (depending on how close to the thing they were standing) and gave him useless tips on the proper way to break through, and everyone who knew him began to refer to Baxter as "Poor Baxter" . . . even Baxter.

He did strange things like taking off all his clothes to wait bare and expectant for a satori when people Dylan-quoted to him, "Even the President of the United States sometimes must haveta stand naked." He didn't do it to blow minds. He did it because he actually thought people were trying to tell him something that would help him out.

If someone did something he didn't approve of, or if too many things went wrong, or if scenes got out of hand, he'd say in an authoritative voice, "Baxter humbly but wisely vetoes this entire section of the film. We shall take it from . . . ohhh, about scene 3,398,278," and then he'd go on about his business with whatever displeased him neatly spliced out of the tapes. He told me once, however, that everything he spliced out simply fell into the wastepaper basket of his mind and was, therefore, never really lost.

Baxter kept his hair cut just above his shoulders, and sometimes a thick full beard would appear on his face as if by magic, overnight, and then disappear just as quickly and mysteriously. He wore a mustache that put every other mustache I'd ever seen to shame. When he combed it down over his lips (using it as "a bullshit strainer") it hid everything except a small portion of the very end of his chin. He was six-foot-three and strong as an ox, but never used physical strength on or for anything. He owned one pair of floppy old worn-out high-top shoes, two pairs of faded pants, two or three lumberjack shirts, and a light jacket that he'd found in one of his chicks' cars. Besides a huge pile of books that he stored at his mother's house, that was the extent of his personal belongings. He never had a wallet—seldom had any money to put in one. He carried his driver's license and draft card (1-Y due to an injury to both knees) in a little plastic bag in his back pocket.

It was great to watch Baxter move. He walked like he was on stilts made out of springs, big strides, arms swinging, his light brown hair opening and closing like an umbrella over his head.

Baxtor was well-read and his powers of retention were incredible. He could supply on command information (which, when checked out, was always correct) concerning nearly any given subject. He considered it a useless gift, and pointed out that a parrot or a tape-recorder could do the same thing.

"Games. So many games," he used to say, and then, "However, one must do *something* for the amusement of the cosmos. Otherwise, there are the inevitable *burns*, which are frightening, not to mention painful."

He also said, "Freaks. The psychedelics have spawned cults of freaks. You realize, of course, that the society won't stand for it. They're nearsighted fools if they do. It is wisely prohibited for individuals in highly technological and complex civilizations to lift the reality curtain and gaze upon the naked beyond. Think what would happen to the bees! Once this is done, the individual sees that the social-game and the civilization-game actually have no goals . . . no ultimate goals that is. They're only guide-lines for the contest . . . to make things appear to move in an orderly fashion . . . to give the ego something to do besides work on the self-defeating problem of itself. Forever discontent with (being aware of) the absurdity and energy waste of horizontal movement, the frustrated (and frustration breeds revolution, friends), the idealistic individual turns away from the acceptable patterns of society and searches for the tempting 'Something more,' contributing from that moment on absolutely nothing of value to the perpetuation of the society or civilization game, which, therefore, makes this individual utterly useless in the eyes of any right-thinking, hard-working, American (or any other —an) dreamer, which means, when all is said and done, that he may be called quite truthfully—as we call ourselves, and as many clever law-men are beginning to call us—a freak."

Taking a double hit off the ever-present joint, rolling to his back on the floor of my apartment, holding his bare feet in the air by pinching his big toes between his thumbs and forefingers, he exhaled with a long, resonant, "Bow-shaaaaw," (Baxter's special, all-occasion way of saying bullshit), regarded his toenails carefully for several seconds, then mused happily, "I wonder where they'll put me? I hope it's warm. Not too warm. Just nice. If it's nice and warm, I'll go quite willingly." It was winter, and Baxtor hated the winter. He often stated that man's soul was at its lowest ebb during the long, gray time of rain and cold.

On a trip to Berkeley, Baxtor introduced me to his old high school buddy and one-time college roommate, Bill Preston, a math major at Cal, who, protesting, resolving, refusing to return to college every summer and then changing his mind at the last minute every September, rationalizing all the way, and facing seemingly impossible odds such as a twenty-five joint per day weed habit, a reoccurring crystal habit, a healthy acid appetite, and friends who hated to see him bring himself down by studying, had made it to his senior year with only one spring-semester drop-out spent reteaching himself how to pass for sane.

I dug Preston instantly. He wore faded old cord pants, frayed but clean (though unironed) white shirts under gray, tan or green V-necked sweaters—engineer's boots for a while, and then (in his rustic period) desert boots. He rode a motorcycle for a time, with his blond and sometimes bearded head encased in a shiny white crack-hat, which, I often told him, "only cuts down on a bike rider's freedom, and also shows an unheroic concern for life," to which he would reply, standing back and regarding me through narrowed eyes, "Ah yes, the old outlaw *sickle* rider raises his hideous head," nodding mock-seriously and examining his helmet. "It *is* a rather chicken-shit thing to do, I would suppose. Especially when I realize that were I to actually collide with any worthy object while piloting that ridiculous machine, or even like just sort of fall off on the freeway or something, I would undoubtedly fracture every bone in my fucking body, and if anything, be thoroughly pissed off at myself for being asinine enough to tuck my fucking *head* in a fiber-glass *egg*," holding the helmet at arm's length and bobbing it along on an imaginary head, speaking now as if to himself, "Although, the egg concept is good. Riding around with your head inside an egg. That is pretty fucking *nice*. No wonder people wear these things. There's a lot of security attached to sticking your head inside a fucking egg." And he would, of course, go right on wearing the helmet, which typified Preston's actions on all levels fairly accurately.

Preston was (save one dark period) perhaps the most quick-minded and articulate member of our tribe. Rivaling and, upon occasion, even surpassing the astounding Baxtor, who would often sit to one side and play straight-man to Preston when the two appeared together at a sizable gathering of the tribe.

Preston made grand, sweeping, theatrical gestures with his arms, his whole body, when he spoke. The more stoned he got, the grander his gestures became. As an evening or day wore on and more and more joints dwindled to ash between his fingers, he would wave his arms like a flagman or clutch his head with both hands, arch his back and say, "Can you *believe* it? Can you fucking *imagine*?" when something said or seen struck him as being too much to hold.

He would throw himself heavily and sprawl grotesquely on a handy sofa or on a bed if one was available (even if it was occupied by someone's chick), on the floor or just wherever he happened to land when he finally reached the end of his endurance and felt like sleeping. No one and no thing could wake Preston up when he was really into sleeping.

Preston had a novel way of saying the (extremely popular at the time, second only to "bullshit") expressions "fuck" and "fucking." Rather than slurring out "fug" or "fok" or "fuckin," as it was usually said and heard, he enunciated carefully, like a kid who'd just got hip to the word, saying, "Fuck-ing," at every possible occasion and with undiminishing satisfaction. He had a great fondness for the sound, tacking its four-letter form onto the beginning of countless, by themselves, simple little words such as bag, head, and dog, and onto the end of others like pig, mind, and ape, greatly extending their meaning and coloring his speech with imaginative and seemingly endless variations of the image-evoking expression.

He wore his hair long and always erratic—for a week or so, held away from his face by a headband until it broke and fell into the ocean while he was on acid, evidently showing him something about headbands that kept him from ever putting one on his head again. At home in Berkeley, he took time to comb his hair exactly right, standing in front of a mirror, combing and re-combing until it conformed to whatever he had in mind, then he'd put the comb away and shake his head like a wet dog, jump up and down several times, look in the mirror and walk away running his fingers backwards through his hair in case any of it was still in place.

Preston smoked, as I have mentioned, unbelievable quantities of weed, frightening newly-turned-on visitors by supplying them with an unending flow of joints until they refused to smoke any more (which meant that he'd skip them for that round, handing it to them again within seconds) or until they passed out and wouldn't respond to his nudges and kicks. He would drive fifty miles to buy a lid if he felt that he was in danger of running out, and never went anywhere without a sizable stash on him or stuck in a special box neatly hand-lettered, "WEED," which he kept in the glove compartment of his VW bus.

He once drove around for two weeks with two entire keys under the seat, six lovingly cultivated female weed plants in a wooden flat in back, his weed box full of rolled joints in three different types of papers (licorice, yellow rice-paper and white rice—for street use), five caps of acid, a little bottle of Librium and Thorazine, a dime-paper of crystal, a square-lump gram of hash, and a black lump of opium in an ornate, blue bottle, clearly marked, "OPIUM."

To celebrate a key he bought after a long hassle in the middle of a tight-time, Preston rolled a huge weed cigar, bigger than the fattest, most outlandish old-man tobacco cigar, and sat contentedly puffing and smiling on it for nearly an hour, while happily breaking up and cleaning the brick. Everyone else in the area was mashing seeds and grinding stems and sweeping under rugs to put together sad little half-lint, cut with tea, emaciated joints in the grip of the terrible weed famine.

When I think of Preston, I always see him as I did one perfect August night at the hot springs, lying totally submerged, with the exception of his beaming head, in the steaming, sulphur-water-filled, giant stone tub, a joint glowing merrily between his grin-exposed teeth, gazing in complete satisfaction and contentment at the Big Sur black night studded with balls of white-light star, saying in a soul-felt sigh, "Ahhhhhh . . . *this* is my double nut. Pax. The world is good." Big Sur and weed were his two most faithfully worshiped and never fading true loves.

One summer, he devotedly labored to forever incorporate the two by raising young weed plants from seed until they were "strong enough to face the cruel reality of a world that has the audacity, not to mention the low-level of reverence, to forbid, under penalty of being jerked out by the *roots*, the existence of the sacred marijuana plant." He hiked all around the beautiful Sur forests, transplanting his pampered sacrament flowers, hoping that they would, as he told us, "tune in to the vibrations of Sur and grow utterly *huge*, with fat paisley flowers hanging maybe seven feet off the ground, and leaves the size of elephant ears." Considering it thoughtfully, "Or even the size of tobacco leaves. That'd be all right. As a matter of fact, that would be *nice*! Can you *imagine*? You tramp into the forest and walk up to this prehistoric, monster weed plant and pull off a leaf, roll it up, hold it out in the sun for a few seconds to kind of dry it out a little, then torch the fucker up and stroll on to the next plant. And if the fucking *bees* screw around with them, they'll start popping up all over! *Now* I can dig old John Appleseed's trip."

He carried water to the young plants for months, stalking out of the trees once to where Beau Faulkner and I had made a camp, scowling and mad, saying, "Some swine-nose-pig-fuck stepped on one of my weed plants. How could anyone *be* such a fuckhead? If you're in Big Sur, you ought to fucking recognize a weed plant!"

He had to sacrifice and smoke all of his surviving plants during a hard autumn spent in the forest. Sitting inside a fire-gutted ancient redwood, ocean fog swirling all around us, listening to a little creek polish rocks, I smoked a tarnished brass pipeful of Preston's harvest, uncured, sun-dried, tiny yellow stems and roots and all, and it was truly beautiful weed. It made us realize how fine weed could be if we were able to grow our own with love, for the sole purpose of smoking it and getting high and digging the vast world, instead of having to buy the leftovers that Mexican or American crooks threw together to sell to Yankee dope addicts.

Preston hated all cops with a passion. "Scourge of the earth," he called them. "What sort of a ruined mind would want to be a fuckbag cop?" He explained that on any reasonable scale of values, cops were always at the very bottom.

"Down there with pimps and winos," I agreed.

"That's rather unkind," said Preston. "A pimp merely fills a need that the government sees fit to ignore. And a cop is far, *far* below a wino. A wino is a relatively *desirable* person in comparison with a cop. What does a wino do to bug anybody? A wino just drinks wine and tries to stay out of trouble and out of the way. But a cop! A cop *has* to be warped. I mean, they even ride around in a classic hell-world, right out of the Book of The Dead! The *colors* . . . black and stark white. The *sounds* . . . wailing sirens and moaning, garbled voices over their radios. The *sights* . . . flashing red lights, smoke from the exhaust and from their cigars. Guns and clubs everywhere. It all fits! The hell-world. The world of the psychotics. Cops are doomed by their own hand. They should *pray* for a rebirth as a wino."

Much of this hatred sprang from early encounters with a fat, gross, bigoted, small-town cop who constantly rousted Preston as a kid, telling him, "All right now, punk, we got an umbrella up your smart little ass. All we gotta do is open it, and we can make you mighty uncomfortable, son," demanding that Preston confess to doing things he'd never done, showing him the jail and saying, "We got a special cell for wise-ass punks in there."

Preston never forgot and never forgave this cop, and he never met one who brightened up his image of the police.

A beautiful dark-eyed, black-haired, quiet, intelligent, part American-Indian girl named Sharon was Preston's chick. She was gentle, easy to be with, faithful to utterly undeserving Preston, and a magnificent soul-mate for anyone lucky enough to attract her. I believe Preston sincerely loved her, although he took great pains to conceal the fact and never talked about her unless it was to grumble about some hassle she'd caused. They lived together off and on for years and, as I write this, still do—more off than on, however.

Preston ran at full speed always and all ways. Journeying from his shared-sporadically-with-Sharon-cottage in Berkeley to Sur to Mexico to New York where he was born, back to Berkeley and from there back to Sur and back to Mexico again in his rattle-putt-clanky VW bus, bringing back dried devil fish, saying, "Look at that *face*!" dangling the creepy shriveled dead ray before our eyes, "Ah, devil fish indeed!"

Preston and Baxtor became my contemporary intellectual leaders. I looked to them for great things.

It was Preston who, in search of acid in The City, took me to meet Lyla, the world's star crystal freak. With a kind smile she told Preston that she just happened to have a great connection for some totally pure and truly beautiful acid. All we had to do was take her to the Fillmore and pick it up.

Four hours, seventy miles, and an uncountable number of barren stops later, we bid the still smiling Lyla goodbye and drove away acidless. It turned out that Lyla had been mad at Preston for somethingerother and had made him drive all over the City in search of non-existent acid as a form of punishment.

Lyla ran endless, elaborate, complicated games that no one understood (including, probably, Lyla). But, if you could ignore that, she was fun to talk to and good to have around—provided you weren't on acid and somehow involved in one of her intricate games. She'd been to college for a while, had lived in New York for a while, had whored around for a while, had balled Preston, Baxtor and several others for a while in "the old days" before I fell into the scene. She was living with Barry Larkin when I met her.

Lyla's full name was Lyla Barbara Spede, and she lived up to her name far better than most of today's Masons or Smiths. She once took some insane dose of speed, got wired into action, cleaned the shower, then the bathtub, then the tile around the doors, then the window sills, the sink, the toilet, and finally the entire bathroom clear into the kitchen with a piece of hand soap and a toothbrush. She really dug speed. No one could stay around her for any length of time without picking up the habit. She was the Typhoid Mary of crystal.

Lyla also ate any other kind of pill she could get hold of—mixing them all up, speed and downers and all imaginable variations, popping whole handfuls into her mouth or putting them in solution and shooting up to flash out and then lay around sick for days, then fading back in to make lists and try to remember exactly how much of what she'd taken so she'd be able to do it again.

On a summer night, with everybody gathered at Zad's shack, spaced behind acid or at least vast quantities of weed, after everyone else was preparing or hoping to drop off and come down, Lyla decided that she wanted a magical seventh hit of crystal and another of acid. She wanted to take it with Barry who was, as was often the case by this time of the morning, in a death-like stupor—six feet into gone.

Barry was an old friend of both Baxtor and Preston. He'd spent a good bit of his school days driving ancient automobiles off cliffs, into trees, walls, other vehicles and such, every month like clock work. He was never hurt and the automobiles were never salvageable.

For one solid year of high school Barry didn't say a single word to anyone. Not teachers or fellow students or his parents or the doctors they ran on him in squads. Everyone thought he was retarded and his parents were about to send him to a special school when he surprised them by saying that he'd just as soon they didn't, and started talking to people again. He explained that for that particular year he'd had nothing to say to anyone. Baxtor told me that shortly before I met Barry he had talked non-stop for months, holding long discussions with Roy Cage (who comes later) in which they resolved all the questions of the universe and discovered that they were actually the two halves of a schizophrenic god who, once united, would be Him—God. But when I met Barry he was quiet and kind of withdrawn, having spent three long months praying and weeping in a bare, one room cabin, hallucinating bullets ripping through the door and the walls, afraid to smoke a cigarette for fear it would get him high, writing in a diary he tried to keep, scrawling with a pencil stub across the pages and onto the top of a barrel he used for a table and even on the walls when the whole cabin became part of the diary, writing things like, "its too big its too big its too big i cant keep it all in place much longer the universe mind is too big to keep in order and i must get some rest," until he finally saw something that he never told anyone about, walked out of the cabin as a pale, greenish, sunken-eyed, bearded, whispering skeleton, drove his seatless, hoodless, windshieldless '49 Studebaker to Lyla's apartment and rejoined the tribe.

In happier times he leapt from impossibly high, dangerous places into freezing winter ocean for whatever small change his friends could scrape up and agree to pay him for the spectacle. "Come on, Barry. A quarter."

"Nope. Nothing under a half dollar."

"Well we only have a quarter."

"It's not enough."

"A quarter and a joint—two joints?"

"Awright." A deep breath . . . arms back . . . arms forward . . . arms back . . . leap . . . "wow" . . . splash, far below, and then wait for the head to appear . . . no head . . . "Ah yes, there he is. He made it again. Whatta jump. We gotta find a higher place."

Barry was good at running amok . . .

"What were you doin outside naked?"

"Running amok."

"Oh. Well, the neighbors called to complain."

And he was good at falling into a "Death-Sleep" halfway through any evening that he wasn't wired on speed. He'd sit like an old drunk, with his head on his arms, curly reddish hair spilling over his wrists and onto the table or chair or whatever he'd crashed on, responding to nothing. You could holler in his ear, pound him on the back, shake him, leave and come back and he'd still be there . . . dead. He responded to nothing . . . except . . . a burning joint. Whether out of a sense of duty, force of habit, conditioning so powerful that it was the last thing to go, or out of a genuine craving for weed, magically, mysteriously and *still* unexplained, when a lit joint passed, no matter how quietly (and we experimented), his hand would quiver with an unearthly life of its own, suddenly dart out and snag the joint, convey it to the slowly turning but still reclining and eye-shut head . . . joint reaching its destination . . . mouth already in position . . . quick intake of breath . . . joint passed to the right (always to his right) and Barry continued to be dead. If you were really hard up for a laugh, you could play a game with Barry and try to fool him with straight cigarettes (which he never fell for) or tobacco rolled in wheat-straw to look like a joint (which he sometimes accepted).

On the summer night I'd begun to tell about while introducing Lyla, Barry was well into his death-sleep. Lyla watched him with mounting frustration, shook him . . . nothing, kicked him . . . nothing, so she took out her set of works, mixed up a dime paper of crink, filled the dropper and began to tie Barry off so she could hit him with the crystal in order to wake him up before she hit him with the acid. In a way, it was the humane thing to do—much softer than simply waking him up with a jab of acid. Those who were watching this action and were still capable of reaction felt, however, that it would be better to let Barry sleep. They told Lyla to let him alone. She fumed, but had to be content with hitting herself up with just the crink, then rapping for hours to Brian about the brain-rotting and cell-destroying properties of LSD for the benefit of those in the room who were on it.

Lyla had brown hair and green eyes and was not at all bad to look at—even beautiful at times. I always felt that she had plans and goals no one else knew about.

Lyla, Barry, Preston, and Baxtor were all linked in one way or another with Zad who, as I've already mentioned, sold me my first cap of acid. With the exception of Lyla, the whole crew had been drinking-buddies as far back as high school.

Zad's parents had named him Tounouse Lawrence Zad, so

everyone called him Zad or The Mad Arab. When I first met him, he was a semester away from a degree in business administration, and maintaining the scene nicely. The training must've come in handy because he was a successful independent dope dealer and generally had merchandise when no one else did.

Zad ate only macrobiotic food after he read a book that convinced him he'd very nearly poisoned himself by consuming hidden chemicals. He lectured for hours on the horrors of chemicals, neatly ignoring the fact that LSD, DMT, DET and most of the other drugs he ingested at a fantastic rate were also chemicals. But that was part of the beauty of Zad—pulling for purity and truth, tied to flesh and self.

Like a holy far-eastern hermit, (or a crazy western hermit, depending upon how you look at it) Zad had thick, jet-black hair that hung over his shoulders and down his back, an even blacker beard that was trimmed when it got in his way, an Arabian face, olive complexion, and completely mad eyes. In Zad's eyes I was to see a reflection of an unknown Buddha upon two occasions.

Zad's chick was a little doll-sized blonde named Nancy Kitchner. She worked as a secretary to support herself and Zad, lived with him in a tight apartment, then a cabin, then a two-room shack, then a VW bus, (when they were both taking too much acid to work)—would eventually marry him, returning to her parents' house long enough to bear Zad's daughter, then back to the bus after a short stay at a Zen commune.

For a month or two Zad and Nancy lived in the hills with a guy on parole named Bob Levin. When Zad brought him over to my apartment and introduced him as "Big Daddy Bob" it was the beginning of a great friendship. I shook his hand and said, "Good to know ya, Bob," then handed him a fat joint. He lit it and turned the whole thing to ash with one huge unbelievable toke—just a tiny roach left between his fingernails.

I thought, "now there stands a true weed-smoker," as I rolled another joint for me and Zad.

Bob was before our time and still happening. He was ageless. Sometimes you'd swear he was forty-eight, and sometimes he couldn't have been older than twenty-two.

An ex-con who'd done three years for possession of nine marijuana seeds, Bob was big and good-natured, soft-spoken, often unpredictable, however, and prone to "strange words and actions" such as reciting a string of numbers when he knocked on your door late at night.

"Who is it?" you'd ask, fogged and suspicious.

From the other side of the door, "Eighteen twenty six one oh three six twenty five minus seventeen oh five five eleven."

And you'd go through nine thousand changes wondering what it all meant . . . which is probably why he did it.

Bob sometimes gave out homey little pieces of advice about how to be better people, which everyone ignored and probably shouldn't have. He was famous for rushing to work in the morning, drinking a glass of chocolate milk with one hand while hitting his wake-up crystal with the other, all in one smooth operation, tied off by his strange little quiet seventeen-year-old wife Sally—gulp, jab, gulp, pinch the bulb, pull it out, glug—through the front door at a dog trot, into his truck and down the road to the gas station.

Christmas came and Bob played Santa for all of us, handing out little gift-wrapped lids of weed in front of his skinny bent Christmas tree. "For you, Zad. Merry Christmas. And for you, Nancy. Merry, merry Christmas. And for . . ." A Santa in light green shades, stoned and quietly jolly, playing Christmas carols on his guitar after midnight, telling us stories (Preston called them "Levin Pen-stories") around the fire—stories about his three years in prison where he'd known a dude who'd practiced every night for seven years until he was able to perform fellatio on himself. Then stories about Christmas in jail, and how they ate Vicks inhalers to get ripped.

Later that night, or rather, early that morning, Christmas Day, I sat by the fireplace coals all tired and happy, and I talked to Bob about Christ and said that I'd only learned to dig what He was putting down in the last year or so. And Bob said yes, and that so few people ever really did, and that Jesus was one of the great Buddhas, and there was soon to be another one, if He wasn't already here and just not being listened to.

Bob had a dog called Christannabella (who everyone but Bob called Annie) and perhaps thirty cats around the house, one or two of them always in his arms or on his shoulder. He loved animals and the outdoors and trees and creeks and especially high mountains. He always said (and I always knew) that they'd never get him back in a cell.

Not more than a week or so after that first acid Christmas, Beau Faulkner, a long-time friend who I'd lost touch with during The Night Rider period, appeared at my door dressed in the 1800s semi-Western outfit he'd adopted as standard dress. He came in without a word, but I knew instantly what he'd been up to. His straight brown hair had grown to touch his shoulders and he twisted a waxed whip mustache like Simon Legree. He was attending an art college in Oakland but assured me that it was, "just until the revolution." He turned out fine pottery and several fair canvases while he waited.

Beau came from a restless, violent, hell-raising, pistol-carrying scene, almost accidentally into the psychedelics and abruptly into a sincere love thing. It was hard on him. But then, it was hard on most of us. We'd all been squeezed out of some sort of heavy role.

In a rare moment, with his nearly perfect guard down, Beau told me of the time he spent in hell-worlds struggling to kill the hostility and distrust he felt for the citizens, for the world in general, and of the peace and beauty he'd seen and tried to embrace, and of the tight times he'd teetered on the brink of bottomless, endless insanity, praying for the return of even a token semblance of stability so he could try harder to make it by.

And there were perhaps a hundred, probably three hundred others who flashed in and then out of the scene with stories and ideas and fantasies and hope, each with a lifetime behind the Now in which I met them.

Great times. Sad times and confused times and painful times of not enough time and misunderstanding and working out personal hangups, but beautiful times. Salvation was just around the comer. Everything was soon to be all right now that so many people had discovered the key to *where it was all at*.

"You mean, we really know where it's at now?" I asked Ted one cold bright winter night.

"Yup. This is where it's at, man," he assured me.

"You mean, this is *really* where it's all *at*?"

"True as true. This is what's happening, man. Now we just gotta hold tight an wait for the others to catch up."

"Yeah . . . but this isn't where it's really all *at*—I mean, *finally* . . . I mean, *ultimately* . . . enlightenment and like that."

"Well no. But this is the *road*. This is the beginning. This is where that's all at, and we're on our way."

"Great! That's really great, cuz that's what I want. A road. A path. Just a road to somewhere. Just some assurance that this is all going somewhere that makes a difference."

"Mmhmm, this is it, Abel. This is what you've been looking for. This is what we've all been looking for."

CHAPTER EIGHT – THE QUICK DEATH OF JULIA CAIN

Even while I sat engrossed in long dialogues, monologues or shouted rambling verbal circuses led by Preston or Baxter or some mad person I'd only just met from The City or Berkeley or LA or just back from Europe or New York, Julia was always somewhere in my mind. I saw her as The New Woman—spring-colored beautiful. I saw myself as one of The New Men, trying to see the Truth, starting all over again from ground-floor basic, willing to learn from all life—a pioneer, leading the way, breaking trail for the many New Men soon to follow.

It seemed like the whole world was excited and aware of impending changes. Big loud discussions erupted and burned for hours and miles whenever a number of heads found themselves together. I listened to, "It's *growing*, man. It's not just California, it's the world! People are tired of the plastic bullshit conspiracy. They're starting to *think*. More an more of em are looking around an flashing on all the confusion and pointless noise. It's growing, man."

And I heard, "Sure, but so's the opposition. The money and power-people have an enforced monopoly on the current reality production. It's gonna cramp their trip if everyone checks out of the rat race, quits going to war when they're supposed to, quits buying or even producing the shiny trinkets manufactured by the money-power-people factories. They're not about to let that happen."

"They'll *have* to, if enough people get behind it!"

"Yeah, but the majority of the people won't get behind it. They've been told since birth that everything's cool and under control. They think things are all right the way they are. They don't even think anything exists beyond the TV-bullshit-money reality production."

"That's all right. As long as they let those who do think there's something else happening live outside their structure."

"But they won't, man. If freaks live outside the structure and *make* it, then it subtracts from the validity of the structure's reality. If you're playing by all the rules and going through steps a, b, c, d, e, f, g, h, i, j, k, in order to get to l, which is living, and then some freak comes along and ignores all the steps and just picks up on l, it makes your game look stupid and it probably pisses you off. That's the way straight people think.

"Besides . . . straight people have been told that freaks are a threat to their society . . . to their whole *thing*. Like Gypsies. And they're probably right."

"Okay. We have to turn em on."

"How? Somebody's been trying to do that since the beginning of Think."

"We have to keep tryin to tell em . . . show em what's happening."

"And how do you get through to them? Whatta you tell them?"

LaMer used to insist "Freaks haveta stand in the streets an holler, 'Wake up, people!' I mean, we gotta actually run into schools an business offices yellin 'Everthing'll be *oh* kay if you kind folks'll only open your eyes!' Cuz, man, we're *all* gonna haveta go through this segment of the fuckin film forever an then forever some more till people fin'ly *wake up*! Right? *Awright*! So you get hundreds a freaks doin it—stoppin straight dudes on their way to work, sayin, 'Scuze me, friend, but I represent a growin horde a madmen an I got this message.' An then you tell em that society—their in-flexible liddle ole idear of society—the society-game they're hangin on to so hard an demandin everone else dig—you tell em it'd be *pitiful* an even *laughable* if it wasn't for the fact that it hurts an warps people an is, on account a that, *hateful*!"

More than once I heard Andre's friends reply, "At which point they either bash you in the mouth for bein a Commie, or call a cop an have you busted for disturbing the peace." But Andre, who'd already done his share of mouth-bashing, was pushing for communication. "No, man!" he'd yell, shaking his head and looking exasperated. "You ain't given em *any* credit. Just cuz they never been *told* before don't mean they're all utterly *ignorant*! You gotta talk it out with em, man.

You gotta point things out to em!"

"They won't listen. You talk abut the structure as though it were a separate thing in itself. It isn't. They are the structure. They're into it . . . they're behind it all the way. They worked hard to get there—to be part of it—and they're not going to let it dissolve after they spent their whole lives feeding it."

"Hmmm. Yeah, I can hear that. Hmmm. Okay, so then I say that's sad. I say I'm sorry. I'm sorry you fed your life to a greedy vampire machine, but if you've gotta cling to it—if so much of *you* has become *it* that you can't abandon it—at least don't ask your children to perpetuate its existence. Don't ask me to feed my brand-new life to it. You can ask me, but don't try to force me. An then you nudge em an smile an say, 'Hey, man, wake up. Open your eyes. Abandon the hungry, fat, doomed machine. Let's try something new. Aren't you tired? Aren't you ready to move up an out instead of horizontally an in circles? Wake up, man."

"That's been said. Saints and Gurus and Prophets and wise old hermits have been saying that sort of thing for thousands of years. A few unfortunate malcontents like the followers of Christ listen, but nobody else does. It's against society and society has people by the balls. That kind of talk doesn't make any sense to them."

"Give em some acid and it sure as hell will."

"(Strange choice of words, man.) They won't *take* acid. They're afraid to. It's a drug, and all drugs are bad. They know that for a fact because they've been told all their lives that drugs are bad. All drugs except those manufactured and taxed by the State are evil. The ones who look past *that* are still afraid acid'll change them and they don't wanna be changed."

General opinion was, "It'll take a long time."

But a long time takes a long time—especially if you're right at the beginning—especially if it's all so obviously right and big and real and good. There were soon glorious plots for a fullscale blitz NOW. At least once a week someone would suggest putting acid in the water supply. God only knows why nobody ever did it. It would've been easy enough, and there was certainly sufficient acid around. Maybe it was because of that big Jesus voice, the voice of understanding reason, in the back of our collective heads, saying, "No, you just have to keep trying to do your thing . . . quietly, honestly and without bringing anyone else down. Don't try to push your trip on anyone else. That's what makes the problems—people trying to push their visions into other people's eyes."

In San Jose, a fast young crystal freak friend of LaMer's jumped up all hot to trot and yelled, "It's time! We do it *now*! We all gotta rally round the cause, man!"

In a sudden blast of ego-involvement, Baxtor put him down with, "There aren't any causes. Rally round the cause is just the same as rally round the flag. A flag is a piece of cloth. A flag is to look at. People should wave flags rather than having flags wave them. Flags should be fun. Nobody ought to push a flag on anybody. No more symbols. No more boolshid. Let's get down to the real thing."

"What's the real thing?" I wondered.

Bob Levin smiled soft and said quietly, "That's what we all should be looking for."

Julia took part in none of these discussions. "There's only beauty in the world," she told me. "Anything else you find, you put there yourself."

Mmhmm.

Julia was staying at Carl's cabin because she was a friend of Sherry's and Sherry didn't want anything to happen to her. Julia was so far from the "real world" that it was sometimes dangerous for her. Not that she'd walk off a cliff or poison herself. She recognized and automatically avoided natural dangers. She didn't, however, recognize (or admit to) the danger of other human beings. Uncool, not in the least hip, but Julia had long since dropped out of the hip-game.

I learned from Carl that Julia'd been raped in Berkeley when she'd wandered past a frat home-coming party and accepted an invitation to come inside. Sherry found her on Telegraph and brought her home.

I completed a physical love thing with Julia only once, and then never tried again. I didn't miss it. There were other chicks around, and Julia was something different. Besides, with Julia, whenever my thoughts turned toward flesh, my head would fill with a vision of her being raped by beer-drunk cold minds, and I'd go mentally, as well as physically, limp. I told myself it'd come. Eventually everything would line up and fall in and be fine and it'd come and be good. Until that time, it was best (and I was content) to walk with her and hold her and sleep beside her in the sun or under the stars and listen to her soft songs and watch the world through those great clear eyes of hers—eyes that saw only weightless happiness. I'd step inside her aura and feel myself slow down, grow calm.

Everyone loved Julia. Even cynical Curt, although he once told me, "She's beautiful, yes. I love her, of course, but when I'm high and too close to her I feel kind of . . . uneasy. I start to think about how far away from what's really happening she is, and it makes me uneasy."

I jumped to her defense with, "Whadya mean? She *is* what's happening! Or *should* be happening!"

Curt nodded and shrugged. "Yeah. Well, it's some personal hangup of mine, I suppose."

Thinking back now, I realize (probably did long ago) that, were I a psychiatrist, I would've pronounced Julia utterly insane. One finally did.

I ate a lot of acid in a short span of man-time. No one had any preconceptions as to how often it could or should be taken, so we took it as often as we could—as soon as we recovered from the previous trip, which is to say as soon as we decided we were "down." Zad sometimes decided he was down four hours after dropping five-hundred mics, so he'd drop five-hundred more as a booster, putting himself in places that made him sit in a corner staring with huge amazed eyes at his circus, playing a single note top-volume on a Cee harp for a whole day and night, returning to babble ecstatically about how BIG it was and how he'd actually stood face to face with the true final IT.

While psychologists were carefully researching the effects of a hundred and fifty micrograms of LSD on test subjects, Zad was trying to "rip away the curtain" with a thousand, Baxter and Preston were anticipating "astounding results and revelations" with two-thousand, and I was eating three-fifty to five-hundred every two days—a day in between to sort things out and try to draw a few conclusions—and the conclusion was always. "Take more acid."

It was almost impossible to conceive of the old world, the straight world, the Victorian hangover, surviving the engulfing wave of The New Madness. It was all so simple. The world was being turned on. The dark stumble ages were drawing to a close. The world was going to stop, reorient itself, and start spinning it the right direction at last.

The old world didn't stop. We waited for the bang or the whimper, but it didn't come. We devoted our energy to rising above. "It'll come. Anytime now. IT will come." In those days we all had a lot of faith.

I'd known Julia for perhaps two months (a short calendar-time—a long, long lived-time) when I returned from a week in Berkeley and rode up to see her at Carl's cabin. Ted and a chick named Lynn met me at the door. Inside, Sherry was crying.

I asked what happened as Ted motioned me away from the door. I didn't connect it with Julia. "What's the matter with Sherry?"

Ted shook his head. "There was a big bum scene up here, man. They took Julia."

"*Who* took Julia?"

Ted's hands were actually shaking. There was a cigarette between his fingers and I'd never seen him smoke. "Ah, phew . . . man, it was really grim. Her parents came up here with a cop. If Carl hadn't spotted the uniform and flushed his stash down the john we'd all've been busted. The cop had a warrant an the whole works. He stomped right in the front door and said . . .

"Why'd they bust Julia?" I demanded.

"Completely shitty. It was because of her head, man. Her parents wanted to put her in an institution. They had the papers an everything. They even tried to bust Carl for contributing. Big hassle about that—everybody yelling an running around. God, it was really bum. Julia freaked when they tried to put her in the cop-car an she ran for the woods, but the cop grabbed her an Carl ran over to help—all happening so fast, y'know—an Julia's old man grabbed Carl an ripped his shirt. Man, just *bad*. Julia was crying and screaming an she tore off her dress while they were holding her. Phhhh."

The whole scene flashed bigger than life behind my eyes. I could see now Julia saw it and how her parents saw it and how the cop saw it and how ugly it must have been for all eyes involved. *The mad girl. Insane*. "Where'd they take her?" I was trying to pull together some half-assed plan for a showdown Robin Hood rescue.

"Carl's trying to find out now, man. He left about an hour ago. Fuck. Sherry crying an all. This thing really brought me down. I don't know, man. It really brought me down."

I worked it around in quick fast circles, hoping I could somehow make it come out right, knowing there was no chance. Done. Reality closed in like a strait-jacket. "Oh no," well aware that it was oh yes. Gone. Just like that, Julia's gone. The System got her. Thwarted long enough, it stepped right in, sent out agents and snatched her off for correction. Nothing you can do about it. It's too late, too complex, too powerful. Confront it and it'll get you too. Gone. Frustration and loss covered by red anger—"Why'd they wanna take her away, man? She wasn't hurting anybody! Goddamit, she was *happy*! She was happier than any of *them*!"

Ted's cigarette had gone out but he took a drag off of it anyway. "That's the way their minds work. She wasn't playing their game. She wasn't even pretending to play their game. That's the important part. Julia wasn't even *pretending* to play their game on any level. They call that being insane, man, and it's grounds for putting you away."

So Julia went to an institution, a "hospital," and stayed there until there wasn't a Julia any more. Sherry got to see her a couple of times; once after they'd given Julia shock treatment (shock "therapy"). Sherry didn't tell us much about that visit and none of us pressed it.

When Julia'd been in the institution for three months . . . a whole summer . . . her favorite time of the year . . . Sherry went to see her, came back and told me, "She wants to get out and then go back to school and get a job. She says she's sorry for all the trouble she caused. Her parents were there and they told me not to come see her anymore."

Much later, I heard that Julia's parents had taken her to Detroit where an Aunt lived and owned some sort of business—dress shop or something. I knew that Julia wasn't coming back, but the realization only gave me a twinge of sad that passed in a single afternoon. Julia actually died in the institution.

Now hear this the way I'm trying to get it heard: Julia was a prism-minor of a crystal-clear chapter of the acid saga. Everyone knew Julia and embraced her or loved her or screwed her in their own way. This is important. Julia's death was the death of a way of life—the end of the first beautiful phase of the psychedelic revolution.

CHAPTER NINE – CONDENSING A PERIOD OF ELASTIC TIME

If someone is actually reading this . . . if the utterly unlikely has somehow come to pass and it's gone *that* far . . . if someone, for unknown reasons, is actually trying to get behind this stumble-dance of words, honestly trying to hear it and follow it through, then you've got to imagine that seven months have passed since the quick death of Julia Cain. Seven months, and you've been with me while they fell away. A whole winter, complete with a winter's worth of everyday hours and events, plus its memorable minutes and meetings and thoughts . . . gone. And now, you and I are reviewing the recent gone-past, saying "phew!" at the understanding in one another's eyes, trying hard to believe it.

Because, after what was, I presume, the proper length of time, a winter slowly dragged itself by so fast (if you know what I mean) that it was suddenly gone. I realized it with surprise one night and understood why old people see time so much differently than children, and I grieved over the death of my child-time-concept.

A winter vanished into invisible memory-bank vaults, leaving only small change to testify to the deposit. Acid was being taken by greater numbers; the authorities were hip to it, calling it "frightening" and "a serious threat"; weed was being smoked in conjunction with beer at frat-houses and was no longer considered a reliable gauge of awareness; new friends had appeared, old friends had disappeared; San Francisco was being called "The Psychedelic Center of the Universe," and people were calling us "hippies," but so much was really the same—especially the important things.

In fog and moonlight on nighttime beaches or sitting around

fireplaces or apartment wall-heaters with year-older friends, I heard them all say the same things that were in my own mind: So much "lived-time" used up in so little "clock-time" and the world still pretty much the same and us still pretty much the same except for having grown even farther away from the straight-world and its children, having grown hairier on the outside and older-younger on the inside because of the passage of so much lived-time—lived-time dotted with visions and experiences like the revelation at Sur when I saw the sky part to reveal the patient Void as a voice roared "TIME WAS," and I grabbed at the concept with a greedy mind while still holding fast to ego, and the concept was so vast that, under an oppressive cloud of ozone, all my circuits burned themselves out with the incredible overload, and the Me-Earth-Time-Life-illusion blinked off, leaving nothing . . . for Eternity . . . and then everything had to be reconstructed in both directions from and to "Let There Be Light" until both ends finally met with a flash on a beach at Sur where I was sprawled on my back, staring open-eyed at the sun, having just tried to grasp the concept of the void.

Eternity had elapsed since I'd last had a structured thought, so it was difficult to remember tiny details such as where I was or what had happened. I tried, and when I couldn't I suddenly felt afraid. The landscape, my body, everything around me changed form and color and validity so rapidly that it was useless to move in any one direction. There *was* no direction that couldn't shift without warning. I vaguely remembered a man named Admiral Dewey and then, with absolute clarity, a portion of the Book of the Dead. Wise teaching which applied perfectly to my situation. I began to meditate on the protective figure of Admiral Dewey . . . with poor results. Gray smoke crept in to cover everything. A horrible stench filled my nostrils. "Burning brain cells," hissed a coiling energy snake, encircling my left leg. "There's *no* business like *show* business!" sang Milton Berle, accompanied by a brassy band composed of mummified fire-men, plucking strings, tapping keys and pushing valves with brittle brown french-fried fingers.

The edges of the wing and drop reality set were swinging from side to side with increasing speed, billowing and twisting, ropes dangling, frame-work ripping through canvas. It was getting ready to disintegrate again, and I remembered that it had taken eons to reconstruct it only seconds or perhaps hours or maybe days or possibly years ago. I felt that I'd learned a very great lesson concerning something-or-other, but I wasn't terribly anxious to go through it again. "Not just yet. I'm very tired and very wise already, and I gratefully but firmly decline to accept another lesson. I have no say-so in the matter? Very well, I'll relax and let it go. It's easier if you don't resist. Float . . . drift . . . wait! I might have to do this forever! That's *it*! It takes *forever*! But! . . . phooom . . . and I slipped back into forever where I didn't exist.

LET THERE BE LIGHT. The world slowly formed . . . life evolved . . . the world aged . . . man evolved . . . man aged . . . thought pulled itself together . . . slowly . . . slowly . . . no way to hurry it along . . . slowly it got around to me, sprawled on my back, staring open-eyed into the sun, on a beach at Big Sur, and then . . . wham . . . and I slid right out of existence again, back to the beginning . . . for twenty-six separate-inseparable eternities until I fell into time again and saw the illusion of ocean-sky-sand and me, and I waited and it held and I said, "Whew. I'm down. That was one long, long, extra-long trip." I breathed in . . . out . . . and in, then out. I shook my body and listened to the reassuring badump-badump-badump of my heart. The sun was in exactly the same place as I'd last seen it. I looked out over the ocean and followed a gull's flight which led my eyes across the horizon, then dropped them in a cloud where, in mocking psychedelic poster lettering I saw written . . .

END OF INTRODUCTION * NOW! THE TRIP!

BOOK ONE

PART ONE

CHAPTER ONE

-START HERE-

. . . and fear tried to rip my mind but found very little left to rip as I realized that all that had happened was only the first flash, and that the real *body* of the trip was yet to come . . . the peak unreached. It came, and it's useless to try to say anything about it. If it has happened to you, then you know what I mean. If it hasn't happened to you (that you can remember), then nothing I could say would even begin to explain it.

I left the beach at three in the morning, hitch-hiked home and slept for two days, waking up only once to take off my pants and brush sand from the sheets. In my sleep I had a dream in which I saw myself sleeping for two days, waking up only once to take off my pants and brush sand from the sheets, while I dreamed of myself sleeping for two days, waking up only once.

When you're doing that maybe twice a week (for one incredible period, seven days a week) you put in a lot of the aforesaid "lived-time," and everybody I hung with was doing it to a larger or slightly lesser extent.

"Decrepit, old, tired minds," said Baxtor, "being carried around in twenty-year-old bodies. A ludicrous spectacle. People have been conditioned to expect some sort of body-mind correlation. How will they react to the sight of a drooling, senile twenty-five-year-old being wheeled into the park by attendants? What excuse would you give? You couldn't say, "Well, there's nothing really *wrong* with him. He's just old.'"

While we waited for senility we made treks back and forth, from San Jose to Sur, to San Francisco, to Berkeley, to L.A. and into Mexico (where I can still see Zad, high on thirty bennies, two reds, a fat yellow and a half bottle of tequila, leading an expedition of American college boys in search of marijuana, getting more and more stoned as it started to rain, until he fell in the muddy river of the gutter, sick and unable to move, looking so wretched and pitiful that an American tourist turned to Preston and said, "That man is dying! Does anyone here speak his language? Do any of you speak Spanish?" We all laughed, and the man walked away indignant. Preston poked soggy Zad with his toe and said, "Keep it up, man. You've become local color. Stay there till that guy gets his camera."), and back to San Jose where we sometimes went to school or got jobs and then quit or got fired.

We talked for whole nights far into the next day, about experiences and religion, Zen, Tibet and the Tao, prison and our friends in it, philosophy and the stars, insanity and music, new drugs and ancient drugs rediscovered, love and cops, bullshit and its universal appeal, poets and dictators, power and the cosmos, and it was all so real and new.

Ted and Baxtor and I started a shop and sold posters and little hand-printed books of poetry by local poets and things that other freaks made and sold to us. We tried to run the only honest business in town, charged only cost and gave things away until we went broke after four weeks due to unforeseen circumstances. Money-people set up shops shortly after, installing clean plastic hippies behind the counters, advertising flower-power accessories in tri-color ads, charging a dollar for buttons that said "Free Love," and needless to say, these shops flourished.

Something is happening. Something is gonna happen. What? And how much longer do we have to wait?

We visited our friends in jail, cried for the ignorance of civilized man, searched for the spirit of American freedom among sadly civilized American Indians who drove pick-up trucks and wore cowboy hats and wanted to be white men. We hunted for apartments and cabins that would rent to "hippies," identified with the plight of the American Negro, wondered why so many of them wanted to be white men. We tried to set up independent tribes in the forest and got kicked out by property owners, cops, the board of health, forest rangers and Smokey the Bear, and returned to the cities where tension was building by the second. Something is happening. Something is gonna happen. It's gonna be big.

"It's catching on. It's growing faster than we ever expected," I said or Zad said . . . someone said. "More and more people are turning on."

"Not as many as you might think," Baxtor pointed out when he was in that particular mood. "We tend to believe that everyone who smokes weed or drops acid is *turning on*. That isn't necessarily the case. How many of them are merely taking dope?"

"But that's one way of turning on!"

"Well . . . maybe. It can be, I guess, but how many new dope takers are actually looking at it that way? How many of them are just doing it for kicks? . . . a new way to get drunk? The majority of them do it because it's becoming the ultra-in thing to do. You know . . . if you don't smoke weed your friends'll make snide remarks about you after school and draw funny pictures of you on their binders. Wait'll it *really* catches on. When it really starts to hit the high schools and then the junior high schools and ultimately, the old people—like the twist did—then I'll lay odds that it'll become the ultra-in thing *not* to smoke weed or take acid. The psychedelics will once again fall into disfavor with the jet set. Acid will be outdated and square. Only us old acid freaks will still be taking it . . . if our minds hold out. The "swingers" will be doing something else. Heroin's probably the next big fad to sweep the fast crowd, or possibly a re-kindling of interest in Zen meditation and thought-games, or perhaps a rebirth of hard-core capitalism."

"No, man. That won't happen. Even if you start out taking acid for kicks, eventually it'll get to you. It'll turn you on."

"Only if you let it. You know as well as I that even now people drop acid a few times, then draw a bad experience, or at least an experience that they interpret as negative or 'too far out', and then they either pull out of the scene all together and write articles for teenage magazines about how LSD nearly ruined their lives, or else they turn to crink and burn themselves out in six or seven months, or fall back on smack or some comfortable downer. Acid isn't instant enlightenment."

"Of course not. But it is a step in the right direction."

"There isn't any 'right direction.' All direction is only in your mind."

"Aw . . . words."

"Ah, yes."

"Aw . . ."

" . . . bowsha?"

"Aw, pass the joint and shut up, Baxtor."

And time passed with the joints. Our hair got longer, our eyes redder. The world wasn't swept by a tidal wave of love, but the glorious love movement began to grow, and, as it did, like the story of the tower of Babel, we began to lose touch with one another and lose sight of the original goals and lose faith, and *our leaders* (the ones that the mass media assured us we had) began to compromise and we found ourselves laboring under the weight of the inevitable fringe element, the hangers-on, the money-makers, the angry misfits, and those who sought constantly the "in-thing."

The winter sent us wandering down the countless divergent ego-paths of bullshit, regretfully admitting that stark reality must go on. And so, of course, it did. I sold a column a week to a local newspaper and got money from my over-generous father who made me feel guilty as hell by never even mentioning the fact that I should be. On the crest of the wave of sudden interest in Hell's Angels, I sold a story I'd written a year and a half before to a man's "adventure" magazine. There wasn't even a single gangbang in the story, but it sold anyway. The money was comfortable to have, but it went fast. The sale shoveled fuel to my fasting ego, but that went even faster. I gave up all serious attempts at writing when I realized that there was nothing to say. There was no time—no reason to try to fold it all into words. That isn't life. That isn't living. That's just recording, or bending things to fit into tight little morals. It's nothing.

I was buying grape-colored-something at a Dairy Queen, searching for the extra penny tax I'd overlooked, when an amazingly small old man—white hair and a long white beard, a paisley tie and a flower-print vest, gold watch-chain and all—tapped me between the shoulder-blades by reaching as high as he could, peeked at me through octagonal specks that rode on the round, red tip of his nose, cleared his throat and said, "Is simply is. Is is. And is is Is, as is is. Is is Is. Is *Is*. Do you understand?"

"Yes. But it's only words."

"Exactly right. Exactly right, man. I wish you luck in your search." He gave me a penny, patted me on my elbow, walked out the glass doors and crawled into a huge camper-truck, made the gears growl and grind their teeth, and lumbered off into the street. A little old man, definitely tiny and probably strange all his long life, alone for years and years in a world full of busy straight people, finding other strangers who he could talk to at last, and now there's nothing to say.

Walking home, I remembered a theory of Baxtor's and decided that the old man was probably only twenty-six and had just had his hair burned white and his body shriveled by putting in too much lived-time.

CHAPTER TEN—HOT SPRINGS

The sliding glass, quilt-covered door of my studio was saying *bam*, and also *bam-bam-bam-bam-bam*. I covered my head with a pillow and listened to *bom-bom-bom-bom*. I crawled out of the twisted sheets and threw open the door in hopes of making it quiet. Sun-power made me blind as Zad (who always knocked on doors in one continual stream of heavy fist-pounds so that if anyone was behind the door, even if they were pretending not to be, they would open it or face going deaf) followed by Preston and Baxtor, pushed past me into the room, saying, "Clothes, Abel. Get dressed, man. Wake up. We're going to Sur."

"Sur beckons," confirmed Preston, lighting a fat joint and sticking it in my mouth. "The call of Sur is heavy in the air today. Not to be ignored."

Still misted over from sleep and dreams, I pulled on pants, boots, shirt, and grabbed a jacket to jump into Zad's bus and clatter off in a cloud of exhaust-weed smoke toward Monterey and, eventually, Big Sur. Three weeks since I'd last dug the dark forests and clean, white beaches. Big Sur did indeed beckon.

A good day. Cold, but the sun was out and it was early yet. Springtime everywhere, telling us how great summer was going to be.

"You remember," Preston was saying to Baxtor as we crossed the Santa Cruz mountains, "that time we saw the flying saucer land on the beach? And all those hand-painted bugs crawled over our sleeping bags? The same day that we took acid eating breakfast at Redwood and you had this vision later that convinced you that you were karma-destined to walk the beaches of the earth forever."

Baxtor rocked and nodded. "Why didn't I?"

"Pure sloth on your part," said Preston. "And also you ran into that sheer cliff face, and then we got hungry and had to go back to the Lodge for something to eat."

"Ah yes. Thwarted again by the greedy cravings of my body."

"Hey, let's stop in Monterey and get some burgers," I suggested from the back seat.

"Plastic shit," said Zad, who was currently on his macrobiotic diet and down on anything that wasn't an organically grown vegetable—preferably a grain. "How can you eat a chemically treated piece of dead cow?"

A big argument about whether or not man was supposed to be a vegetarian lasted all the way to Carmel where we finally stopped so I could buy a salami and french rolls and a chunk of cheese.

"The bread and cheese aren't *too* bad," said Zad, "even though they're full of chemical preservatives that will slowly kill you . . ."

"So will life, man," cutting into the salami with my hunting knife.

"But don't you *realize* that the last thing an animal feels before it's slaughtered is *fear*? The fear of death! All those meat cells are full of death-fear and you *eat* it!"

"Yup," I said, biting into my salami and cheese sandwich, "and I like it. If I let myself think about things like that, I'd starve. Lots of animals would eat me if I let em, and that's okay with me. Worms are gonna eat me when I die, and they're welcome to me. Everything eats everything else. It's too bad, maybe, but it's the way things *are*. I feel just as sorry for carrots as I do for cows."

"Meat-eaters . . . they'll never break through," Zad grumbled, piloting the bus past long, white-sand beaches.

"It's good," I thought to myself, looking out the window and smelling ocean air. "The earth is good and these friends are good and the day is good and even this piece of dead somekindof animal is pretty good. Sad, kind of, but pretty good." And we zipped along the high coastal cliffs, over the hundred-foot drop into clear, blue ocean, while I recited guilty Indian prayers to the spirit of the animal I was building my body from. "Forgive me, dead animal. I hope you won't be waiting for me with sad eyes at the gate of the Void. I hope I'm doing right. I sincerely hope I'm doing right." Past Redwood Lodge, past campers with backpacks, past Robin Hood clearings protected by no trespassing signs, up the last grade where we can see mountains blanketed by trees that go on forever, uncut, unburned, untouched by straightedge, rip-saw, iron-nail, concrete man.

"Look at those fucking seals!" shouted Preston after we'd bounced and banged down the rutted dirt road and climbed out of the dusty bus at our special beach. "How I missed those seals! Why do I ever leave this place? Everything you could ever *hope* to want is right *here*! This is beyond any possible shadow of a doubt it." Taking a long, noisy hit on his perpetual joint (Preston once outraged Sharon by driving her mother to the airport while he smoked joint after joint which he maintained were "well disguised as Camels," meaning that he'd rolled them in white instead of brown paper), "Ah, what a set!" He turned and, with one of his characteristic expansive theatrical gestures, said to me, "Just *think*! At one time this whole fucking coast-line was like this. *That* must have been *fat*! How could those fuck-dogs have wiped it out? Civilization is obviously an evil state to attain, or, for that matter, even *work* toward attaining. Look at this set!" and he threw himself onto the sand, clutching the beach like a man clinging to a disintegrating raft in heavy seas.

A truly beautiful set. Cool, dark redwood-pine-cypress-and-unknown-tree forests coming right up to unbelievably white sand beaches that slide into cold blue waves broken by jagged, black, patterned rocks. No high-tension wires slice up the sky. No fake prop poles stand in front of trees. No monster signs tell you what to get drunk on, or what to clean your toilet with.

When the fog comes in, it comes in fast, and you can see long gray arms of it reach out to you on the darkening beach from far out to sea. Timeless sea, timeless sand, timeless sky, timeless mist and fog, "There is no *time* here. No hungup minutes or hours or years," says Preston, standing on a huge boulder with waves smashing into wobbling ovals and hard, round diamonds, and rainbow vapor all around him. He and Baxtor applaud the waves, shouting words of encouragement. "Up now . . . UP! Ahhhh. You're such great waves." Zad crawls like a happy crab on the rocks, saying things like, "Ah . . . wow . . . yes this is how I'd build a rock. These are the finest rocks in the cosmos. The best of all rocks. Ah . . . lookit the patterns of holes . . . wow." *Whump*! *Tchssshhh*, and Zad is lost in white diamond spray, emerging drenched and smiling to shake water from his hair the way a glad dog does, climbing even farther out on the rocks, inches from the breakers.

By noon, two or three families had set up umbrellas and transistor radios on one comer of the beach. Preston showed his indignation at the sacrilege by stripping to his tattered, barely existent jockey shorts, and leaping from rock to rock ape-fashion. One family packed up all their anti-beach material and left, but the others seemed to know that he was harmless and stayed on, ignoring him to the best of their ability. Preston climbed to the highest boulder and pissed into the ocean. The families pretended not to see, and I felt embarrassed for Preston, us and them.

"Come on, man. Don't do that. Those people can see you." Preston smiled down at me, finishing with short, powerful spurts. "I'm only pissing in the fucking ocean. You sound like ole Barry. We used to come here and I'd have to take a piss and he'd look at me and say, 'How can you *piss* in the face of all *this*?' I mean . . . I'm not pissing on it *maliciously*, for chrisake. I just have to piss. Don't *you* ever have to?"

I walked down the beach with Baxtor and he told me, "Preston and I spent whole weeks down here a couple of summers ago, taking acid and stumbling through the woods. I was having good trips then. Beautiful trips." He pointed to the seals that played on the waves. "I used to sit all day on the beach in the sun trying to swap minds with one of those seals."

"Would they actually trade?"

"Of course not. Don't be ridiculous. Seals are much too smart. I never found one who wanted to trade a perfectly good seal-mind for a useless, hungup human-mind. I worked at it though. Flies would land all over me, using me for a sun-deck and snack-bar, but I didn't want to shake them off. I saw that since I had a finite amount of body-area, I could only accommodate a finite number of flies. If I continually drove them off, however, then there was no limit to the number of flies that could land on me—in shifts—taking turns. So I decided to allow my exact number of flies to land on me and stay, in hopes that I'd get to know them and then they wouldn't bug me so much. Until one time this chick walked up, looked at me for awhile, and said, 'You're covered with flies, you idiot,' and then walked away."

I laughed at the picture I got of Baxtor, sitting mindless and cross-legged in the sand, staring out at the seals, his body covered from head to toe with thousands of flies, all of which he knew by name. "The Lord of the Flies," I said.

"The Buddha of Bullshit," sighed Baxtor, side-stepping a spoiled jellyfish.

Preston and Zad had climbed to the top of the beach's highest hill, along the little goat-trail foot path, and they were now waving their arms and jumping up and down like sun-crazed ants in the distance. Preston still wearing only his shredded shorts, holding his shaving kit full of weed in one hand. Baxtor and I waved back and they disappeared to the far side of the hill.

For some reason, the thought, "Where do you suppose it's all going?" as I tossed a purple starfish into the water.

"Where do I suppose *what* is all going?"

"Oh . . . us . . . and the acid freaks in general. You know . . . the whole thing. Or anyway, this whole tiny part of the whole thing."

"If we can learn anything from history (and I'm not necessarily sure that we can)," replied Baxtor, "then the answer is probably 'nowhere.' Aside from the chemical catalyst of LSD, we haven't really come up with anything startlingly new. There've always been small minorities of drop-outs, forsaking the obvious games of society and retreating into sub-cultures, or no-cultures to contemplate their navels. They see and say the same old truths and change nothing."

"What's the use then? Why are you in this thing?"

Baxtor hung his head in mock sorrow (perhaps not so mock in view of later developments), "Trapped by acid," he said. "Once it alters your mind, you can never see things in their proper perspective again."

"Well, what *is* the proper perspective?"

Baxtor shrugged his eyebrows. "How the hell do I know? My mind's already been altered. I'll never be able to trust it again."

"Man! You work with some dark thoughts."

"Yeah. I wonder why I had to see that? Everyone else seems to be taking acid and tripping around comfortably, having a great time. Doesn't it seem that way to you?"

"No."

"Ah," said Baxtor, stroking his mustache, "But then . . . my failure to grasp the truth undoubtedly causes a good deal of incidental confusion."

By late afternoon we'd all gathered on a big, flat boulder, five feet above the thudding breakers. Zad and Preston had taken acid on the hill-top and were falling down, overwhelmed by the force and power of the setting, clinging to handholds in the pitted rocks, saying, "Wow . . . wow . . . WOW!" with every new wham of the waves.

A group of fair young chicks had set blankets on the beach about a hundred yards away, and we peered at them from behind rock cover like a gang of bandits. "Lookit the chicks, Preston," and his eyes lit up at once.

"They have fuck-me written all over them," he said happily. "Maybe one'll come over here."

"You'll be reborn on the animal level," Baxtor reminded him. "My favorite level," said Preston.

Zad, smiling and obviously somewhere else, weaved over to squint at the chicks, saying, "Nice," and staggering back to watch the ocean. Uninterested in matters of the flesh.

The chicks stripped to bathing suits and a collective sigh (minus Zad) went up from the rocks. "Now *that* makes my mind water," breathed Preston.

I watched them kick sand and giggle and run like wild colts into the shore foam, shaking their hair and squeaking in girl language to one another. I tried to imagine what they were like and what they would do if I walked up to them, shaggy-bearded and red-eyed, asking them to talk about themselves. Just to hear them speak, because I loved them.

The most graceful of the chicks (all of them equally lovely in the flattering distance) suddenly pointed our way. The others looked, and then there was a flurry of action as they brushed sand from their legs and gathered up clothing and towels. I glanced up and saw Preston high above us, unencumbered by even the questionable covering of his underwear, waving and smiling at the chicks. Realizing suddenly that they intended to leave, he began to scramble down the rock like a shaved monkey. His intentions were all too clear, and I yelled, "Preston, cut it out, man!" but he paid no attention. I thought about running after him, then changed my mind and decided to pretend that I didn't know him.

The chicks were pulling on sweaters and sandals when he reached the sand and started toward them at a trot. They grabbed at towels and headed up the beach to the parking area. Preston broke into a full run. He looked like a sheep dog scattering a bunch of strays. The chicks ran in dead silence, not even taking the time to make female eek sounds.

When it became very clear, even to Preston, that these women were emphatically against meeting him, he changed course and sprinted down the beach parallel to the ocean, splashing into it finally and running back to the rocks with his head back and his arms outspread. Ulysses, rending himself from the magic grip of the Siren's song.

"What drama," said Baxter.

"Let's make it," said I, envisioning legions of armed cops bearing down on the scene of the attempted mass rape, and anyhow, it was late.

Preston was reluctant to leave, grabbing on to the biggest available of the huge boulders, shrieking, "No! I wanna stay! How can you even *suggest* going back to the temples of mechanical crap?" but we pried him loose and scared him with stories of impending cop retaliation, until he agreed to put his pants on and followed us sullenly to the bus.

"Purification rites must be held at the hot-springs," announced Zad from his distant zone as we bounced onto the highway, Baxter behind the wheel.

"You have to have a reservation," I argued.

"It's eating meat that makes you so down-headed," said Zad quietly, putting his hand on my shoulder in sympathy.

"Back to the beach! Back you dogs! Back, I say!" yelled Preston, his face pressed against the rear window, eyes watching his beloved beach receding in the distance.

"We can try to get into the baths," from Baxter.

Outvoted, I said, "Let's at least wait till it's dark," hoping that when the sun went down we'd all be better able to handle any hassles that might come up when we confronted the hot-springs' management.

We pulled off the road behind a grove of trees and smoked weed, waiting for the sun to disappear. Preston ate a cheese sandwich and Zad ate little turd-shaped globs of brown rice wrapped in dried seaweed, while a sky-fire sunset happened all around us.

It was after nine when we parked the bus beside the main house and got out like a box of spilled ping-pong balls. Next to us, a man climbed out of his Corvette, locked the door and started for the bar. Zad stood in his path. "Hello," smiled the zoned Zad. The man scowled and said nothing, put his hands on his hips and waited for Zad to move.

"Hello to your Buddha inside," Zad extended his hand.

"Get out of my way," said the man, and went into the bar.

Zad smiled harder than ever and sat cross-legged in the gravel. "The right answer," he assured us. "That was a very wise man. A Bodhisattva if ever I saw one."

Baxtor talked to some people and returned to say, "'Only those with reservations will be permitted to take baths,' in the words of some official personage."

"I have money for them," said Zad, holding up a handful of tightly crumpled bills.

"Zad, don't sit in the middle of the parking lot," I warned him.

He got to his feet. "It's eating meat that does it to you. I'm not hurting the parking lot. The gravel doesn't mind if I sit on it."

We didn't know what to do, so we did nothing. Baxtor and I were stoned and tired. Zad and Preston were just stoned. The four of us sat on a bench, smoking cigarettes and fidgeting, watching people go in and out of the bar, wondering what to do.

I'd say, "Aw, let's go," and Zad would say, "We're supposed to be *here*. We're going to take sulphur baths. It's our reward," and Preston would say, "Let's just go down there and *take* em," and Baxtor would say, "Well . . . we might as well wait a little longer. Maybe something'll happen," and I'd nod grudging agreement, and fifteen minutes would go by and I'd say, "Aw, let's go," and Zad would say, "We're *supposed* to be *here* . . ." and this went on until a chick wearing shell-beads over a sweatshirt tucked into ragged Levi's walked up to our bench and asked if we were waiting to get into the baths.

"I have money for them," said Zad hopefully.

The chick nodded to Zad. Zad nodded back. We told her about the reservation hangup.

"That's a bummer," she said, pushing dead brown hair from her thin gray face, motioning into the darkness of the parking lot where car doors slammed and gravel crunched and a pack of dusty, wrinkled people shuffled toward us. A round chick with limp black hair, a young looking guy shivering in a T-shirt and barefoot with a wispy Chinese beard, a tall greasy cat with a long gunfighter mustache and tiny gray eyes behind thick, finger-printed glasses, and a ratty little maybe eighteen-year-old blondish chick hidden in a big Mexican poncho all filed out of the shadows nodding and mumbling, "Whasay man . . . whas happenin . . . wow sure cold . . ." and other stock greetings.

Now there were nine of us standing or crouching around, smoking cigs and fidgeting, wondering what to do. "We're supposed to be here. All of us," said Zad. "Something will happen." We were surprised when something did.

A straight guy, wearing an expensive cardigan sweater, stepped out of the bar and spotted the thin gray girl. "Susan?"

The girl turned and studied him.

"Aren't you Susan?"

"Yeah . . .

"Didn't you go to (something) College of Fine Art?"

"Yeah."

"Don't you remember me? I'm Claud . . . the guy with the two bull dogs who used to . . ." and rapid talk and happy recognition and "Oh wow . . ." and, "What've you been doing?" followed, and it turned out that these two had known one another some several years ago and the guy was now a minor commercial artist living in

Carmel, and why didn't Susan come in with him and his wife on their bath reservation?

"What about my friends?" asked thoughtful Susan.

"Sure. How many?"

"Uh . . . two, three . . . nine. Nine."

"Nine?"

"I don'wanna go," said the greasy gunfighter.

"You *have* to!" said Susan.

"I don'wanna an I don'havta."

"Eight," said Susan.

Claud looked at all the raggy bodies, swallowed and said, "Uh . . . well . . ." and I felt sorry for him and sorrier for his unseen and unsuspecting wife. I was going to say forget it, when he nodded and said, "Okay. I'll go get you some towels. Eight?" and he went back into the bar.

Towels in hand, we marched single file down the little dirt trail to the bath-house with our benefactor, generous Claud, and his good looking, dark, worried wife in the lead holding white candles to light the way. I could hear snatches of whispered conversation from them. Wife saying, "Did you . . . (whisper) . . ."

Claud saying, "It's all right, honey."

"But . . . (whisper) . . ."

"No, it's all right."

" . . . (whisper) . . ."

"No, they're all right. They're good people."

Into the bath-house where Preston and Zad jumped into the first stone tub, plosh and ploosh, immediately, and I realized with a twinge that they'd undressed on the way down.

"I'll leave a candle for *your* bath . . ." indicating the majority of the naked or getting naked bodies " . . . right here on the edge," said Claud tactfully.

"Thanks, man. Thanks a lot for everything . . . you know." I wanted to tell him more—impress upon him how much he really deserved our thanks—but I knew that I'd only blow it (as usual) if I used too many words. Why is it so hard to talk—really *talk* to fellow humans?

"Spa-lash!" went the big white globe that was the round chick. Her thin young bearded evidently boy-friend stepped in beside her, saying, "Wow. This is *too* much. This is really too *much*!"

The air was cold enough to make mist from our breath. Spirits danced in front of mouths. Beyond the shiny-wet wooden railing, straight down the rocky cliff-face, the ocean smashed with a rhythmic deep rumble. Nothing else but the black, black, incredibly black night sky spattered with unblinking pin-holes into pure white light, in front of millions of billions of flickering lesser sparks. Too beautiful to fully appreciate, so you don't really, and soon accept it as merely "the background."

In the very center of the cosmic light-show was the little bathhouse, jutting out of the sheer cliff, full of candle-lit, pale bodies in the unbelievable shapes and sizes that only a nudist can view without an inner gasp of astonishment in this age of cloth covering.

I put my clothing in a dry spot and stepped into the big tub of super-hot sulphur-water between Zad and Preston—Preston staring at the round chick with unconcealed wide-eyed wonder.

"How is it?" asked the thin Susan, standing over me and looking like the pictures of concentration-camp Jews waiting for their showers. As pitiful as that, and also as beautiful as that.

"Hot," I said, trying not to let my eyes rest on her grape-sized breasts, but evidently failing because she folded her arms over them and turned away. Blew it again. The whole universe, full of traps.

Claud, in the other tub, said something to his wife and left the water to fumble in his pants-pocket. Preston watched him with hungry weasel eyes, seeming to know instinctively what he was after.

Claud held out a bent little joint. "Would you like some pot?" Preston leaped from the tub and ran to his jacket where he'd stashed his shaving kit. Claud had made the first move. The question, "Should a freak offer a straight looking cat a joint?" had been answered.

Joint after joint rolled from Preston's nimble assembly-line fingers, swamping our startled new friends who smoked them at Preston's insane pace to avoid offending him, or possibly to prove that they were all very hip and could inhale as much weed-smoke as the mad stranger who evidently had the approval of his three equally mad friends.

Zad sat in full lotus position on one of the tables, silhouetted against the holy stars. Steam rose from his wet body, his head was thrown back and his mouth hung open as he drifted through no-time and endless space. I saw him as a god-sent vision of an ancient Tibetan monk, gazing far beyond his eyes at the wonder of enlightenment. He fell to his back, arms flung wide, legs still crossed, a sound between an om and a low cry of pain or ecstasy rising from his gaping mouth and mingling with the steam that rose from his body.

Preston, reverently irreverent Preston, said, "Go you dog," as he rolled another joint.

Zad twitched once all over in a spasm of approaching ego-loss, and Preston laughed. Baxtor and I laughed too, but the others were somewhat shaken by this display and began to whisper among themselves and such-like.

With the hot baths, the steam, the Big Sur narcotic night-air, Zad's vibrations, and many joints, everyone was soon totally ripped and having a good deal of trouble communicating on any verbal level. The solution to this problem is to simply quit trying to communicate with words, but some of the members of our bathing party either didn't know that or had forgotten it. There was considerable confusion. The round chick, submerged up to her mother-nature watermelon breasts, began to pick up uncomfortable signals from Preston, and the evidently boy-friend started eyeing us all suspiciously, so the little blondish thing got scared and it showed on her face, which caused the thin Susan to think something was happening that she wasn't in on, and she stood up fast and it turned out to be *too* fast and she fainted. Not a sound out of her. She just stood up and wilted . . . plop, on the stone floor.

The beautiful wife of Claud, who had been worried about and unsure of the situation from the beginning, freaked openly. Claud saw the scene getting out of hand and, realizing that he was very high, became worried himself.

Soon everyone but Zad was aware that things were turning strange. Zad was blissfully unaware of anything taking place around him, reviving only once or twice to leap into the hot sulphur-water and then out again to resume his position on the wet table-top, "O OOOOOOOOooooowwwwmmmmm . . ."

The thin Susan fainted again after only two or three seconds of consciousness, and Claud carried her into the shower room followed by his wife.

I got dressed, as did the round chick and her (I had, by this time, decided) probably boy-friend, while the blondish chick went into the shower room to dress. Baxtor got out of the tub and pulled on his pants, but Preston only rolled another joint.Zad lay full length on the table, his eyes and mouth as wide as they could possibly get, gone. Just "OOOOOOoooooaaaaauuuuuooooww mmmmmmm," now and then whenever he got the feeling.

Claud came out of the shower room and said, "Time's up," politely, tapping his wristwatch as a visual aid.

"Is the chick all right?" I asked.

"Sure thing. No problem. Too much steam."

Preston handed him a recent joint and he took it automatically, then handed it back, saying, "Uh . . . no thanks. I'm feeling good."

"Hah!" said Preston, "Not as good as old Zad," which seemed to strike Claud as an odd thing to say or, perhaps he read something into it, because he looked perplexed, started to say something, changed his mind and said, "Time's up," then turned and walked away.

"Hey Zad. We gotta go now," I called.

Zad didn't move. I shook him and said, "Hey, man! Our time's up."

His eyes swam into focus. I could see the little Zad-pilot waking up and stumbling to the controls, flicking switches and pulling knobs at random. Zad rose to his feet, "Very good," he said, and jumped into the tub.

"Atta boy, Zad," said Preston, jumping in himself.

It took awhile, but eventually all four of us were dressed and following the six other bodies up the trail.

G'bye to everyone when we reached the top of the hill. Zad waved goodbye to us and started to walk away.

"Not you, Zad. You're with us."

Zad trotted back and said, "Let's go down there and take a bath in the hot-springs."

I told him that we already had. He said, "Ah," and climbed into the bus.

"Well, crew," said Baxtor, sliding in behind the wheel, "Back to magic San Jose, the jewel of the West."

"No!" yelled Preston. "Back to the beach. I reject any and all suggestions pertaining to a return to San Jose. This is home! Baxtor, you low dog, how can you even say something like *San Jose* after that bath experience? Have you no sense of decency? That was by far the most fattening two hours I've ever wallowed in. Zad, you want to stay, don't you?"

An amiable nod from Zad who was understanding none of this but anxious to please.

"See? See? Zad wants to stay. Now let us have no more mutinous mouth-noise from you swine. We've only been here for . . .

Baxtor started the car and swung onto the highway, heading for home with heavy dissent from raging Preston who grumbled all the way, saying that the next time he came to Sur it would be with plenty of food and no useless companions and he was staying forever.

"Everything has to come to an end, Preston."

"Only as long as everyone agrees that such is the case."

"There'll be other times, man."

"A groundless assumption. I know for a fact that there *is* this time, and that's the one I'm concerned with. It's the one that has *me* and *now* in it. Back to the beach! Back!"

CHAPTER ELEVEN – OTHER DAYS

In the summer, when the days were long and hot, and often in the winter, to witness a storm, we pilgrimaged to Sur whenever the vibrations were impossible to ignore, sometimes staying to explore the forests or run around the beaches for a week or two, finally dragging ourselves back to civilization when food or energy ran out, sometimes returning simply because the toys and games of civilization and society are novel and even fascinating, and we hadn't outgrown them yet.

Maybe once a week or at least once every two weeks, a bunch of us would get a car and drive to San Francisco to visit Lyla and sit around Haight Street, digging the shops and the people, hunting for happenings, maybe take a wander through Golden Gate Park, or jump over to Berkeley to find Preston, see what he's up to. Many expectant searches for wise old modern Sages we'd heard about, who would usually turn out to be blown acid-dealers-turned-messiah or tired old men quoting faded passages from Salvation Army pamphlets (which might just be where it's at). "There is salvation in Jesus, brother."

"I'm hip. How do I find it and keep it?"

"Accept Jesus as your Saviour, brother."

"How can I accept Him as my Saviour before He saves me?"

"Repent your sins, brother."

"I already have, man. Now what?"

"There is *Sal*-vation in Jesus Christ. Would you believe that I was a wino and a sinner for thirty years?" (I would. You look like a man who has been a wino and a sinner for thirty years) "It's true, brothers! I was a lost and troubled sinner for thirty years! Then I found salvation in Christ Jesus! Praise be to Jesus, brothers!"

"But what about the war, man? And the draft and jail? What

do I do about food and clothing now that I've accepted Jesus as my Saviour?"

"There is salvation only in Jesus, brother. Sal-vation in Jesus Christ the Lord!"

In San Jose, we watched LaMer sweat and jump around naked to the waist and sometimes beyond, yelling entire chapters of the Bible, all mixed up with parts from the Koran and Ginsberg's *Howl*, at jeering crowds of college kids. " . . . and them people that follow the one who come down with that flamin sword in his mouth, them people have blown it bad an are gonna be screwed by the *real* Messiah, cuz the *real* Messiah ain't gonna have no sword, flamin or otherwise, in his mouth! That's like it is! An if it sounds like somethin you heard, it's cuz it is somethin you heard . . . an you didn't listen *that* time *either*!" Shouting the last part over his shoulder as he sprints away, outrunning the Campus Security Cops who have arrived to cart him off for being naked in public again.

Any other day I'd wake up to find Beau or Preston or Baxtor or Tom or all four still crashed in sleeping-bags or blankets on the floor where they'd fallen out the night before. If no one had to be anywhere (and no one ever *had* to be anywhere) we'd start rolling joints, sitting on the floor in our underwear, shouting questions and fantasies and sorrows and joys at one another until it became early morning of the next day and we'd fall out again to wake up that afternoon and start all over for three days and nights in a row or until something came up to break the set.

We tried to take acid the same way for awhile. Then we began to find ourselves in dangerous, mindless situations on the city streets more and more often, bewildered by the lights and horn-honks and hurry-fast citizens, confused, frightened and once or twice busted by suspicious cops, freaked-out in general by the hard, straight, insane city vibes, so that after many mind-rotting scenes we came to prefer taking acid in friends' mountain cabins, in the forest itself, or at relatively deserted beaches (except for special tribal gathering occasions, or when there was no transportation out of the city, or in an attempt to recapture carefree city-trips gone-by, or in an effort to work out a structural environmental problem of some kind).

Many hours, days and nights, spent walking the downtown streets with Preston or Baxtor or in a big herd of everybody, laughing at neon signs and billboards that said, "EAT," "SLEEP," "BUY," "STOP," "GO," "WAIT," "WALK," "DRINK." Preston yelling, "Look at this one!" pointing to a billboard telling people to take the train, which has a picture of commuters' cars jammed bumper to bumper as far as the eye can see, angry faces at all the windows. "When I see things like that I really have to stop and hand it to the straight-people who don't flip out and murder their neighbors with Nazi war souvenirs. No wonder so many of the poor fuckers *do*. Can you imagine facing a scene like that every morning before your actual *work* even started? My mind boggles at the thought! What raw courage those people have."

"Or raw stupidity," says Beau, giving a scowling storeowner the finger.

"Well yes . . . but it's all relative. Courage . . . stupidity. It just depends on where you're standing."

Sitting up late at night, reading Revelations from the Bible with Brian Kelly, high and really behind it. "Wow. Those very wise, very farout ole cats saw what was happening way back then. And they tried to put it all down and turn people on to it. Lookit this, man. John tells about his trip, an then says if anybody messes with it—the story he told—you know, tries to change parts of it or like that—then they'll get the shaft from God."

"Yeah, and now they don't even teach those parts in Sunday school."

"They don't?"

"Nope. They call those parts 'Mysteries.' When I was about twelve I asked this Priest what John was saying and he told me it was a mystery and I wouldn't understand it."

"It's all evidence of the conspiracy to keep people in line."

"Of course, man. Christ was saying don't get hungup in all the bullshit of the *society* and the *You-game* because there's something bigger happening. That's dangerous talk, man. The authorities were hip to it even back then. Jesus got the shaft for saying it too loud and too convincingly."

At Zad's wedding, the Minister stood right under a picture of Christ and said to me, "I'm not going to do anything about it now, but I *will* tell you that you are not welcome in my church." *His* church? Cold. Really cold. The god he represents is a pigeyed, pot-bellied, bigot pimp. Everybody stands around clearing their throats, ashamed, while I say, "What did *I* do?"

"What did you do. You come to this House of God looking like . . . like *that*, and ask me what you did? Look at yourself!" I look at myself—mostly the part that shows because I'm pretty sure that's all this guy can see. Rented Tux, polished shoes, clean finger-nails. "I was told to wear a tuxedo. I thought I was supposed to."

"I'm not talking about your clothes. I'm referring to your hair and that beard. You look like a *tramp*. I won't throw you out, as I should, but you are not at all welcome in this church." Above the Minister's head, Jesus looked down from the cross with sad, holy eyes. Jesus in the hands of ugly old bigot anti-Christs, but making it through holy just the same. A week before this enlightening meeting, Brian and I had decided to visit a Priest—a Western holy man—just to see what they had to say. Now I knew.

After the ceremony, Zad shook his head in disgust and said, "He's no 'Man of God.' He's a used-car salesman." The Minister split right after he said his final words and locked himself in his study so he wouldn't have to look at us. For a couple of days we talked about burning down that house of false prophecy as a service to the community, but ultimately decided that "Vengeance is Mine," says God, and we figured it would all come out clean at the gates of eternity.

Much later, in San Jose, still bitter and suspicious of the clergy, I met "Father" Roy, a Baptist Minister who worked with what he called "the Love-people" (he never used the term "hippie"). He didn't try to preach to us, didn't tell chicks they'd be damned for laying their boyfriends or any of that noise, he just hung around, ran a little coffee house called The Wail, did what he could, and let it be known that he was there to talk to if anybody felt like it. For a long time no one did. He was a nice guy, but who wants to talk to a preacher when you know damn well they're all working for the establishment? Father Roy didn't push it. He didn't try to pull any of that "I'm your pal and it's alright if you say damn around me" crap. He just stayed in the shadows until we were all used to having him around. He never tried to convert anybody or put anyone or any belief down. As a matter of fact, he didn't do or say much of anything—only listened and watched and waited until he knew *us* well enough to know who he was talking to . . . and what he was talking about. Within a year, among the "Love-people" of San Jose, Father Roy became the most respected professional Christian walking the earth. Even hard-core, old-time Zen Buddhists would drop in to talk things over with him. I don't imagine he ever realized how much he was doing for Christ.

He told me once, "There are twisted, bad things going on in the church. I'm well aware of it. Some of the things I see make me absolutely ill—sick to my stomach. But in there somewhere (and I know sometimes it's hard to see) there's a lot of good. There's truth there, Abel. I think you know that. There's truth and love in Jesus' teachings, even as distorted and misquoted as they've become. We're after the same thing, Abel. We're working for the same thing."

Working for the same thing. But working for anything *all the time*wears you down. Especially when you're not completely sure that the "Thing" exists in any attainable sense. A vast number of people assured me that it didn't. Who do you believe?

Talking to old junkies, hiding behind shades and smoking cigs down to their yellow, trembling finger-tips, "You hippies ain't bein cool. You ain't bein atal hip, baby. You makin so much fuckin noise, you puttin the heat on us all. I don't want no revolution, baby, I just wanna get by."

"But that's only turning your back on the real problem, man. We're tryin to make it so there won't be heat on *anyone*. You don't wanna spend the rest of your life groveling for enough bread to score enough dope to keep you goin long enough to run after another fix? Do you?"

Taking short, nervous pulls from the pinched cig, "You cats is just kids, baby. Just a buncha young *kids*. When you been in it as long as I been you'll realize that that's where it's all really at, baby."

"What's where it's all really at?"

Cig so small it's just a hot ash between his finger-nails—squeezing smoke out of it "Just gettin by. Goin as long as you can, as quiet as you can. That's were it's at baby."

"Man, you oughta take some acid."

"Listen . . . I took some a that shit in L.A. You wanna get y'sef spaced *that* way, you oughta shoot up a spoon a battery acid. It's the same trip, baby. I've geezed just about ever'kinda dope there is to geeze. I've eaten it an sniffed it an smoked it an crammed it up my asshole, but I couldn't handle that fuckin LSD. It's pure insanity, baby. Why anybody'd wanna go in-sane on that shit is way beyond me."

Later that night, out on the street Beau says, "And the straights call *us* junkies. Junkies are just sick straight-people who happen to take drugs. Just trying to 'go as long as they can, as quiet as they can' from one dope fix or money fix to the next. Fuck."

"Did you notice that he said we were 'only kids' and so we didn't know where it was all at yet?"

"That line doesn't hold up any more."

"Yeah, but all old people say it. They tell you from birth on that the reason you don't understand things is because you aren't old enough yet—not as old as them. If you don't agree with them, if you don't think like they do, it's because you're still a kid. Even if you hold out till you're eighty, they'll say you just never grew up. What can you say to em? Anything you say in your defense becomes proof that you're not 'an adult' yet."

"Peter Pan was always one of my heroes," says Beau, and I can see that he's tired of the worn-out old conversation, "I always dug Old Pan's trip. Aside from his rather limited sex life . . . which may have been a cover-up on the part of some puritan historian . . . Who knows what kind of weird things him and Tinker Bell pulled off? . . . and aside, of course, from the later-learned faggot symbolism. Although he just mighta tamped a few . . . " something about long nights and the lost boys as we walk into China Town where I eat a fortune cookie inside of which is the message,

You think that it is a secret
but it never has been one.

I ate the message as well, and washed it down with a cup of tea. Can't even trust a fortune cookie anymore.

In Zad's infamous Trip Room, many bodies sprawled everywhere, on mattresses, on pillows and rugs, all under the multicolor tent-structure that Zad erected in one room of his three-room shack. A patchwork tent of Oriental Macy's and downhome rioting, clashing colors, sewed and safety-pinned together, with speakers and amplifiers hidden everywhere, behind the cloth walls, under rugs, inside pillows, controlled by Zad who sits beside a thousand dials bathed in pale green light. With a twist or a flick of his finger he swings sound across the walls, flashes lights, switches to strobe, back to color wheel, runs the audio-visual effects of the circus. Electronic rock is our sound cyclorama. The Trip Room is all flashing lights and sound and hash pipes and hookahs of weed and Zad's little insane dog shitting where you can't find it and sometimes ten people all jammed in and blasted out of control.

Pushed above the environment, my voice, barely audible, "Why are we here?"

"What?" two voices.

Louder, "Why are we here?"

Guitar fighting an organ. Strobe light. One voice above it, "You mean in this room? To get high!"

In between drum-beats, through strobe and color-wheel, "No, I mean like here on earth. You know . . . *here* . . . in this scene."

Another voice, "Same reason, man. To get high."

"Aw come on. That isn't it! 'To get high.' To get high for what reason?"

Maybe Zad's voice, "We're here to have fun."

"Okay . . . why? And how come everybody isn't having fun?"

"How come *you're* always trying to figure it all out? Why don't you just let things go, man? It's the way of the Tao. Effortless. No picking and choosing."

"I just want to have one or two of my many whys answered. It's a hangup, maybe, but it doesn't seem like much to ask."

"They'll all be answered when you're enlightened."

"Only if I keep asking."

"Wrong, Abel. When you *stop* asking."

Another voice, "Read the Koran. Read Allen Watts, or even the Bible. They're fulla nice little neat answers."

"I've read em. All I got was bigger an better whys . . . which I'm not altogether positive that I am thankful for."

"Don't get hungup thinkin, man."

"What *should* I do then?"

"Live, man."

"By what rules? Toward what goal? With which set of rules?"

"Your own. The rules of God and nature. Same thing."

"But you can't get away with that!"

"If you really want to you can. If enough people get . . ."

"I don't think it'll happen."

"It's thinking like that that keeps it from happening."

Is it? and I fade back into the strobe light and moving sound. The music is saying, "Jump on, people! Grab hold and let's go far above and far beyond this frozen world," I climb, using the electronic patterns as ladder rungs, to the peak of the Himalayas and then three rungs more. But every record ends . . . with a scream, leaving you to gasp and crawl back, or with a receding murmur, leaving you right at the beginning once more. Only the memory of the trip. Like everything . . . only the memory.

When I'd get restless or discouraged or doubtful or just sad or tight-jawed and down, I'd get on my faithful old companion bike (grown badly in need of repair—paint scratched and chipped, parts stolen and never replaced) and ride in whatever direction it wanted to go. No better therapy for a tight mind. Wind in your face, the cement blurring by inches beneath your feet, a big engine banging and vibrating between your legs, fast or slow with a twist of the throttle, the thunder-rumble of twin pipes in your ears and tumbling in the street behind you, no decision that you can't handle with throttle, clutch, brake or all three in fast, smooth harmony, and there's mile after mile of scenery flashing past with you in command.

I'd ride in a state of no-thought or simple good-thought until the wind had blown my mind-cloud away or until a cop stopped me and ruined the mood.

Peggy Malory, a cute little round blonde I'd met at college, and Sarah Dennis, small and thin with short black hair and Italian eyes and a head full of printed mysticism, were the two chicks I usually turned to for body comfort and woman-touch. They both lived close to my apartment, had their own scenes going for them and never tried to control mine, which made for a fine, mutually satisfying relationship. Nights I didn't feel like sleeping alone I'd walk over to Peggy's house or, if she was busy, over to Sarah's apartment where I'd smoke weed, she'd drink wine, we'd talk and finally go to bed. Wake up the next day and, if it was Peggy, she'd already be off to work and I'd play a few records before heading home. If it was Sarah, she'd feed me orange juice and cereal and maybe tell my fortune with a deck of cards before driving me home on her way to school. No heavy involvement, no snags, just easy and nice.

Some nights I'd get hungry for a chick I'd never seen before. I'd just want to be with and make love to a chick I knew nothing about—one who knew nothing about me. An unwise practice with the clap running rampant, and an ego-game of some kind, yes indeed, but so are all the others—so are all the others.

When the feeling got hold of me I'd put on a T-shirt, get into my leather jacket and run my bike to The Place or The Wail or wherever I knew there'd be bodies, park my machine and go through "What's happening, man?" with familiar faces, then break away to sit or stand in shadows watching the scene's chicks. Beautiful chicks. Some are ugly all the way down to their hard back-bones, but most are so beautiful just by being chicks. You can't become totally enlightened and still want chicks, and that's one of the things—just *one* of the things—that makes enlightenment so painful-hard to reach. Because chicks are so perfectly female and beautiful. Not toothpaste beautiful, not roll-on deodorant beautiful, not hair-bleach beautiful, not ten dollar perfume beautiful or any of the other plastic ad-man beautifuls you're told to expect and even demand. *Chick* beautiful. Flesh and fur and breath and warm-woman beautiful.

I'd sit in shadows, seeing all this and thinking all this and sooner or later one of the untaken females would magically somehow match orbits with me and decide on an impulse or maybe take awhile to think up an unnecessary opening, hit me with a smile or a practiced mysterious look, saying, "Are you as lost as I am?" or, more likely, "Is that your motorcycle outside?" (old bike being a great chick magnet, probably due to all the nasty stories concerning the evil boys who ride them).

The pick-ups were usually high school girls or a just-out-of-high-school girl who'd been warned about free love, dope and bearded wild-men, and now wanted to get some first-hand experience or had already had experience and now considered herself a hippie in good standing. Sometimes it would be a slightly drunk sorority thing who was mad at her boyfriend or maybe just bored and wanted to be "far out" and "wild" for a night, take a peek at all the action she'd been told was going on so she'd have something to remember college by. Sometimes—the best times—it would be a fairly squared-away, good-headed and hearted chick who was high and lonely and just happened to like me. Never a shortage of chicks, though. Always chicks around, and most of them restless and wondering and anxious to be living and just as confused and tired of their sad little hack-written roles as anyone else. Everybody looking for what's happening or trying to make something happen.

I'd take them for rides on old bike, fast and hard, with their fingers tight on my stomach and their breasts shoved nice into my back. Light words, heavy bullshit if they wanted it, then we'd go to their place or, if they lived in dorms or with their parents, to my apartment and eventually to bed. In the morning they'd be gone. If not, I'd take them home . . . or somewhere, and maybe see them again or maybe not, and it was never important. It's good for the male ego. It's a diversionary tactic, but if you don't remind yourself of the fact, it supplies a release. Tomorrow you might be old and bald and tired and ugly and unloved, (and if you look around you you'll see that that's no-doubt-about-it what's in store) but right *now* you can get a chick just by staying in one place until one of them chooses you.

But the flash fades long before your sex-drive. In no time at all you can't even ball your way out.

Wendy was the name of the chick who brought this minor satori down upon my undeserving head. One night with a young hung chick named Wendy taught me a sad lesson in movement and loveless sex.

It was a Friday night. The San Jose streets were busy with Friday night action—action in search of some action. I was restless, tight, empty . . . trying to bring it all down to a level I could deal with. Bike's rear tire banged against the curb, I killed the engine, toed down the kickstand, peeled off my gloves and went into The Wail where David Anderley and his band were making a flood of electronic sound for wall-to-wall bodies all sitting cross-legged under the music. David stood in front of his amp with his back to the room, working guitar strings, doing something personal and pure. I listened by the door for a couple of minutes, then picked my way through the crowd to the snackbar.

From behind the counter Brady in his black cowboy-hat, a thin black cigar under his Bat Masterson mustache, handed me a mug of cider and said, "Hey'd you know Adriel's back from Georgia?"

I didn't know. "Mmm. Hope to see her." Small memories of an Adriel three years ago—a happy little artsy-craftsy chick doing happy little sculptures and paintings at a time when I was disgusted with nearly everything, art and artists included, drifting into validation with the Night Riders. But I meant it when I said, "Yeah. I'd like to see her again."

None of the available chicks looked interesting or interested, so back outside to drink my cider, sit on my machine, smoke cigarettes and watch the cars that went by at a crawl in search of something worth stopping for. Mechanical traffic noise, muffled electric music from inside The Wail and from passing car radios, neon sign and street-light buzz and blink—stars hidden by the reflected glare of the city. Suddenly it all sounded and looked gloomy and tired. I set the cider mug on the sidewalk, propped my feet up on the handlebars and thought about riding over to Santa Cruz to sit in the sand by the ocean and let the blue mood that was creeping up on me do its thing all the way.

"Would you take me for a ride?"

I turned to see neutral-colored hair, green eyes, pug (too bad, because it's outgrown cute) nose, sweatshirt over small breasts, small ass, legs hidden by oversized Levi's, bare feet. She was seventeen. No older. Possibly younger. She'll say she's eighteen or nineteen because they all do. I said, "Alright," flipping the cig butt into the street. "Where'd you like to go?" Kick, and the engine under me started.

"It doesn't matter," she said, climbing on behind me. "I just want to GO."

I mentally calculated the number of teen-movies I'd heard that line in. Did the movie-people originally get it from the kids, or did the kids pick it up from the movies? Bike's tire said *erk* and the three of us, me, ole cycle and her, rapped down the street, through a yellow light toward "it doesn't matter" which is, of course, the same as nowhere.

Right away hands slipped inside my jacket to finger my stomach. Very hot pants, I thought to myself, cruising along dark streets and admittedly digging it. Hard little bumps nibbed against my back and it felt good enough to pull my own pants tight across the zipper. I wondered how old she really was.

We pulled over at a local park, left the bike and laid on the wet grass. A prowl-car swung by slow and I had to do some curfew paranoia till it slipped away.

"What do you do all day?" she asked—a long blade of grass between her teeth.

"Ride around."

"All the time?"

"No."

"What else do you do?"

"Sit around."

"That's all?"

"No."

My answers sparkled with such wit that she laughed and rolled over to kiss me. A young kiss trying to be an old experienced kiss, so it wasn't too good . . . but it wasn't too bad either. When it was over and something had to be said I asked, "Whaddaya do?"

She rolled to her back again. "I go to school . . . sometimes." She paused for effect, then repeated, "Sometimes."

"Hmm. Where?" thinking that maybe she was actually going

to level with me.

"City College. Money hassles, y'know. I'm transferring to Berkeley next semester."

Bullshit, I said, but only to myself. To her I said, "Ah. Yeh, I got some friends in school there. It's a good house of learning."

"School," she said, "is a drag," playing with my hair and working at making her eyes smolder.

"True." And this was also getting to be a drag, so, "It's prob'ly close to eleven. I'm gonna make it pretty soon. Anywhere you wanna go?"

"Yes. With you."

"I'm just gonna go back to my place . . .

"Take me with you."

This was more or less what I had in mind, but I tried not to be a pushover. I have my pride. "You waste no time," I smiled, pretending to be Paul Newman the handsome drifter.

"I haven't any to waste," she murmured, which ripped me out nicely because it was exactly the proper line, following wild and worldly Joanne Woodward's script to the letter . . . and I should have countered with long, pregnant seconds of meaningful silence before running my ice-blue eyes the length of her graceful body, back to her face for a close-up as a foghorn blows mournful notes in the distance, trailing off to cold stillness (with maybe a little soft ocean sound) at which point I say, "Let's go, baby. We'll run in front of the wind as long as we can. We're that kind of animal. You and I are the earth's wild, free wind-runners. We never touch ground, baby," as mist swirls and defiant waves are heard thundering all around us walking hand in hand down the darkening beach, two sets of footprints being erased by the rising tide, music crashing to a powerful climax as the camera swings up and holds on two gray gulls winging higher and farther out over the sea into racing storm-clouds, and no one moves from their seat . . . the theater is silent . . . each individual stunned by the impact of this soul-freezing portrayal of stark human life.

But instead, for no particular reason, (could just as easily've played it all the way) I broke character and said, "What about your folks?"

"What about them?" she whispered, her teeth touching my ear.

"I mean, what'll the good people say when you're not home for bed?"

She thought I was making fun of her and sounded indignant when she replied, "Oh come *on*! I don't have to answer to my parents." Big exasperated sigh. "I ran away from home two years ago and never went back."

I zipped my jacket and considered this information. Possibly true (many runaways these days). Probably bullshit (many bullshitters these days). But even if it is and she is, what are my chances of getting burned? Let's see, there's always . . .

"You don't have to *worry,*" she assured me in tones that said I was being more than slightly cowardly. "They're not looking for me or anything. They don't care what I do." In a well-done aside, loud enough for me to hear, soft enough to make me think I wasn't meant to, she added, "They never did."

The movie was almost *too* familiar. No room whatsoever for creativity. The only question was, which part should I play? I could be Tire Good-guy and watch over her all night from my place on the floor—a faithful hound, a brother—eventually leading her to the path of righteousness through my lasting moral love and devotion. Or . . . I could be The Bad-guy and take her home and screw her.

I decided on Bad-guy because that role had the rewards I was interested in at that particular moment. "Okay. Stay with me tonight." I kicked bike to life, said, "Hop on," to the chick, and we rolled to my apartment.

On the way, she told me that her name was Wendy . . . which could be either *Wendy* the good little witch, or *Wendy,* Peter Pan's chick who copped-out and grew up. (Wendy only told me her name. I added the rest myself.)

At my place, lock the door, pull off jacket and T-shirt. Wendy flopped immediately on the rumpled bed and I was struck by the thought that perhaps it was too easy. I reprimanded myself for such neurotic thinking. Why should it bother me? I'd never subscribed to the theory that half the fun of balling was the battle. I'd always felt that all the fun of balling was the balling. Unless, of course, you were working some other game on the side, but at the moment I wasn't. So, kick off boots, lie on the mattress beside do-it-smile Wendy and kiss her several times before attempting to remove her sweatshirt.

What are you *doing?*" Shocked-outraged-violated.

"Taking off your sweatshirt." A statement of the obvious, it seemed to me.

My hands were removed from their resting place, the sweatshirt was jerked back over her hips. "Now be good," she commanded firmly.

I leaned on my elbow to review the situation. Could she be that dumb? that innocent? No. Highly doubtful in this day and age. Could she be *that* young? I glanced at her again—objectively. No. Probably not. Of course, it could be a game. At certain ages some chicks feel obligated to play the game of no. Then they can later yield to masculine persistence and feel taken instead of accepted. But after the come-on in the park?

A tongue in my ear while hot hands crawl over my chest, across my stomach and beyond. It's a game, I decided, and kissed her several times and waited till she ground her pelvis into my own before I attempted to remove her sweatshirt—gently, I might add.

"What are you *doing?*" she demanded. We did a repeat from that point through all that took place between that point and that point once again (with insignificant variations) until I became pissed off and left the bed to light a cigarette and grumble.

"Oh, Abel," whimpered Wendy in torment learned from many grueling hours of television study. "I don't *want* to make you unhappy."

"I tell you what then . . ."

"It's just that . . . well . . . I don't want you to think that I . . ."

"Aw come *on*! Stick to one role. Let's get it straight now. What game you wanna play?"

"I'm not playing any *game*!"

I felt like a jerk. There I was, taking it all seriously, sucked right in. "Sorry. A poor choice of words. Let's forget it, huh? Where can I take you?"

"Oh, Abel." A deep sigh of surrender. "Come here."

"No, it's all right. I mean it. I'm not broken hearted. It's your right to say no."

"You don't understand." She dropped her eyes, then brought them up to my face. She pulled her sweatshirt over her head, clutched it to her breast, then threw it on the floor. Her head fell back on the pillow with a plop. Utter resignation. Somehow, the sight of a very common dime-store brassiere failed to set my blood afire. "I don't want to say no," she whispered with painfully evident inner suffering, closing her eyes. The inner suffering was so painfully evident that I nearly vomited . . . but didn't, and simply took off my pants, then hers, and made her from behind with fast cold stabs. Masturbation, really. It wasn't making love. It was just fucking, which isn't at all bad with someone you like, but by this time I didn't even *like* Wendy, so it was nothing—cold flesh zero—nothing.

But a nothing that left me lying on my back beside sleeping, snoring, naked Wendy, while I ran bum thoughts through my head. First, ugly visions of the animal level and lower, and I saw that I was daily blowing my chances for anything higher. Then I worked it down to "why did I screw a not very good-looking teenie-bopper chick who I don't even dig one little bit?" I realized that I was running the risk of getting jailed for messing with an underage thingy, of catching some (why'd I have to think of it?) disgusting disease (the full-color slides of rotting tools that a school health instructor'd run on me leapt to bigger-than-life before my repentant eyes), of getting her (perish forbid) pregnant (she couldn't be *that* dumb . . . she could . . . I was . . . didn't even ask her if she took pills), and it wasn't even fun. No grins. No flash. What's the matter with me? Maybe the stories about long hair and faggotry are true. Maybe I've burned myself out. And now what'll I do for body kicks? Why wasn't it fun? This is supposed to be *The Rebirth of Fun.* I remembered the poster on Sharon's wall: LET FUN HAVE YOU. What happened to fun? Why wasn't fucking the chick fun?

Because we had to play a long, meaningless game beforehand.

Yeah, but a chick trying to come on like a "good-girl" is duty-bound to play that particular game in order to retain her self-respect.

Sure, but it makes the whole works all the more meaningless when she wants to be loved, *plans* to be loved, *asks* to be loved, then insists on playing the game anyway. It makes something that's satisfying and beyond fun look and feel like a zip-chrome trophy for winning a game that any clod can win given sufficient time. It's . . .

No, this is probably all wrong. I'm making too big a deal out of it. I'm tired and tight and confused. I got into her pants, didn't I? That's what I wanted, wasn't it? Having to play the game isn't her fault. She's only doing what *Teener Magazine* and all her friends say is right.

But then, it *is* her fault for not seeing through it and questioning the existence of the game. And it's my fault for . . .

And this rambled into a long, complex monologue that explored all of our guilt for not questioning the existence of meaningless games, climaxing with Society (favorite among favorite scapegoats) proven the source of all evil.

At five in the morning, during the monologue's denouement in which I was being disgusted with myself and craftily transferring the disgust to the chick, I decided to take Wendy somewhere other than my apartment. I figured the easiest out was to simply fling the albatross overboard.

Woke her up with, "Time for school."

She was puffy-eyed and ugly from sleep. Two pig noises and a gurgled, "Nugh, muh . . . mmnot gointaday."

"Sure you are. Come on, get dressed. I've got things to do."

She turned over, blinked, snuffled, saw me ready to roll and said, "Just take me wherever you're going."

"Nope. Nope, it has to be some place of your own. I've really got things to do."

She started to dress slowly with whines and murmured complaints, with no pretense of her earlier modesty, accidentally showing me an infected scab on her elbow that made me cringe in early morning revulsion. She caught my reaction, traced it to its source and quickly pulled her arm in close to her body. Embarrassing for both of us. In the merciless new daylight I saw that her body wasn't good at all—not even terribly clean. Turn away and out the door, down to the car-port to get bike going. Even old cycle was beat-up and ugly. Grease, oil, dust, dried mud—cold and moody and hard to start.

When Wendy came out to meet me, I noticed that she was shivering in the pale morning cold, wearing only her sweatshirt, so I gave her my jacket and shivered myself. Penitence.

"Where to?" over the engine-noise.

"Just drive around for a while."

"Uh-uh. Where to?"

She tucked her hands into my waistband and shoved her chest against my back—a promise. "Can't you just take me with you?"

"No. I've got some things I've gotta take care of."

"Please!"

"I can't Wendy. Where do you wanna go?"

"Ooooouh!" pulling her hands out of my pants, "take me to Larwick Apartments," she pouted. "If it isn't too much *trouble.*"

"No trouble at all." I carried her there and deposited her down the street from a battered building. "Don't go right up to it," she'd cautioned when we swung onto the street—convincing me that it had, after all, been only an exciting story about "running away from home" and an angry mom and dad would be waiting for her with a stiff punishment for having stayed out all night (or maybe with no punishment, depending upon which child-psychology books they'd read, or how much they actually gave a damn in the first place).

I collected my jacket and rode away fast, mad at myself and feeling cruddy. Smog and road-grime, itchy eyes and sewer in my mouth. No bright side. Sexual liberation and psychedelic revolution just new words for young whores and junkies. A very low day—and only just begun. Everything stained with the poisons of no-sleep and bad-thoughts.

Back at my apartment, the night's sins caught up with me for real when I found Al Vaughn camped at the door, reminding me that we were supposed to help build a speaker's platform for a pro-love anti-war demonstration that day. I could see how it all fit. I accepted the weight of quick karma with hardly a moan. Sometimes it comes back just that fast.

CHAPTER TWELVE—BLESS THE HOLY TWELVE. EVEN THE FAKE WHO REPLACED HIP JUDAS ISCARIOT

For a long stretch of time, all of us, Vaughn, Preston, Baxtor, Ted, LaMer (especially ex-Marine LaMer), Curt, Zad, myself and nearly everyone we knew were staunch supporters of demonstrations against the war. We went to every one we could and helped any way we could. We marched along carrying flowers, singing "We shall overcome" and smiling at the poor misguided people who bounced rocks off our heads. It was for peace, and everyone wanted peace. This was before we became discouraged with speeches by people who we didn't necessarily consider our representatives, speeches that said the same thing over and over again getting absolutely no results, peaceful demonstrations that got busted by the cops, where we sat quietly getting clubbed and tear-gassed and dog-bit, showing the world that we stood for love, only to get beat-up at the next "peaceful demonstration," and the next and the next, our women pushed and night-sticked and jeered at by public-minded citizens, while one speaker said, "War is bad," and the other said, "War is necessary," and one speaker said, "We will teach the world to love by loving it and its people no matter what," and the other speaker said, "We will teach you to shape-up by kicking the crap out of you every chance we get," and one speaker said, "War is bad," and the other speaker said, "War is necessary," and the war, of course, went on.

But at *this* time (chapter twelvish and some pages past) we all believed in the anti-war cause and felt that very soon the government would say, "Hey man, they're right! People don't want to fight wars. Let's call it off." One of the pleasanter things that the cops and hawks called us was, "Stupid Pacifists."

—CONCERNING THE OBVIOUS, NAIVE AND MANY-TIMES SAID, WHICH MUST BE RE-SAID BECAUSE IN CHAPTER TWELVE WE ALL SINCERELY BELIEVED IT AND SAID IT MANY TIMES AND IT ALL SOUNDED SO SIMPLE THAT WE WERE POSITIVE THAT SOON EVEN GENERALS WOULD BE ABLE TO GRASP IT—

Do you realize that if everyone simply agreed to stop killing one another there would be no more war? Just think! No more murder, no more billions upon billions of dollars spent devising ways of blowing people's guts out, no more guts blown out, no more legless eighteen-year-olds returning from somewhere-islands, no more bombed out houses, no more sobbing war-widows holding burned-up babies, no more . . . no more any of that insanity. Couldn't you dig it? Why is it so *hard* to get people to stop killing? We have world-wide communication now, why don't people get together and agree to stop killing one another? Nearly everyone you talk to says killing is bad. Then, of course, most of them quote Generals and point out how "we" have to keep killing so that "they" won't take what "we" have, and "they" tell their pacifists that they must realize that killing and war are necessary to stop "them" from taking what "they" have. BULLSHIT. Can't you see what utter, pure, simple, childish (no, *adultish)* bullshit that is? It means that "we" have to keep killing and being killed until there are no more "them" left (the definition of *them* depending entirely upon where *we* are located), then "we" wait until more "thems" evolve and start all over again. You have world-wide communication. Talk to one another. CUT THROUGH THE BULLSHIT.

Murder, including murder sanctioned by the state, is wrong. All of history's wise men have said in no uncertain terms that murder is wrong. Why keep doing it? Why not stop? Tell all of your friends. Tell everyone you meet that you will never kill another person. Tell them to pass it on. Get everyone behind it and killing will stop.

Do you *like* wars and murder? Some of you do. I once talked to a soldier who said that he would pay to get back to Vietnam. "You don't know what it *feels* like to kill a man," he said. There are undoubtedly others who feel the same way. These people are sick, not to mention dangerous. I'd just as soon not be around them, but if this is their trip—if this really makes them happy, then they should be allowed to do it. Everyone should be allowed to do his or her own personal thing AS LONG AS IT DOESN'T INVOLVE TO THE POINT OF BRINGING DOWN INDIVIDUALS WHO *AREN'T* ON THE SAME TRIP.

Let the kill-game people—the pro-warriors, Generals—let them have a whole island to themselves. Let them kill other kill-game people on the island. Let them assemble there and choose sides and then kill and capture one another endlessly, without interfering with the people they call "lamentable civilian casualties." It can be done. Don't you see? It can be done! Get behind it. Just don't give them any boats or airplanes because they'll organize and attack the rest of the world. It's their trip. Let them work it out on themselves.

Everyone who doesn't want to kill . . . stop killing! Refuse to kill. It's that simple. Refuse to kill.

Refuse to kill, as many of us did, and you will discover that you will be put in jail, your parents will be shamed, good, patriotic people will call you a yellow pacifist, and you'll never get a job or find a place to live. Just refuse to kill.

If you are healthy and sane, it's your duty to kill on command. If you are crippled or insane, it's too bad and you don't get to join the military and kill with all the latest equipment. Only healthy, sane people may become soldiers and be allowed to kill. If you are healthy and sane, it is your duty to become a soldier and kill your country's enemies. Your country will point them out to you. All you have to do is kill them. You should be proud. It's an honor. God's on your side. There's a crisis . . . yesterday, today, and tomorrow.

CHAPTER THIRTEEN – COPS (Archaic slang for "Pigs")

In Berkeley, a demonstration against the war was breaking up after an uneventful day of promised hope and joy. LaMer and I walked off the Cal campus feeling high and good because many people were present at the gathering and brotherhood was something real that day and we honestly believed that antiwar and anti-hate sentiment was gaining hold and soon there would be no more war, no more hate, and peace would come to the earth.

Across the street, we sat on the curb eating candy-bars, smiling at pedestrians, digging the sun. "How come Three Musketeers don't have three flavors no more?" said Andre.

"Did they ever?"

"Sure! An you was supposed to share em with two friends."

"Candy-bars were bigger."

"An our mouths was smaller."

"A point."

A cop appeared, stopped in front of us and said, "Get your asses off the sidewalk. It's for *people* to walk on, not for *you* to *sit* on."

We got to our feet, Andre brushed off the cement in case he'd dirtied it up with the seat of his pants, and the cop told us that he'd been at the "peace-nik rally" and was "sorry none of em got outta line. I was hopin I'd get to crack one of those creep's heads."

"Wow!" yelled Andre, holding his head in both hands. "That's the ugliest thing I've heard all day! You're *crazy*! I bet you'd dig bein on the Selma police force."

The cop hitched his gun-belt. "Niggers an these hippies—they're all the same to me. Now move it'er I'll run you in."

LaMer was screaming, "GAAAAHHHH!" as the cop strutted away.

Which brings me to cops, which brings me down, but which

is, unfortunately, part of the scene we all worked with. So Chapter Thirteen is about us and the cops. I might as well get it out of the way.

Everybody I trust avoids the cops like the Black Plague. And this is frightening—this is wrong—this shouldn't be. These aren't "criminals." These are "good-people." They're college students, high school kids, artists, writers, never-hurt-anybody love-freaks, college profs and truck drivers. They dislike cops and are afraid of cops. If a cop decides to give you a hard time, you're in for trouble. What can you do? Call the cops on him? Take him to court? Ah yes. There were those who tried. They went down fighting, they went down following due process of the law, they went down broke and in debt, they went down discouraged and innocent, but when all is said and done . . . they went down.

The police were fuzz, bulls, badges, storm-troopers, blues, laws and The Man, but mostly "the goddam cops" (eventually refined to "the fuckin pigs"). They busted your friends, stopped you on the street, pushed you into squad-cars on suspicion of anything-nothing, and weren't anywhere around when the three drunk football players beat on you in front of a downtown bar. Cops wrote your name down on ominous lists, called you a punk, called you a creep, insulted your chick, broke up your parties, searched your house, and took it upon themselves to remind you constantly that you were a nobody in a society of somebodies and completely at their mercy.

Bitter words. Friends, this is a bitter chapter, written from memories of bitter moments of frustration.

When I rode with the outlaws, I hated cops because it was part of the role, because cops were The Enemy. We raised incredible hell and it was their job to stop us. We hated them and they hated us with good reason. When we got the chance, we jumped on them. It all evened out. We may've burned a cop-bike or two, but they ran over our machines whenever they could, or stole them legally when they arrested us. We'd punch a cop for pushing us, and the cops retaliated by beating us into the ground with nightsticks. Give and take. A fair exchange.

But when I dropped my colors and left the Night RidersI was tired of warring with the cops twenty-four hours a day, tired of being busted and searched and beat on and shot at. I wanted to hunt quietly for some kind of peace. I fell in with people who were looking for the same thing.

Once again I must ask you to remember that this is a chronicle of the past. Even as I write, things have changed—things are going to keep changing. But the early acid-eaters (ultimately covered by the blanket-term "hippies") were the most law-abiding people I ever met. Their one crime was their devotion to substances which, in the twentieth century, were considered illegal drugs. (Perhaps another was their love of love which has gotten people into trouble more than once). They didn't even try to break traffic laws. They didn't want to hassle *anyone.* They went out of their way to avoid hassles of *all* kinds—*especially* cop hassles.

The remainder of this bitter chapter is devoted to:

STANDARD STORIES OF THE PIGS WHICH HAPPEN REGULARLY THROUGHOUT THE BOOK BUT HAVE BEEN SPLICED TOGETHER HERE IN ORDER THAT YOU MAY SKIP THEM IF YOU'VE ALREADY HEARD OR HAD YOUR QUOTA OF PIG STORIES. THEY ARE RELEVANT ONLY AS BACKGROUND INFORMATION. (And as a therapeutic device intended to chase devils from my own hung mind. I'll pay for it.)

"Why do you wanna bug us all the time?" I asked a cop as he searched Ted's car.

"That's my job, buddy."

"*Buggin* people?"

"Protecting people."

"Well what're you protecting us *from?*"

"I'm not protecting *you* from anything. I'm protecting *people* from creeps like you."

Anytime we used a car, we knew that we were increasing our chances of being stopped by the law. On the freeways and highways, cops pulled in behind us and shadowed our tails for miles. Always a sure-fire ticket. If we were in the fast lane, we could pull over and get cited for unsafe lane-change; speed up and get cited for speeding;

slow down and get cited for "obstructing the normal flow of traffic"; stop completely and get searched for our "suspicious behavior"; or we could simply wait for them to pull us over for unstated reasons. (Listen close and you can hear thousands of Bloods laughing their long-time hip brown heads off.)

Coming home late from a midnight eat at the downtown burger-bar, driving up Twelfth Street with Tom Hailey in his old panel-truck (Hailey was an always-hustling little Irish sometimes crystal-taker who I'd known for years. He rode a bright red, thirty-nine hog, turned on finally and became one of the local resident freaks. For a year I considered him to be one of my best friends. He was easy to be with, having a chameleon-like quality that enabled him to blend into nearly any situation that didn't require outright invention on his part. His only really glaring fault, I discovered some time later, was coveting his neighbor's chick . . . which, now that I think of it, was probably a by-product of the aforementioned chameleon-like quality) we were stopped by a cop who demanded to know where Tom had been.

"Eatin at the burger-bar," said Hailey.

"Then how come you cut down Thirteenth Street?" slyly, as though he really had us. I never figured out what Thirteenth Street had to do with anything.

Hailey'd just finished a joint and had forgotten how to come on to cops. "I didn't know it was a bad thing," he said.

The cop straightened up and hooked his thumb in his gunbelt. "I didn't ask for a smart-ass answer, pal. I seen you cut down Thirteenth an then over to Twelfth. Now where were you goin?"

"Well, I missed Twelfth, so I went down Thirteenth an then turned back onto Twelfth because otherwise I'd . . ."

"I asked you where you were *goin.*"

"We were going home . . . *to his* house," indicating me with his thumb.

The cop noticed me for the first time and shined his flashlight in my eyes. "You got some identification?"

I handed him my driver's license and he took it to his car.

"We didn't break any laws, man," I said to Tom. "He's got no reason or right to do this."

"No, but he does have a gun," observed Hailey.

Foolishly, righteously indignant, "I'm not taking any more of this shit," climbing out of the truck with a pencil and a piece of paper in my hand, intending to take down the cop's badge number. Not expecting to do anything with it, just exercising some imaginary rights because I was pissed.

The cop bad-eyed me through his windshield and I saw him grab for his radio. I had a hunting knife in a sheath on my belt and it evidently scared him since he only had a pistol, a shotgun and a club. I was writing his license-plate number when five patrol-cars screamed onto the scene like an opening for M-Squad. Head-lights, red-lights, door-slams, armed cops jumping out of their cars. It would have been exciting if it weren't for the sinking feeling that we were about to be erased by the people's police.

The first cop, who'd been sitting in his car waiting for the reinforcements to arrive, leaped out and shoved me against the side of the truck. "You just stand easy there hot-shot," he sneered, sticking his hands in my pockets, slapping my sides and the front of my pants in a way that only someone with a badge and a gun on you can get away with. I stood with my feet apart, hands on the side of the truck, hoping I wasn't going to be shot.

"Check his boots," barked another cop, "they carry knives in em."

"Aw come on," groaned Hailey, his hands in the air.

"*He* had one!" snapped the cop.

"On his belt! In plain sight!" said Hailey.

"You stand over there in the head-lights an take those boots off," commanded a fat, pink cop. Hailey did as he was told.

One of the cops started to bring a dog out of his car. "Naw, leave im in there," said the first cop.

One cop opened the back of the truck and two others opened the doors. One watched from his car with a hand on his shotgun in case we should try to use karate on the first cop who was busy interrogating us as we stood (Hailey barefoot) in the circle of head-lights. Three others helped search the truck, while one played with his police dog. Nine cops and one dog . . . two of us. It pays to be careful. We might have had armed comrades stationed in the bushes.

"I think you should have a warrant or something," said Hailey to the cop closest to him.

"You have to talk to the arresting officer about that," shrugged the cop.

"Are we being arrested?"

"I don't know a thing about it. I just answered a call." The first cop hurried by, writing in his notebook. Hailey asked, "Are we being arrested?"

"Why don't you just wait an find out, buddy?"

"Okay, but don't you need a warrant or something to search the truck?"

"What's that, pal?"

"Just a passing thought," sighed Tom.

I turned to the fat, pink cop who was pulling up the truck's carpet, looking under it with a flashlight, "You probably know the law better than I do, but . . ."

Fat-pink-cop face suddenly an inch from my own. "That's right, baby!" he fired in a Mike Hammer imitation.

I shrugged and turned away. An almost irresistible urge to make the pink, globular face into a red, flat, pizza-pie face was creeping over me. I knew better than to give in to it. I'd seen too many friends dissolve under cop-club storms. Turn the other cheek, said Jesus. Will do, said I, wondering if I could find the cop alone some night.

"You got anything to say?" demanded the recently saved cop. Not to him, so I said nothing.

"You got an argument?"

"Nope. You got the gun."

"That's got nothing to do with it!"

"No?"

"That's right, pal."

"Okay, give me the gun." A stupid thing to say. I didn't want his gun. I knew he wasn't about to give it to me. And all my asking for it did was make him madder.

"Hey, AH" he yelled to the first cop. "You got this one's name?"

The first cop said that he had, but the fat cop took it again in his *own* notebook. "Uh-oh," I thought, "Now he's gonna shoot me later if they can't get me now." (He never did, so this was purely paranoia on my part. The cop evidently just liked to write down the names of people who gave him a bad time.)

Hailey was saying in a monotone—like a broken record—"You can't do this—you can't do this—you can't *do* this—"

"Any more weapons in the truck?" From cop one.

"Hope they don't find the sub-machine gun," I whispered to Tom. Another stupid thing to do, because cop one heard me and said, "You got a machine gun in there?"

"No, no," Hailey assured him, "He was only kidding. But feel free to search the truck."

Since the truck was already torn apart, feverish searching going on all around us, the invitation to search was supposed to be a joke. One of the cops actually laughed and Hailey and I joined in. It felt like the game was breaking down for a second. I almost expected the cop to say, "This sure is a pile of bee-ess, isn't it?" But instead… "Hey, lookit here!" shouted fat cop, emerging from the back of the truck like a huge, overfed gopher, holding two Fourth-of-July firecrackers in his hand. "Transporting explosives. That's a felony, ain't it?" He placed the felonious evidence in cop one's hand.

"We could hang you good for this," said cop one to Tom.

"They're firecrackers! They're only firecrackers!"

"I suppose you don't know that firecrackers are against the law? You know damn well they're against the law!"

We stood in the center of the ring of head-lights while the cops searched with renewed vigor. Time passed and they got tired of tearing up the truck, so they formed a circle around us just beyond the glare of the head-lights. They could see us, but we could only see vague outlines of them. Un-American, un-American, un-American. All the bee-rate Gestapo films I'd ever seen came to life before my eyes. Trapped. Wolves all around. They can see us, but we can't see them. Questions from shadows—"What're you carryin that toad-stabber for?"

"It's a hunting knife. I just got back from…

"Where were you two goin?"

"We already . . .

"You belong to some kinda club?"

"No . . ."

"Then how come you both got long hair and beards and boots an T-shirts? What's that supposed to mean?"

"It's not supposed to mean anything."

"Well how come you both dress like that?"

"How come you guys all wear blue suits and badges and white helmets and short hair and . . ."

"We get paid for it, buddy. What's your excuse?"

"Why do we have to have one? We do it because we want to."

"Ooooh . . . (snicker, snicker) . . . I see. How *sweet.* Fun and games, huh?"

"Yeah, and we don't even get paid for it."

"Real cute. I tell you what. You wanna play games, we can take you down to the station and play games all night Now, where were you goin?"

"We already told . . ." and we do their thing (no alternative) until they finally have to break for coffee or something, and the first cop hands me back my knife, saying, "I'm gonna give this little sticker back to you, hot-shot, cuz nothin would please me more than to see you turn up with a bullet-hole in your little ole belly."

The other cops chuckle and nod. I've got bad feelings. Bad feelings that are gonna take a long time to wash out. "You don't even *know* me, man! Why the hell do you wanna see me with a bullet-hole in my belly?"

Getting into his car, cop one says, "Just one less for me to worry about. One less creep on the streets." And they roar off in different directions, leaving me and Tom to put the truck back together.

And this sort of thing happened about twice a week, till we all learned to sneak around better. Not many of the acid-freaks knew *how* to act like criminals before the cops taught them.

In San Jose, a cop told me, "I haven't run across a problem yet that *this* won't take care of," patting his revolver and looking stern like Matt Dillon.

One cop informed a being-searched group of us that the best

part of his job was "kickin you long-haired, pink-assed little faggots in the butt." And this man had a gun and a license to use it.

At a stop-the-war demonstration in San Fran, a cop beat Nick Burnard's wife with a nightstick and then arrested Nick for assaulting an officer (after beating him into the pavement) because he'd had the audacity to grab the cop's arm. Nick's wife was charged with resisting arrest.

Dennis Herschberg was an epileptic who made the mistake of growing his hair long. He was at a party in the Los Gatos hills when the cops rushed in and arrested everyone on "suspicion of being in or near a place where marijuana was being smoked." Dennis stupidly had an epileptic seizure, which added resisting arrest to the charges against him.

In San Jose, Roger Pokallus was in a crowd protesting the use of napalm, when a guy in a sweater and slacks hit him in the back of the head. Roger turned around and hit the dude in the stomach. The dude pulled out a badge and busted Roger for assaulting a police officer and resisting arrest.

Lou Alvarez got three years in the can for picking up a sixteen-year-old hitchhiker who had a lid of weed in his pocket. The kid and the cops all swore that Lou'd pushed the weed.

Jan Walters was picked up by the cops and charged with "threatening a man's life" after he told a restaurant owner who wouldn't serve him, "When you die and face God, you'll be sorry for this."

Pat Bollen and Mary Buckingham were busted for smoking what turned out to be a Bull Durham cigarette in the park. They spent the night in jail waiting for the cops to analyze the "vegetable substance."

Ted, Andre, George, Mark, Sherry, Carl, and Craig were all busted at least once for resisting arrest, failure to disperse, or disturbing the peace at various anti-war demonstrations.

Even when you're innocent, even when the charges are eventually dropped, you *still* sit in jail for awhile. And being busted costs money . . . money that none of us had.

Busts all the time. Someone you knew got busted every week. The busts that usually stuck were narcotics busts, because weed was good, tangible evidence and there was plenty of weed around. And if you didn't have anything in the house, the cops could always plant a joint or two, or produce a handful of seeds or a roach or some pills or the hookah you never thought about or maybe just a pack of papers, but something . . . there's always something.

At first—when everything was a big secret, everyone pretending they'd never heard of weed, people burying their stashes in the backyard or keeping them in elaborate hiding places—when a house in the area got busted we'd all go into fits of paranoia and cringe behind locked doors for weeks, waiting for The Man to bang on the door and haul us away. But after awhile we got so used to hearing about friends being busted that when it happened we just shook our heads, lit a joint, and hoped we wouldn't be next. (Fighting back came much later and has nothing to do with this time-period.)

Okay, not all cops are bastards. Okay? Some are good people, sincerely dedicated to keeping the peace, or just trying to do their job so they can feed their family. But if you're not breaking into a house or robbing a bank or raping an old lady or pulling off something along those lines, you aren't likely to meet the dedicated cop. He's too busy earning his pay, trying to catch crooks and keep the peace.

Cops, busts, the draft, landlords, rent—all minor hangups when you think about it, when there're bigger things trying to happen. It's all just background noise. Background for the search.

CHAPTER FOURTEEN – GOOD OLD CAGEY CAGE

I slid the door open and Preston grinned at me, match already to joint, thrusting a newspaper at my face with his free hand. On the front page the headlines announced, MOTORCYCLE DOPE-RING LEADER ARRESTED, and below and to the right of the heavy black words was a fine photograph of our old buddy, Roy Cage. "They got ole Cagey," said Preston. "Motorcycle dope-ring leader that he is."

I read the article while Preston made himself a cup of instant coffee. Cage had been arrested after he'd foolishly befriended a teen-age, flower-child chick who was later picked up for "being in danger of leading a loose and immoral life," freaked out and pointed the finger at Cage as the source of her corruption and a big-time dope-dealer. "They got good ole Cagey Cage."

I finished the newspaper story, which stated that Leroy David Cage was a member of the Hell's Angels (untrue) and the leader of a state-wide dope-ring (also untrue), turned back to page one and studied Cage's picture. Cage with his hair and beard all snarled and wild (they broke into his cabin while he was asleep), looking like a wise-guy Christ on the cross, his shoulders bare, mouth a tight line but his eyes prankster-smiling the way they always did, gold chain around his neck with just the top of its crucifix visible in the photo. It's Cage all right.

"You realize, of course, Preston, that Cage isn't going to stand for this. He's undoubtedly let it go this far only because 'They know not what they do.' "

"Right," said Preston, gulping his coffee and passing the joint, "I just hope he doesn't go too easy on the fuckers." The rest of the day was set aside for heavy sacrament smoking and reminiscing in honor of captured Roy Cage.

Cage was a mountain-boy who ran full tilt, head up and grinning, through a fast early teens of stealing cars and smashing them into trees with the law in hot pursuit over winding mountain roads that Roy knew far better than any sheriff. He bought an old '39 Indian motorcycle when he was about fifteen, and rattled over hills and highways at unbelievable speeds, flying off embankments and into fences regularly, having a good, mountain-boy time in general.

He turned on to weed before long, and then turned all of his Okie and hill-folk pals on to it. For an impossible couple of years, he and his wild followers did things like getting drunk on wine, then high on weed to drive their lumbering old Cadillacs, Buicks, Chevies and worn-out Studebakers into a parking-lot where they'd hold destruction derbies, driving foot-to-the-floor-flat-out and howling with mad laughter into one another until all the cars were dead, then they'd hitchhike home.

Cage gave up stealing cars, wrecking cars, and berserk activities when he became fantastically devoted to marijuana. He once had a photograph taken of his '52 Chevie covered with all the weed he and his friends could get their hands on (nearly a hundred keys), while he stood on the top with a pitchfork in one hand. He wanted to have post-cards made from the picture to send to friends, but then decided that they might fall into the wrong hands and "tend to criminate" him.

When acid became available, he took it and arrived at the conclusion that he was God. His mountain-boy followers (as well as a few hip city people who took acid with him for a laugh and got more than they bargained for) became his disciples and actually sat at his feet while he told them how nice it was going to be when they finally all got together and broke on through to The Kingdom.

"Can I have me a '63 Cor-vette, Cage?"

"Anythin you want, Russ. You jus want it an it's right there."

Once, he just dug in with a tablespoon and ate some unknown and unbelievable quantity of acid that was sitting in a bowl waiting to be capped. When it came on, he started controlling the universe. Days passed with Cage bringing the sun up on time, making it go across the sky, pushing it down behind the hills and calling for night, lighting all the stars, seeing that people and animals went to sleep and continued to breathe while they were unconscious, tending to the wind, making trees and flowers grow, causing the world to turn at just the right speed.

On the fourth day, Cage got tired and wanted to sleep himself, but by now he had too many obligations.

"There wasn't hardly no moon las' night, Cage."

"I know, but I got a lot on muh mind. You're lucky there was a moon atal."

On the sixth day, Cage was so tired that he decided to let the universe take its chances for a few hours while he rested. He closed his eyes, started to drop off... and his heart stopped. When his heart stopped, so did the universe. To start his heart—and thereby keep the universe in order—he had to walk. One step—one heartbeat—one breath—one click of the universe-cog. Another step—another heart-beat—exhale—one more click of the big cog... for five hours, and then he got panicky.

"Well... I wasn't really *panicked* like. I wuz just kinda concerned."

Wracking his very busy brain for a way out, he hit upon the idea of calling the Stanford Research Center on the phone.

"I knew there wuz alota smart people up there cuz I read about it once."

He had to march in place while he was on the phone.

"I tole em what mah problem wuz an said they'd better help me out if they wanted to keep on wakin up in the mornins, but they jus tole me I'd been messin where I shouldna been an to go to sleep. They wuzn't so smart as I read they wuz. They almos ended the whole world right there."

Luckily, Cage discovered by himself how to put "the whole works on remote-automatic-control," and he finally went to bed. Unfortunately, "remote-automatic-control" was "only good for maybe eight hours. Then she heats up." The universe was still in his hands.

Cage got all of his pals high on acid and then delegated responsibilities by granting them special powers for a limited amount of time.

"I knew I could do it, cuz one time I said 'Norm, you got the power to go get me a drinka water' . . . an he done it right off."

"Fred," he'd say, "I'm gonna let you work the sun for awhile. Now don't you go screwin it up." Fred would sit down immediately and carefully concentrate on running the sun, honored by Cage's trust in him and well aware of the importance of this cosmic task. Then Cage would give other jobs like wind, earth-turning, clouds, etc. to other responsible disciples, watch them for a while to make sure they had the hang of it, then slip away for a quick, much deserved nap.

Even those of us who didn't necessarily believe that Cage was God and in control of the cosmos (although he might well have been) liked to go up to visit him. His exploits had, by this time, made him almost a legendary figure among local psychedelic pioneers.

"I read where you can buy this pickled head," he told Baxtor and me. "I'm gonna get me that head," he said slowly, rubbing his bearded chin and working out the details as he spoke, "I'm gonna put it behind these . . . like curtains, see? An then maybe put all kindsa screams an moans on this tape recorder. Then I'm gonna get a buncha mah partners together an give em all a big dose a acid an sit em down in fronta these curtains an tell em this story 'bout the head an how there's this curse on it an anybody who looks at this head goes nuts right off. Then I say that *I* got the head an here it is right here, an then I pull back the curtains an play the screams an stuff." He chuckled his deep, Cage chuckle, visualizing the scene. "That'd sure put a few of em in the hospital. Yessir, there'd sure be alota blowed-out minds aroun here if I done that."

Cage began reading for the first time in his life after he took acid. He read whatever was hanging around—comic books, novels, magazines, old textbooks, anything, because it was all new to him. Somebody left him some books on Tibet and he devoured them in one sitting, shooting crink to keep his eyes open.

"I think I oughta go to Tibet," he said a week or so later. "I wanna meet up with one a them hermit monks I read about. Ya know, they can jus make anythin they want outta thin air. Jus . . . zap . . . an it's right there. They wear these robes an that's how they get em. Right outta thin air. I'm gonna go to Tibet an look one a these cats up an have im take me to their hang-out an get em all t'gether—maybe lay a couple a caps a acid on em—an tell em I got alota power an wanna join up with em. Then I'll say, 'Let's see what you can do' an ask em to make me up a robe outta thin air. Not jus *any* robe. I'll tell em to get me Christ's robe. I'd sure like to come on back from Tibet wearin Christ's robe."

Baxtor pursed his lips and said, "I don't know, Cage. Those monks are pretty clannish. They might not accept a Western sage."

Cage considered this unforeseen hangup, squinting his eyes and scratching his beard. "Well," he said, "Then I'll haveta start up mah own buncha hermit monks an wipe them other ones out."

Cage grew quieter and deeper as time went by and he digested more and more acid. Too old and wise at twenty-three to steal and punch cops and raise hell or even get drunk with his partners, he settled down to selling weed and acid, reading books he found and developing "The Power." He quit worrying about making a profit on the dope he sold and gave it away or passed it on for pretty much what it cost him. "I'm jus spreadin the word," he'd smile. "I ain't no dope dealer. I'm a missionary . . . workin on bein a Messiah."

"I always knew they'd eventually get ole Cagey Cage," said Preston when we'd gone over Cage's countless adventures for the third time, "Remember when he had this plan to get the smallest man in the world—some little dwarf he'd read about in one of those magazines of his—and put him in a glass case so he could watch him and smoke weed with him? And then he was going to invite the tallest man in the world over for dinner and introduce the two freaks to one another to see 'how they hit it off'."

I remember. I also remember, "That time we all went to the beach with him to dig that eclipse of the moon, and the whole thing really got to ole Cage an he wrote that message in the sand—huge letters, saying, 'GOD . . . IMPORTANT. GET IN TOUCH WITH ME . . . ' with his phone-number under it."

Preston picked up the newspaper and looked at the headlines and Cage's picture again. "*Motorcycle dope-ring leader.* It *is* rewarding. Local boy makes good."

Roy Cage, missionary working on being a Messiah, went to

prison and wasn't to come out for two years.

So many friends sent to prisons and work-farms and jails as felons for owning ounces of dried-up weed. People walking around free on the outside, plotting ways to cheat their neighbors, planning wars, making money on alcohol-drug and diet-drug and nicotine-drug, polluting the oceans and rivers and the air, lie-makers and hate-makers and walking-death-merchants all free to come and go, seeing nothing but one side of their green-paper-money blindfold, while inside prisons gentle friends are made to stare at steel bars and gray stone walls because they took it all seriously and wanted to talk to God.

CHAPTER FIFTEEN – COP OUT NOW – UNCLE SAM NEEDS YOU

To cop-out or not to cop-out. That is the question, (or at least one of the questions . . . at times it seems to be The Question). Whether tis better to live honorably, following your heart—your own visions of truth—thereby offending and generally alienating straight-society, to suffer the slings and arrows of their crap-barrage retaliation—or to cop-out and do things their way, follow the accepted pattern and squeak-by invisible on their simple little trip—pleasant, low-level validation from all sides—comfortable. It would be so easy.

Jesus looks sad when our thoughts turn to copping-out, and Buddha smiles his knowing Buddha smile.

Monday evening at my apartment in San Jose, treading brine in the wake of the crystal-ship disappearing over the horizon after a seven day cruise.

I been up all night
leanin on the window sill

Highway 61 Revisited spins slow and already scratchy from hard use on the tired record-player. Dylan farther out than ever. Everything moving in that direction . . . but not as fast as Dylan.

I'm flat on the floor—wasted—drained—saying, "Good old Dylan. Good ole psychotic, visionary Robert John, king of the lot. Ahhh, man. Puttin it down in back-home, rhyming words Dylan. Pure genius. What was it like before Dylan? What was it like without his word-images in our heads? I mean . . . Many Dylan-saturated heads nodding right along with me.

I went to tell everybody
but I could not get across

"Were we ever without him?" and Brian passes the last squeezings from our dead lid to Baxtor, shoeless and blasted, sitting like a deflated rubber doll on my blanketless bed.

Reaching back as far as I can, "I guess not. He was always there."

No more talking while we all hang behind the message of one of our Saints, waiting for the chilling, familiar flash of . . .

Don't say I never warned you
when your train gets lost

"Wouaw . . .

"That's right from way down in there."

"If only he'd come up with a solution."

"Fug. You don't deserve what he gives you."

Silence all the way through *Ballad of a Thin Man.* The record-player shuts itself down and no one says a word for half an eternity. Then, "What ever happened to euphoria? Remember euphoria?"

"Only vaguely these days . . . only vaguely."

"Everything passes, man, as The Dylan says."

"I'm afraid that he wasn't the first," says Baxtor. "Everyone ignores his blasphemy."

"When we discovered euphoria—re-discovered euphoria—I thought it was here to stay."

"It *was* nice."

"No shit. Sitting around, laughing our asses off, digging everything like it was all new . . .

"When you turned-on, all of the bullshit stood out so well and looked so Mickey Mouse that you had to laugh at it . . .

"And yourself."

". . . and yourself, right. Wow, those were great days."

"The proverbial 'Good-ole-days,'" mocks Baxtor, and is again ignored.

"Remember how . . . how *great* everything looked? Solid hope and fields of fun in all directions. I thought something was really starting to happen."

"Yeah. The flash of recognizing the bullshit was a good one. Like waking up and finding out that the quicksand you're caught in's only a dream."

"But it didn't last."

"Nothing does, man."

"Remember that time Preston told us automobiles and airplanes were obviously phallic-symbols . . ."

" . . . and right then, a huge, silver, noisy, dick-shaped airliner roared over the shopping center and we all broke-up laughing right in front of Macy's and that woman thought we were making fun of her dog . . ."

". . . and everytime some down-headed, cigar-smoking business-man honked his super-horn at us, pissed-off . . ."

". . . we'd see him driving this hideous, tail-finned, chrome prick, with a brown one in his mouth!"

"Man, we did a lot of laughing."

"When'd we stop laughing?"

"When we saw that the joke was on us."

"No man . . . I saw that right away. That was all right."

And Baxter supplies the capper. As usual. We've been waiting for it. "No one can laugh forever at the same thing. You see some old codger fall on his ass and your first reaction is to laugh. But if he's your grandfather—someone close—or if you watch him do it fifty times, you only feel sorry for him—or disgusted with him. We laughed ourselves right off the edge."

"Very profound, Baxter."

'Very much bullshit," he replies while endeavoring to put his big toe in his mouth, "Ugh. Can't do it. I used to be able to do it when I was four."

Everyone stares past walls. No conversation. It's all been said.

A freight-train leaving the yards honks at cars and rattles the apartment building. I get up to put another record on.

"It's always sorta sad when we reach this point," says Brian.

"Yeah, I know what you mean. Nothing left to say."

"There was nothing to say in the first place," smiles Baxtor.

The record-player does its record-changing-thing. Click-click . . . plop . . . klikit . . . tsssssss . . . then sound . . . bedow-dudum-bedow-dow dududu dum clash.

"It all got so fuckin serious," says Beau (who I thought had been asleep).

"Real serious," yawns Brian.

"Time to move," says Beau, swaying to his feet.

"On what level?"

"I mean, just change the stage—move to another set."

"Like where?"

I suggest Zad's place—no one has a better suggestion, so Zad's place it is—bodies move, searching for coats, fumbling for cigarette-straight-world-shields—"I'm too stoned," says someone, but the complaint is lost in the shuffle and forgotten, even by its creator.

"Zad's prob'ly in bed," putting on my jacket.

"He doesn't sleep," says Beau.

"The hell he doesn't."

"Not when *we* are demanding his attendance," as we stumble out the door and down the stone steps, stoned and into Brian's Packard, packed. Me and Brian in front, Baxtor and Beau slumped in the back. Four door-slams, one right after the other and it sounds so solid that we open the doors and do it again—wham-wham-wham-wham. "They built em solid an tight in them days. No planned obsolescence."

"Where's the keys?"

"Key hangups. Always a key hangup." Fumble—hunt.

"In your pocket, man."

"Nope. I took em out." Fumble—search. "Aw shit. I didn't leave em in the apartment, did I?"

"Did you?"

"No, Gawdamit, where are they?" Hunt-fumble-search.

"Hey, speaking of keys . . ." says Beau, who is presently dealing full-time, making enough money to buy art supplies, food and antique guns on the side, "I got one lined up for fifty. Anybody wanna go halfs?"

Brian's interested. "When do you pick it up?" The car-key hunt comes to a halt.

"When-ever."

"Well, how about if I . . ."

"Hey, come on. Find the car-keys!"

Brian looks on the seat and on the floor. "They're lost."

"They're in the ignition, you cretin," says Beau.

"Ah. Step one. Now, on to step two—starting." And starting isn't much of a hassle and neither is driving once Brain switches to pre-programmed skill, and we pull up eventually in front of Zad's little flat-black with construction-orange-trim, plywood shack (which has mice and even rats, or at least *one* rat who appeared one night to give us all a mean, red-rat-eyed mind jab, then grab a piece of dog-biscuit before waddling back to his hole).

The shack is on the outskirts of Campbell, right next to a white-brick church, the congregation of which will soon see to it that Zad and his offensive chunk of Sodom and Gomorrah are removed. But not this particular night. Now the church is dark and empty and truly God's, so it watches us with holy stained-glass eyes as we pile out of the Packard to ring the bicycle-bell that's nailed to the orange door of Zad's dwelling, which is actually a dwelling within a dwelling, for it contains "The Trip Room."

The shack also contains Zad, his chick Nancy and their dog, who is also named Zad, and is white, looks like a dust-mop, fucks a toy dog (or your foot), barks constantly and is partial to crapping where people can sit or lay in it. We can hear fourlegged Zad yapping hysterically as we ring the bell and kick the side of the house.

Two-legged Zad opens the door, stark naked and squinty. "Greetings, brother Zad. One side," as we bumble into the shack dispensing joints and noise. "Were you asleep, man?"

"Yes. Yes. Very asleep and very stoned. I've been fasting," says Zad, searching the cluttered floor for a pair of pants.

"Where's your head at?"

Zad has settled for a long-tailed shirt because it's within reach and his pants're not. "A good place. My head is happy. Far out. Far from the earth."

"Very good. Glad to see you're doin your part. Have some weed." Beau sticks the joint between Zad's lips.

"Ah. Thank you, thank you," bowing and puffing like a Chinese opium-head in just his green shirt with his legs and behind bare, suddenly spotting his pants crumpled under a chair, "Mmh. My pants. You see? Everything comes to pass perfectly if you just let it happen. Whatever works, works." A light rain and howling wind compete with the stereo, while Zad adds a half-gram of hash to our heads and four-legged Zad barks at the evil demons that followed us in. "Get em, dog. Keep em off our backs."

Nancy, in a sweatshirt-nightgown, joins us for one quick round of hash—nodding and quiet, finally dropping off to sleep sitting upright in a chair. Zad carries her back to bed and returns to answer the door-bell—the rest of us preparing to eat all of the dope on the premises at the first glimpse of a business-suit or badge.

Peering through the Cost-Plus bamboo curtains, "Preston!"

"And . . ." says another voice.

"Barry!" finishes Zad, opening the door.

Preston and Barry are in the shack, taking in all the faces, nodding heads all around, Preston saying, "Ah. No wonder the pull of Zad's shanty was so fucking powerful tonight. A tribal gathering, eh?"

"Baxtor, you dog, you're out of school again I've been told."

"Yes. One semester a year is more than sufficient."

"One semester a year is actually overdoing it. God-all-holy-fuck, if I don't drop out soon, you can expect to read about a raving, mad-dog killer running amok through Berkeley, murdering people at random with an abacus."

"Do I detect the evil odor of exotic hashish?"

"All gone, man."

"Swine! You get not so much as a *taste* of my opium."

"Forgive us, Preston."

"Never, you dogs. However, since I seem to have lost my fucking pipe, I'll relent on the opium if you have one in the house."

"Your choice," Zad indicating a wide selection in a box under the writing-desk.

Selecting and filling a brass and bamboo conventional, Preston encourages the dog with, "Go, son of Zad! Drive that fucking Sow-headed goddess from our lives. Ah, look at that dog! You've driven that dog utterly insane, Zad. It's obviously deranged. Although it is nice to have something on the job, keeping the Wrathful Deities in line."

Blue vapor from the black dot. Demons scurrying to skulk in the bobbing candle shadows. Serious power in gear.

I'm upstairs kickin the gong for . . .
Euphoria

But it's gone so far past that.

In the needle-point rain, hair on end and snapping like whips in the banshee wind, on Zad's roof at five-thirty in the morning, seven spaced and drifting souls trying desperately to launch the collective conscious into the void.

"Hare, Hare, Hare Krishna, Hare Krishna, Krishna, Krishna. Hare, hare, hare Rama, Hare Rama, Rama, Rama . . .

"Almost! Almost! This time we break on through!"

"Hare, Hare, Hare Krishna, Hare KRISHNA, KRISHNA, KRISHNA . . . with faith—with feeling—with shrieking tonsils—with *soul.*

In the house across the street, three pairs of wide eyes peek from between venetian-blinds. Ma, Pa and kid, wondering what the hell those crazy beatniks are up to now. That's what happens when you let them weird-ohs move into a neighborhood.

"HARE RAMA . . . RAMA . . . RAMA!!" and this time it's gonna happen. This is the break-through. Hysterical power almost knocking us down . . . actually knocking Zad to his knees where he keeps on chanting like a spirit-of-God-filled, old fashioned Negro Holy Roller. "HAH REY HAH REY HAH REY KREESH NAH HAH REY KREESH NAH KREESH NAH KREESH NAH HAH REY HAH REY HAH REY RAH MAH HAH REY RAH MAH . . ." Dripping wet and blinded by the rain—screaming hopeful magic into space—Barry jumping up and down, putting his foot right through the roof—the wind rising and trying to help us lift off—the whole cosmos spinning itself closer and closer to the tiny zero that opens into the exact center of the All—"HAH REY RAH MAH RAH MAH RAH MAH!" until we are sure that the sun, although hidden by wet, gray clouds, is undeniably up and in working order and, "We failed again."

"You're looking at it in the wrong light, Abe. We got the sun up didn't we? We made another day."

"We didn't break through to the other side."

"Almost though. Almost! Whooo!"

an if I don't make it
you know my baby will. . .

Dylan's moaning inside the shack.

no break-through
and no baby to break through without me
but oh yes they're all my babiesas i am theirs
and i wish them all a quick death and no more time in
game existence

" . . . little speed to keep it goin, man. We can't just fucking stop now cuz we're almost there."

Follow Captain Preston—split two dime-papers of crink many ways and swallow colored pills—the beginning's lost and the only way to find it is to catch up to the end—

the sun travels across the sky
once like a comet
watches and clocks spinning to keep up
once like a snail
all docks frozen nearly solid
once not at allsuspended outside the illusion of time

whoooooeeeeee . . . the whole fuckin lids gone . . . soze the hash . . . no opium left . . . time for some acid . . . we re almos there . . . we re almos through the curtain . . . shhhhhh-hhhh . . . it . . . god high . . . fuhhhhh . . . this is high . . .

cansa caliba munelfen neo porlis

i make nothing of anything you say man—help me god—grab my hand—i am truly reaching as far as i can—beyond words—beyond me—beyond us—beyond

-fade out-
-fade in-

". . . an so's Preston an Barry. They went back to Berkeley." It makes no sense. It means nothing. Oh yes, this is Zad's house.

"What day?" struggling to structure a visual reality. "What day they left, or what day now?"

"What day now."

"Uh . . . Wednesday. No. Yeah, Wednesday."

"It's Thursday, Zad," says Nancy from the bedroom.

"It's Thursday," says Zad with a shrug. "I'm gonna take some yellows an crash. You wanna sleep here, Abel?"

"No." Watchful devil eyes peek wickedly from the woodwork. I can hear their claws scuttling and ticking.

"Well . . . do whatever . . . you know. Wow. A binge. An old-fashioned binge. See ya, Abe."

Hours later at my apartment, I watch walls until sunrise, then fall into something like sleep and clock-hands spin or jump while I'm gone.

A bad, very bad, cold and lifeless re-entry. Maybe no re-entry at all. Nothing clicks. Six long days in a row I wake up to ugly and say, "I have to get *back.* I'm too far out. I have to get right up and cut my hair and shave and graduate from college and get a good job and get back to what's considered by all those good people out there to be acceptable time- and life-filler. This has gone too far. Sooner or later there's going to be a large, painful burn to face. Maybe tomorrow or the next day I'll find myself to be forty-five years ancient and no

closer to solving the mystery of why and I'll have to fall face down and crying on some flop-house bed in between wine-vomit spots and flea eggs and admit that for this life (which is perhaps the only one we ever get) I am only a poor old bum."

Innocently, friends and people from early college greet me with simple things like, "Well whaddaya know, Abel! How've you been there, fella? I hear you're out of college now—another one of those drop-outs, eh? Hah hah, yessir. Well whaddaya do with your time these days?"

And what can I say to them? Shall I say, "Well now, I've been trying to become enlightened by meditating on the void, searching my cluttered-up soul, running around mad with insane wild people and eating a lot of LSD and other drugs that from time to time fall into my hands." That's not the answer they want to hear. Unless they're cops. And, of course, they all could be—and even if they aren't genuine badge and handcuff cops, they could probably bust me.

No. This is just a period of paranoia. Why would they want to bust me?

Because I'm taking illegal drugs which is a red-pencil no-no in any straight-shooting, apple-pie American's book. Although perhaps no one is that terribly concerned.

And in all honesty, I don't know. Gone too long. I gotta get back and find out. I gotta get back to the security of the straight-world. If only I could remember what the straight-world is. Did I ever know? I did. I'm sure I did. It's all simple and easy and maps are for sale on any street corner . Don't think about it, pattern your existence after *Time* magazine and newspapers and TV commercials and do what everyone else does and you're in. You're in the "real world," playing the game and everyone's happy, even you, if you can just remember the number one important ingredient which is *don't think about it.*

Only now it's too late and I can't seem to forget the smell of bullshit—can't erase the holy vision of the first beginning and the final end from my branded brain—can't bring myself to cop-out and let the patient, calling cosmos down. Besides . . . they probably have vast detection machines monitoring those who are faking it.

I walked onto the street bundled up in an old army coat with my hair tucked into the collar trying to look inconspicuous to face the grumble-growling moving busy outside city, and almost the very second my feet step on public sidewalk a car full of teen-age hot-rodders zooms by and one of the passengers yells, "Suck my dick, hippie!" as I hang my head in humble fear sliding in and out of rage, shuffling along, wandering aimlessly trying to think.

Past used car lots full of lazy salesmen leaning on three-hundred-dollar bargains with their arms folded and filter-tip cigarettes stuck in between big gold rings on their fingers, down the road which is now a snarling nightmare gigantic crawling ant-path of purposeful, angry Omega-day insects hurrying to and from vast, complex skyscraper-hives.

On Sixth Street a black and white, thousand-eyed (two of the eyes red) beetle-monster halts beside me and its parasite pilot sticks his head out of its belly, calling for me to come closer. I follow orders because all of this is real.

"You got any identification?"

I search through my pockets hoping that the papers I have somewhere are the correct ones to cover this situation, wondering how they saw through my disguise so easily, realizing now that the monitor-machine actually does exist and function with lightning speed and precision, find my wallet with all the signed and validated and state-sealed and numbered cards and pieces of paper tucked into the secret pocket which is so dog-eared and fat now that it's not very secret anymore, pull out the worn driver's license with the long-ago unrecognizable clean-cut-me-picture on it, and with uncontrollably shaking hands turn it over to the uniformed power representative. It's only a cop, I tell myself, and any other day I'd take a cop hassle in stride, but on this day it scares me and validates my wretchedness and outstanding lack of acceptability.

"What are you shakin for, buddy? What've you been up to?"

"Nothing. I'm cold."

The mechanical keeper smiles down at me scornfully, his hands on his weapon-hanger hips. My eyes fall on and stick to the network of belts holding ominous cases and bullets and handcuffs and black pistol and short club. He's fully equipped to kill me and *could* actually kill me or at best or worst simply haul me off somewhere never to be seen again and it would be all right and within the law because he's a cop who's allowed to do that sort of thing in the interest of public decency and I'm only a "hippie," which everyone knows is the same thing as a commie or a dope-addict, if not—and probably is—both.

"We'll just run a little file-check on you, pal," says the cop, returning to his host-machine where I can see the shotgun bolted to the dash, "You stand there where I can see you."

Obey. Because this is real.

I push down fear and trying-to-rise anger by holding visions of too-intelligent Negroes being hip and keeping their cool in the face of an entire continent of slave holders and ex-slave holder bigots, and of early, before-the-church pure followers of Christ taking shit and even death from the law-abiding citizens and soldiers of Rome. But I unfortunately also know that all their humble pacifism won them absolutely nothing, except . . . possibly (and how can I be sure) an eternity of peace.

I wait on the curb while the cop code-talks to his all-seeing radio controller as businessmen and housewives drive by shaking their heads because another one of those deviates has been apprehended doing something evil and illegal, or they smile to see that justice is being done in this land of law and freedom where everything's under control.

The file-check takes its unhurried correct time, then the cop motions me over with a sharp nod, hands me my evidently valid license and, "Okay, pal. Take off. We just like to keep an eye on you people," roaring off to join the moving ant-path.

You gotta get back. Remember when the machine ignored you? Remember when you were invisible? You gotta get back. Review the rules of the straight-world, find out where it's at and what it demands, and fake it.

Downtown I start to read—then feel guilty and buy—a paper from an old man who frowns over a counter and a chewed cigar-butt at me. The old man says, "Gumph," tossing my dime (now his dime) into a beat old cash-register. The paper says, "THIRD DAY OF RIOTING IN L.A." (picture of a uniform holding a night-stick at the base of a bloodied Negro's skull).

"This is real," I say. The old man chomps his cigar and turns away.

The paper says, "HUSBAND MURDERS WIFE AND TWO CHILDREN" (picture of a blank-faced, weary husband crying in his hands) . . . "72 VC KILLED. 30 ALLIED CASUALTIES" (grim, determined GI leaning on his rifle) . . . "GIRL RAPED IN PARK" . . . "WAR WITH CHINA?" . . . "FIVE HELD FOR POSSESSION OF DANGEROUS DRUG" . . . "MOTHER CONVICTED OF BEATING INFANT SON TO DEATH" (sobbing, wild-eyed, but mother-looking mother) . . . "POLICE OFFICER ACCUSED OF BURGLARY" . . . "ACTOR DIES OF LUNG CANCER" . . . "ARCHBISHOP CALLS WAR 'A MORAL TOOL'" (puffy old bald man in a white collar—resolute—his god is with him) . . . "DRUNK DRIVER KILLS STUDENT" . . . "CHURCH-BOMBING VICTIM DIES."

This is real.

A drunk stumbles out of the bar I'm passing and, seeing me, roars, "Well if it ain't Jeezuz Krize hisself! Hey! Hey, Jeezuz! Bless me!"

"Bless you."

"Haw haw HAUGH!" slobbers the drunk and reels back into the bar yelling, "Cumon out here! Jeezuz Krize jus blessed me! Haw haw! Lookit out here, lookit!" And I hurry off, hanging my head as a crowd of afternoon drinkers gather to hoot and yell at my back.

"Oooooohoooo! Jeezuz! Hey hey come on back here an save us sinners! Have a drink, Jeezuz! Come on back here you mutherfukker! Ahhhoooo!"

It's doubly pathetic because for all I know they may be serious. They may be calling for salvation in the only way they know, and I'm unable to grant it—unwilling to stop and try.

Caught up in these thoughts, I cross the street without neon consent and step right into a cop waiting on the other side. Another file-check, and I walk away with a ticket for jaywalking which means a court appearance and a fine unless I simply pay the fine by mail . . . which means money, and I have no money, which means I'll have to make some, and no one will hire freaks, which means I'll have to sell dope, and I don't want to sell dope because that means that, like so many other dealers I know, I might get caught and then have to sell much more dope in order to pay lawyers to keep me from going to jail for selling dope.

A sky-filling billboard says, "YOU'RE IN THE PEPSI GENERATION," but none of the twelve-foot examples look like me or any of my friends. The next billboard tells me that if I *really* want to be happy and free, I must buy a bigger-n-better-n-ever new car, and the billboard next to that one lets me in on the secret of secrets . . . "THE GOOD GUYS ARE ALWAYS ON THE WHITE HORSE" and you can pick up a bottle at the comer liquor store for just a little more, but then, it's just a little better.

This is real. This is what I've gotta get back to.

Through Ant City, hurry-fast to my apartment, lock the door, roll and quickly fire a joint and fall on my bed, whew. Mother-of-pearl and holy smokes and lasting name of zot, that was reality! "That was *reality*!" to the walls, and they're not nearly as awed by the realization as I am. "That was reality as controlled by the super plastic and asphalt time-merchant conspiracy in power today. That wasn't just my *projection*! It really *is* that bad!"

"The eternal cry of the paranoid psychotic," says Baxtor later that evening when I finish telling him of my bad day and dark revelation, "'This isn't just my paranoia! It's *really happening*!'" he quotes, then laughs till the noise turns to, "Bowsha bowsha baughshaaah. Do you want to go to the city tonight?"

"What's happening?"

"Marion's having some kind of thing. You ever been to her place?"

"Once."

"You know what to expect, then. Preston'll come get us."

"Okay. But, Baxtor . . . it really is that bad, man."

Halfway out the door, he turns and says, "I know. See you in a couple of hours, Abe."

CHAPTER SIXTEEN – THE BABY OIL EXPERIENCE

Gatherings at Marion's apartment in The City were memorable for two reasons; Marion and the apartment. Marion being a crazy twenty-two-year-old topless dancer with pillow-sized breasts and an amazing sense of indecency. The apartment being the most expensive and movie-set lavish that any of our poor tribe had ever been allowed to enter—fat thick carpets that you felt bad about stepping on, furniture from old Doris Day movies, a telephone that would bring anything outside almost immediately inside upon request, and a wall-sized picture-window that framed the entire city. Marion sometimes undressed in front of it for the kick of standing nude before all of San Francisco. At night you looked out and down on a movie-blinking-flashing-changing-blazing sea of lights.

Behind a lavender-satin-padded door, quietly secure in its unchallenged elegance, yawned a huge, sunken bath. A bath that was to play an important part on this particular night at Marion's.

Baxter and I rode to The City with Preston, who had driven all the way from Berkeley to pick us up and made sure that this fact was well stamped on our brains. "All the way from Berkeley to cart you dogs up to The City. All that way through straight-land and freeway-land and cop-land. Greater love hath no man. And am I rewarded for my efforts? Do you guide me to the clear-light? Do you lay a cap of acid on me? Do you set me up with a piece of local ass? Hah! Thankless lot."

"One must practice charity with no thought of reward, Preston."

"Mmhm yes. Smoke these and may you become so mindless that you follow your own foolishness," handing us his box of weed.

When you rode anywhere with Preston, your chances of reaching your destination before reaching your weed-medicine saturation-point were poor . . . non-existent, actually.

The City. The bus got parked, its doors opened and the three of us popped out in a line to zip up the elevator like a pin-ball machine and into Marion's mansion-apartment without offending or even seeing any of the class residents.

Zad and his small blonde wife, Nancy, were already there, along with Barry and Lyla (both strung-out on crink), Sharon, Bob Levin (who Preston was currently mad at for telephoning Sharon mysteriously one night to tell her not to marry Preston . . . although Preston didn't necessarily plan to marry her in the first place), and a skeletal freak from New York whose name was Bruce.

Marion had mixed fifteen caps in a bowl of fudge that sat on a marble-top coffee table in the middle of the room. A terrible way to eat acid, but it was novel and holidayish so we all had to dig it. Zad, Nancy and Bob had already eaten a square or two of the fudge.

"H'sit come on yet?" asked Preston.

"Mmmm . . . said Zad, after a long moment of careful consideration, "Not yet. It must be still fighting its way out of the candy. Refined sugar, you know. Ugh."

We all ate sticky chunks of the powerful fudge.

"I can taste the acid," said Baxtor.

"You can't taste LSD, man."

"You can't, maybe, but my Baxtor mind can." (Baxtor once got a psychotic reaction from standing too close to a table where Beau and Bob were capping acid.)

"What's it taste like?"

Baxtor swallowed. "Like electric spark smells."

"Even through the fudge?"

"I can't taste the fudge." Another sign (ignored like all the rest) that Baxtor had outlived his acid-life.

The acid's eaten, the stage is set—and as always, this is the beginning—point zero—the tiny piece of action that will be lost, found, re-lost, grabbed for, clung to, repented and marveled at in the hours to come, when all cause and effect melt into a mental kaleidoscope.

For six or seven months, Marion had dreamed and talked of dropping acid with a mob of freaks, then taking a baby-oil bath in her big sunken tub. She got the idea from an underground film or something. Tonight she decided to do it. It took me awhile to summon the courage to ask, "Why?"

"To see what it's like," replied Marion.

Good a reason as any. Who knows what variables must be lined up for the Break Through? Remember Archimedes and the bath that brought enlightenment. And remember Archimedes I do . . . but not very well.

We all contributed what money we had to spare, and Barry and Lyla volunteered to go get the baby-oil. While they were gone, we ate the psychedelic fudge and smoked weed and some DMT that Bruce had with him.

"You ever shoot that stuff?" asked Bruce (a confirmed needle-man) when we'd recovered from the second round.

None of us had. "What's it like?" from Zad—his mind watering visibly.

"It's big, man," said Bruce. "It's awful big. You only shoot-up a little bit, and *man* is it big! You look right into raw energy. You lose hold an there's no stoppin it. You can't hold on."

"I gotta try that," said Zad (and did, two weeks later. He shot an eighth of a gram twice in one day and never did it again. He recommended it to everyone, however).

Bruce had eaten Sacred Mushrooms in New Mexico and we all wanted to hear about it. Psilocybin was available, but none of us had ever had—or knew where we could get—Sacred Mushrooms themselves.

"You rip the skin offa the top," explained Bruce, "then you soak em in vinegar so they won't poison ya. The ones I had was dried already. I got em from this weasely liddle old scrawny Indian who ate em all the time. Really a farout old dude. Whiskey an mushrooms was his whole thing. All day—all the time, man—drinkin whiskey an eatin them mushrooms."

"How much does it take?" asked Zad.

"This Indian ate like whole big hanfulls of em, but I just ate two an it was pretty scary. I thought I was gonna die sure. Hot an cold flashes like I never had before on anything, an I seen this white angel an all kindsa black death scenes. Mostly I thought I was gonna die an it seemed like the best thing that could happen."

"Wow. How long gone?"

"Ah, it screwed me up for days, man. I just laid aroun that ole Indian's shack, shiverin an seein all the answers an waitin for the end to come."

"Wouldja ever take em again?"

"I dunno. I guess if I ever felt the need."

Barry and Lyla returned with a bag full of baby-oil bottles. The acid hadn't come on yet, but we were all ripped high and low from the weed and the DMT as we filed into the bathroom.

Twenty-four bottles of baby-oil but, as Bob pointed out, they'd only put a slippery film on the bottom of the gigantic tile tub. "You'd fall an break your ass."

Marion was disappointed. Her baby-oil orgy fantasy, so close to being a reality, was bogging down. "We havta stay sitting down is all."

"We could pour it over one another instead of right into the tub," Lyla suggested.

Bruce decided against the whole thing (I figured later it was because he knew something we didn't) and went back into the living room, saying he'd wait to see what happened. Sharon didn't want to try it either and she followed him, which made Preston narrow his eyes and say, "I detect hanky-panky," but he shrugged his brows and started to undress.

"Light on or off?" asked Bob.

"Uh . . . off I guess," decided Marion, "It'll make it softer. Leave the door open so light'll come in from the living room—yeah . . . like that."

We climbed into the Mad Emperor Nero tub, nine of us holding bottles of oil. A strange scene. Baby-oil started to flow and it certainly *was* a trip. All legs and hands and slick bodies, with everyone trying not to be too sexual, and then the acid started to come on and things went from strange to stone-solid, hard-edge weird. We talked and laughed and squirmed for a while—everyone lost or getting lost and afraid to admit it—the tiles reflecting sun-bursts and circus freaks—faces melting and bodies shifting like soft wax. I saw that all these people were merely *tulpas* of my own creation. Tulpas created in some forgotten past, gone out of control. Or was I merely a tulpa granted existence by one of them? All of them? Or (even more likely) were we all tulpas, forgotten and left to our own poor sad designs? The room grew suddenly brighter and I took this as a sign that I was close to the truth. Then Baxtor, higher than anyone else, did something to Nancy that drew a negative response from both her and Zad. The vibrations became noticeably tighter—motion slowed down—finally stopped—dry-ice hot-cold frozen. We sat still, covered with oil, feeling our hyper-sensitive bodies and remembering how unpredictable acid could be as walls began to billow and eyes dilated to black, bottomless holes. Purpose and plan forgotten. All laughter a hollow fake. But it could be just me . . . so ignore it. But then again, "This orgy lacks a certain elusive something," said Preston, putting his hand on Marion's earth-mother breast. She looked at it. We all looked at it. She looked at Preston. We all looked at Preston. Preston looked at us and we turned our heads so as not to stare. What role to play? What's expected of us—of me? Should we all be fucking? It is, after all, the basic dance of life. But do Saints and Sages fuck? Did the . . . but then . . . of course . . . in this . . . I want . . . oh no I don't . . . oh yes I do . . . webs get tangled in . . . should we be talking it over? . . . should I confess? . . . confess what? . . . confess to all this separate existence and the fact that I have been known to dig it . . . we should be trying to work it all out.

"Is something wrong?" I asked in a whisper.

"Bowsha," said Baxtor, and, "Bowsha bowsha bowsha."

Marion turned on the shower. "Maybe we should wash this oil off."

A sigh of relief. Water to wash it all away. The solution to whatever had been going wrong is found—is discovered—is taken care of—we're in control again—it's all fine and cool. No, it's warm. The shower made everything even more slippery, then steam filled the room, giving the acid material for constructing complicated patterns and conflicting dimensions, which added to the general confusion and growing insecurity, which was compounded by Baxtor who suddenly freaked-out and tried to stand up (a difficult maneuver to execute on oil and water-slick tile). He fell on Nancy, pushed Zad aside and stepped on Lyla, slipped again and crashed into Bob who attempted to grab him and, of course, couldn't, could only watch as Baxtor fell out of the tub with a squashing thud and crawled through the open door as fast as he could, which looked to be about four hundred miles an hour. An explosion of speeded-up cartoon movement—rinky-tink music and all—frames sticking, action flickering—Bosco squeaks and exclamation points over everyone's head.

Over the shower noise we heard Sharon's voice saying, "What's *wrong,* Frank?" and then Sharon herself followed the voice into the bathroom, looking worried, and saw us all looking probably scared and she took a towel from the rack and went back into the other room fifteen radical scene-shifts in swift succession and fifteen to come and none of them real or worthy of notice or having anything to do with what is happening which could be absolutely nothing but I think not.

"What's happening?" whispered Nancy to Zad.

"Did I do something?" Zad asked us.

I *knew* that I'd done something and felt myself bumming-out. The feeling you get just before a very bad trip starts to happen, and you realize it's coming and recognize the signs but there's not a thing you can do about it because you know that it might have already happened and you're just going to have to catch up to it and live it out or else stay hung on the brink of it for an eternity. Nothing you can do. Even praying's a joke.

"Baxtor freaked out," said Lyla. "It was just Baxtor."

It wasn't just Baxtor. A flash of senseless shame and an ugly vision in which I saw us all as depraved worshipers of the golden calf—angry Moses watching in disgust. All my friends and all my soul lost in a mad Hieronymus Bosch-garden of delights. Not just as Bosch painted it, but as Bosch *wanted* to paint it. "We're taking a bath in naked hot baby-oil! It's all just fleshing around in a stupid illusion and we won't admit it! It's sick! It's nothing."

"Hey, hey, easy man. Stay cool, Abe," soothed Bob, and I was instantly sorry for having spoken foolish words. But a bath in baby-oil was no longer a fun thing so I crawled out of the tub and dried off a little before putting on my clothes.

Preston said, "Bah," when others began getting dressed. Dancers. Dancers in the dance macabre—the dance of life—the downhill dance to death. "Be neither attracted nor repelled." Easy to say. Hard to pull off. Hard to pull off because it's the easiest thing to do and therefore anti-life.

I went into the living room and the light showed me how high I was. Steam rolled from the open bathroom door. Dante's inferno. Naked, glistening, damned souls struggling with bewitched garments in the vapor and brimstone.

Baxtor was sitting in a warped position on the sofa, staring wide-eyed at the bathroom door, the towel that Sharon had given him draped over his drooping shoulders, Bruce offering him a pair of pants and getting no response.

"Is he all right?" I asked Sharon.

"Everything's all right. Nothing's wrong," she replied, which I took to mean that I should calm down, which meant that I was freaking out, which meant . . . I turned away and tried to stop thought. Everything was all *right.* Baxtor'd just flipped out for a second. I couldn't quite make myself believe it. I tried harder, remembered not to, and let my mind drift.

The others came out of the bathroom, blinking in the glare, reprogramming for the new environment, the acid really doing its thing now. A few attempts at verbal communication, which all ended in babble and then, "What?" and "What?," "What?" from those who had been talking or listening. Impossible to remember the beginning of your own sentence—of your own thought. We retreated into various corners of the room, watching one another and naked, unmoving Baxtor, with only an occasional flare of, "Maybe we should . . ."

"Huh?"

"What?"

"I asked, What?"

"I was . . . never mind."

"No, go ahead, man."

"What?"

"I just . . . never mind, I lost it."

"Well, wait . . . oh I see," and then silence as we slipped back into ourselves to wait it out.

Waiting out a bad trip takes forever. It does eventually come to an end (you tell yourself) but that's not much consolation when you also know that it takes forever. Your knuckles get white and your brain gets so tired it starts to hurt from holding on—holding on forever, waiting it out.

It was an hour before sunrise when things finally leveled off a bit—for everyone but Baxtor. Baxtor still hadn't moved.

Preston walked around the room in a tight circle forty-two times (I counted his completed circuits, thinking that perhaps the number would be significant), smoked exactly twenty cigarettes and a joint, ate a banana, then turned to the Baxtor-body and said, "All right, you dog, enough is enough. Have you no sympathy for our poor bleeding minds? How long must we be forced to look at your hideous naked carcass? Let's have no catatonic trances, eh boy?"

Baxtor said nothing, and he said it so loud that I shuddered.

Marion made some coffee as the sun came up, and we all drank it sitting in front of the picture-window, feeling better because it was such a normal average thing to do, while walls slid into place and everyone eased over to the smooth side, except, of course, for Baxtor who still wouldn't move.

On the window-wall, the San Francisco picture was waking up for the day. Amazing. People piloting their Buck Rogers cars off to work, totally unaware of the ill-fated baby-oil party trailing off to safety above them. Another day. Just another day.

Bruce and Bob left after hitting speed to keep them going through gas station jobs, Sharon stayed awhile longer, then kissed Preston and went home to sleep and prepare for her afternoon class. It was time to split.

"Come *on*, Frank!" pleaded Marion, "You can't sit around my apartment naked all day. I gotta work this evening!"

Baxtor didn't even blink his eyes.

Lyla decided that she could pull him through with sex, so we went into the bedroom to drink our coffee while she gave it a try,

Preston grumbling, "You'd think we could at least watch. I mean, that useless lout could at least provide us with a little stag show. Marion, why don't you make some popcorn?"

"Gah. I can't think of a more perverted 'finale.' "

"It's too bad you don't have that German shepherd anymore. We could get the three of them to do it in front of the window. Brighten-up ole San Fran."

"Preston, shut up."

"Old age is taking its toll. If the public ever finds out what a bunch of puritans the acid-heads really are, we'll never live it down. Don't you read the papers? Don't you read magazines? Hippies take acid and have indiscriminate sex orgies. It's a fact. Right down in black and white. We're disgraces to the uniform."

A half-hour later, Lyla appeared in the doorway and shrug-sighed, "No response. He just sits there. It's disgusting."

She'd only frightened him more. Now he lay curled up in a fetal position on the floor.

"He did it," I thought with a dark mind, "He's gone. Baxter broke his mind. He really did it."

Zad and Nancy got ready to leave for San Jose and I almost went with them, but then felt guilty about deserting Baxter and decided to stay. "It's just one of Baxter's ego-games," said Zad from the other side of the open door. "He'll be back in a day or so." The door closed, leaving Preston, Marion, the Baxter-body and I to work it out.

"I gotta be bright-eyed, big-boobed an dancing at six," moaned Marion.

Ten minutes past noon, a mechanical voice said, "Take me home."

"It talks!" exclaimed Preston.

"Home," said the voice from Baxter's body.

"You might consider getting dressed first," said Preston.

"Home."

Marion handed Baxter his clothes. He looked at them, and then at us. "Home." I knew that he feared a trick of some kind—another deception—one more false out. "It isn't a trick, man," but as soon as I made the words I knew that in the land he was walking through—drifting through—being dragged through—someone saying, "It isn't a trick," is only one more voice chanting lies.

"Go ahead. Put em on," prompted Marion.

Baxtor suddenly reached out and snatched them from her hands. He turned his back on us while he dressed, stopping every couple of seconds frozen solid again—starting with a jerk—stopping—starting—putting a leg through his T-shirt, taking it out, studying the problem, turning his shirt around and around, looking for an opening, finding one, sticking an arm through it, taking it back out again, until he was finally dressed. "Home."

"Ah yes, he's going to be great," said Preston. "We may even be able to teach him how to feed himself."

"G'bye Marion. Have a good day at work." Just something to say, because I was standing at the door and felt that something had to be said.

"Blah. Dirty old men an pinchy dykes. Hope you feel better, Frank."

"Home," insisted Baxtor as Preston and I guided him out into the hall, put him in the elevator which was unfortunately occupied by an elderly woman and a poodle who both regarded us in eye-lid stretched horror.

"Mental case," said Preston. "You may have read about him. Chopped up six old ladies with a rusty straight-razor."

"Home," said Baxtor.

The woman pushed a button and hurried out of the elevator. The doors hissed shut and we continued our descent to the street where we put Baxtor in the bus, removed the parking ticket from the windshield and left The City.

A long ride with sandpapered nerve-endings and Baxtor saying, "Home . . . home . . . home," every mile, while Preston said things like, "You realize, of course, that you're attracting bullshit exactly like the huge bullshit-magnet that you are, Baxtor?"

"Home."

"No, we've decided to drop you off at the nearest madhouse."

"Home."

"Preferably one that specializes in prefrontal lobotomies."

"Home."

"Keep a sharp eye for a very gray, prison-like insane asylum, Abel."

I said things like, "Come on, Preston, he's really into something heavy."

"Bah! Why is he a special case? We all took the same acid." Shaking a finger at Baxter, "You'll pay for this. The cosmic judge is on to your devious bullshit."

It was the first time I'd seen Baxter in the grip of the "Baxter-catatonia" I'd been told about and it scared me. Like seeing a great man sick-drunk . . . only worse, because being drunk is nice and safe and acceptable, but being insane has all that deep-rooted Bedlam and screaming fear and lonely empty eyes behind it. The acid was already faded and gone, its visions only pale phantoms that made me wonder just what was so awe inspiring about them in the first place, but Baxter was still trapped somewhere back in the gone-past-Now—still hung there, right in it—maybe for good. "This is serious. Everything's getting so serious and . . . I don't know, serious and heading for final or something. It's not like it used to be."

Preston was smoking a joint, slumped over the steering-wheel the way he always drove, like a dead man at the controls, swerving back and forth over the white line, his chin on his hands, nose three inches from the windshield. "A mire," he said. "Admittedly a mire. But then, what can one expect? Being born into the lowest ebb of the Kaliyuga and all."

"What's the 'kaly-yooguh'?"

"That, Abel, is what we are trudging through. The Kaliyuga. The lowest ebb of the Kaliyuga, to be exact. The murkiest, nastiest, darkest point of the darkest age. Of all the Yugas, this is the shittiest. A few Yugas ago, there wasn't even fucking. Not even the *desire* to fuck. Now *that* must have been a fine Yuga! But we (sad dogs that we are) are in the hideous *Kaliyuga*. The age of darkness. Our only consolation is that when it worms its way to a close—the show's over." Preston cranked the wheel and swerved to miss a station wagon as he handed me the joint.

"No thanks, man."

"Slacker. How can you face the Kaliyuga straight?"

We took Baxter to the house in Saratoga that he shared with his mother and younger brother from time to time. He shoved open the door, stumbled down the dirt path without glancing back, and disappeared.

"Should we have let him go like that?" I asked as we drove away.

"He'll just go to bed." Preston swerved back onto his side of the road just in time to miss a potato-chip truck. "I've seen him in considerably worse states."

In front of my apartment, I said, "Poor Baxter," meaning it sincerely and understanding now why I'd heard it said many times before, "I hope no permanent damage has been done to his head."

"It was permanently damaged at birth," yawned Preston, "He's probably working out some past sin, that's all." The standard moments of parting silence, then, "Well, I've gotta get back to Berkeley," and he raised one hand in salute, worked the gears and drove off.

"Wow," as I drag my numb feet up the stairs, "May I never have to work the same thing out," knowing—or maybe at this time only suspecting—that I most certainly will.

Ah. Have faith. Have courage. Let it ride and it'll come full circle sooner or later.

There was a time when a baby-oil bath on wonder-drug would have been a great idea. I would have dug it. There was a time.

There was a time when going to school to learn how to make countless dollars and then going on to learn how to count those countless dollars sounded like a worth-while time-plug.

There was a time when God was just a game for old people looking for a reason after all the others had fallen by the wayside.

There was a time when I was me with well defined boundaries and simple little clever thoughts about my many tomorrows in which I would have a better and better time by following the leaders who were pointed out to me as shining examples of successful, important, happy individuals, and I never even considered disappearing into the forest to fast and pray and come to some kind of terms with the universe of my mind, and "identity crisis" was just a joke that people told on sullen teen-agers, and "meditation" was just a game that skinny old Fakirs and unwashed beatniks played at, and "cogito, ergo, sum" was Latin gibberish too obvious and silly to waste a moment's thought on, and the all-encompassing question "Why?" was too general to apply to anything I could see or touch and was, therefore, completely irrelevant, and all I had to do was walk close enough to the line to pass inspection, play my role by the easy-to-follow rules, and everything was going to be fine.

There was a time. I remember it well. There was time at that time, and it proceeded in an orderly fashion, regulated by unquestionable clocks. There was a time.

"I do believe some head-straightening is in order," said I, locking the door and crawling into bed.

CHAPTER SEVENTEEN – MORGAN'S ACID TEST

I stayed home alone for two days and practiced do-nothing, slowing down at last to only a couple of notches past normal, at which time I slept.

On the morning of the third day I woke up to a holy quiet that brought to mind visions of post-card Christmases and gently falling snow. I savored the peaceful hum of silence and almost convinced myself that during the night the end had come and now, outside, the world was reverent and at peace and saved. I heard a diesel on the highway, but it sounded a long way off—droning along slow—an honest, satisfying rumble in the distance like I used to hear them late at night when I was a littler kid, lying awake warm and secure, wondering where they were going, dreaming myself inside the cab driving all night till sunrise on the road in some rough, He-man place like Montana, where I would get out of my truck (named *Road Eater—a* name I'd heard from a friend whose father was a trucker) at a truck-stop and greet all the men inside, who knew me by my reputation as a hard-drivin-man, and smile my craggy smile at the beautiful Spanish waitress (who also knew me well) and drink my coffee and smoke a slow cigarette while trading stories of Deadman's curve and burned-out brakes with the other hard-drivin truckers before climbing back into my dusty rig to drive a hundred miles an hour all the way to probably Texas or Wyoming. The diesel honked once to say goodbye and I rolled over and put my feet on the floor, no longer a six-year-old hard-drivin man.

Why is it so beautifully quiet? I pulled the heavy curtains aside and looked at a drifting wall of solid cloud. The entire outside world cushioned in thick, white fog. So thick that it even muffled the street sounds. A day made up of nothing but soft edges. Cool and soft.

I dressed in coat and sweater, walked out into Sherlock Holmes' London and strolled along with just my boot-taps for company, pretending that I was on the water-front—a lonely sea captain at home in the fog—actually hearing waves lapping on barnacled hulls and fog-horns calling to one another. With every step I took I could feel the depression that had been sitting like a fat toad on my brain rip itself loose one suction-cup finger at a time—like sinuses opening—until, when I reached Tenth Street, the toad fell off with a final croak of surrender and dismay, and I saw with absolute clarity that everything was fine. Only my own hungup mind that produced conflict and confusion. The universe was in perfect harmony. Everything was fine.

Walking back to my apartment, zigzag and really just wandering glad, having met no one in the miracle-healing fog and having been passed by only two or three cars driving slow and quiet with their lights on, I thought of Adriel who loved the fog and the rain and the wind as much as she loved the sunshine, and who, I realized suddenly, I wanted very much to see again. Adriel with her black hair and wide green eyes, paints and poems, shy smiles and hellos, speaking with a sweet southern drawl when I first met her at seventeen. And then, when I re-met her at twenty, I discovered that she actually had raven-black Spanish-Oriental silk-fine hair that touched the small of her back and shrouded her tiny body when she sat like a sleek Siamese cat, her always bare feet tucked under her beautiful little behind, watching me quietly or just eye-drifting into deep space. Raven-black flashing blue hi-lite hair that agonizingly perfectly circled and framed her pale little-girl face with its huge sad eyes that always looked as though they were on the verge of clear tears even when she was laughing and honestly glad.

So much had happened since I'd seen her last—since she went to Georgia to visit Grandfather and cousins and home where she was born, writing only one strange letter to me in a year, a letter that told about Negroes grown sad as she hadn't remembered them, and sticky heat much hotter than when she was five years old running barefoot through the dust, and people all red-faced and uptight and narrow-minded although they used to be wise and friendly and good.

The letter'd rambled on for pages about social reform and the South being so different from the North—written in her lacy feminine hand but sounding nothing like the big-eyed naive little Adriel who used to worry about me dumping my bike or being arrested, whispered "be careful, please" and touched my arm when I'd stop by to see her on my way to a Night Riders meeting or headed for a big club-run to somewhere, and who was sincerely sorry for me and my discouragement with the (in my eyes hopeless, in her eyes hopeful) games of life.

A long time since I'd seen Adriel. It seemed much longer than it really was. I felt that I understood and could appreciate so much more of her than I had before.

I wanted to see Adriel, but just then I didn't know where she was and there would be plenty of time to find out and anyway it didn't matter because the universe was in perfect harmony and everything was standing fine and there's my apartment hiding in the slow-flowing white cloud and that's beautiful . . . and inside, roll a slender symmetrical joint and light it while putting all existing Dylan albums one right on top of the other on the thoughtfully automatic record-player and sit down in front of the glass door with the curtain pulled open to get spectacularly high watching the infinitely deep oh so beautiful swirling white outside while mystical Mister Dylan magically adjusts his music to the fog and its special vibrations and comes on from exactly the right place. Perfect. All the world so strange and multi-level intricate, but so perfect, so beautiful, so fine, so good, so *perfect.* Ah, how can anyone possibly fall into hate or worry or hangups or sadness when all the world's so perfect-fine-beautiful-good? Today I'm so fine-glad-perfect-happy that if the worst of all Hell-sent hideous bads burbled in and grabbed me by the spine I'd be able to smile it into submission. And I *am* Abel. Yessir, I'm Abel and everything's perfect and gooder'n'good.

I surely do wish I'd been able to hold that state of mind.

Later in the week, a search for acid brought me to Rob Tilding's saggy old brown house on San Fernando. Rob met me at the door in a pair of unzipped wrinkled tan slacks, his wild curly dark hair exploding on his head, eyes all bloodshot and blinky from a long run of book-study and paper-write with black coffee and white bennies and no sleep, two days' stubble on his usually clean-shaven jaw, finger-tips stained orange from a hundred chain-smoked Camels. I followed him to his room where he plopped on a straight-backed wooden chair beside a portable typewriter surrounded by reams of typing-paper in neat stacks and crumpled piles all over the floor. Ashtrays and coffee-cups-become-ashtrays overflowed on his desk in between, under and on top of open textbooks. A truly classic slaving-student scene.

"Mid-terms?" I asked, adding a used cigarette to one of the butt mountains.

"Mid-terms," said Rob, stretching with a groan, rubbing knuckles into eyes. "Four papers due next week and an exam in every class."

"Hey, I'll leave you be, then."

"No. No, I was about to knock off anyway," fumbling through empty cigarette packs for a smoke. "Whattayou been up to, man?"

"Right now I'm lookin for some acid. You still got any of those clear caps?"

Rob yawned and shook his head. "I've got some new stuff though. I was thinking of dropping one tonight myself . . . blow out some of this mind-clutter I've been diligently accumulating." He got to his feet. "How many you need?"

"Uh . . . three if you've got em."

"Sure," as he went to the kitchen.

Footsteps sounded on the wooden porch, the front door rattled open and Baxtor strode into the room, leaping back in stylized W. C. Fields surprise when he saw me. "Aha! Abel! What a tiny cosmos it is. I was just on my way to see you."

"Baxtor!" glad to see him. "How's your head, man?"

He pursed his lips, shoving his mustache over the tip of his nose. "Ah yas. You mean following that freak-out at Marion's. I'm truly sorry about that scene."

"Hey, don't apologize to me. What happened?"

Shrugging his shoulders and speaking as if I already knew—"I became ensnared in a network of elaborate games. I realized that you were all calling hopefully for my successful death from the entrance to the Void and I foolishly rebelled against the inevitable. It's this ego problem of mine. Yas. It took me a few days to work my way out of the hole I dug . . . Hiya, Robert," to Tilding, an old friend of Baxtor's from long before I came on the scene.

"Nobody's out for your death, man," said Tilding, smiling and counting out acid caps on a glass-top table.

Baxtor gave me a knowing look. "That's what they all say. But don't worry. I've nearly got it worked out. I won't hold things up much longer." He turned to Tilding and said, "Rob, you'll be interested in this. Ben Morgan is holding an—and I quote—'Acid Test' at Muir Beach tonight."

"I heard about it," said Tilding. "What's the word on that anyway?"

"Ben Morgan. Acid test. That's all I got."

Ben Morgan was a young underground film-maker-artist who'd recently won fame and moderate fortune with a disturbing cinema experiment called, *Home Rule*s—a great film, honest and so totally involving that it was bound to drive you insane at the very least. We all looked to Morgan for big amazing things to come.

"What'll it be like? I mean, a party or what?"

"I can't imagine," said Baxtor, "but it's obviously not to be missed."

I said, "Are you sure we can get into this thing? Morgan doesn't know us from Adam," accepting three caps from Tilding and handing him a five-dollar bill.

Baxtor informed us that, "Steve Lewis who's one of Morgan's crew and an ex-card playing acquaintance of mine, told me this morning that *all* freaks are invited. If we don't fit into that category, then I hardly know who or what does and, if nothing more, it will be interesting to witness a gathering of those who consider themselves invited to an all-freak, organized acid test."

Rob and I both wanted to go, of course, and I phoned around to see who else could be found. Only Brian Kelly was at home and he promised to meet us in San Jose. I was supposed to see Gina that night (a chick I'd dated for some time and wouldn't be ready to appreciate for at least two more years) and I asked her to go along.

"*The* Ben Morgan?" she squeaked.

"The same."

"Can you get me a cap of acid?"

"It's already got if you want it."

"I do. Come get me."

We met at Tilding's house where everyone but me (because I'd volunteered to drive and recalled bad experiences driving while acid-stoned) dropped small red caps of brand-new, untested but reported to be deadly acid and piled into the big Galaxie 500 that Rob had borrowed from his brother. Then we were zooming down the freeway, headed for Muir Beach and unknown what.

We'd only gone about ten miles when Baxter said, "Hmmm. I'd forgotten how *fast* this stuff comes on." The last words he said all night. In time to come, I will often wonder what messages and astounding truths we would have attributed to that statement had it been the last he uttered in his life.

Maybe eight miles from our destination and completely lost—me unfamiliar with the territory and the others too spaced to give directions—when a sign materialized in the beam of the headlights blowing our collective mind. "ACID TEST" it shouted in big red letters with an arrow pointing the way (which was up) tacked to a telephone pole.

"It's a hallucination," said Brian.

"It's for real," said I.

"Now that's what I call having absolutely no fear," marveled Rob, who, like all of us, dropped acid in as much secrecy as possible and in constant fear of being busted by the nebulous "Authorities," although acid wouldn't actually be illegal for another five months.

I know it's a joke of some kind, but I followed the signs . . . "ACID TEST" . . . "CAN YOU PASS THE ACID TEST?" . . . "THE ACID TEST" . . . to a lodge-like building, where I parked among an unbelievable number of cars, almost positive that at any second people would pop out of the bushes with cameras, yelling, "Caught ya!" since it was becoming more than obvious that we'd been lured into a trap designed to snare unsuspecting, gullible acid-heads as part of "Operation Clean-up." I even reflected that it was a clumsy and childish trap which no one in their right mind would fall for, then realized with a mental groan that five of us just had, and I sighed because the statement was still true.

"Are you *sure* this is the place?" Brian peering over the car door and out the window in disbelief. "There aren't that many acid freaks in the whole world."

"It's the right place," Rob assured us, taking the initiative and leading us, "Come on, Baxtor," single file to the door of the building which is wide open, so inside, look around, and it's a kitchen.

"Hey man, this is somebody's home," I whispered, sure that we were stomping into some poor unsuspecting citizen's beach-house.

"It's okay," said Rob, and he seemed to know, so we followed him down a shadowy hallway, turned a comer and walked into a huge dark room full of what seemed to be hundreds of bodies all sitting or standing in every square foot of available space, watching a movie that was being projected on one entire wall. The movie was now a swirling vortex of vivid color, now a black and white study of a man motioning for us to come forward, now color again—bright—moving—spinning—and a chick is dancing through party balloons and flashing lights while a bleary old derelict ogles her from an oozing rainbow bed. "There is no real," says a loud, amplified voice, "Only the movie is real and it's certainly not real now is it people? But it's the movie children that must be accepted or else where then there can any of us possibly seek . . . refuge . . . in . . . this . . . chang . . . ing . . . veh . . . ree . . . veh . . . ree . . . holl . . . oh and cold-and-lifeless-and-dark-and . . . ahhhhhh . . . only in the movie sad people of this sad scene . . . find joy in the movie . . . we must get into the movie . . . we must GET RIGHT INTO THE MOVIE!" and a real chick (distinguished from the chick in the movie) is clawing at the wall, trying to obey the command. The film is suddenly being projected on the ceiling, then the audience, then the wall again, this time upside-down, now sideways, now rightside-up but the film is running backwards. A dying sun is racing across the walls, "Follow the sun . . . wheeeeooooooh . . . follow the sun . . . wheeeeeoooo . . ." sang the sound track.

The lights flashed on, I blinked, cleared my eyes, looked around me and thought, "Tonight something will be revealed." The room—a huge barn-sized enclosure—was packed to overflowing with freaks. Baxtor, Rob, Brian and I—who couldn't appear on a public street without causing heads to turn and cops to come unglued—were among the more conservative of those assembled. A cat in a white jump-suit, his face painted green, was passing out caps of acid from an ornately carved, crystal punchbowl. A midget dressed in a purple cape that trailed along behind him and a top hat that covered the upper half of his head passed by crooning, "I can't follow the sun. I can't follow the sun yet, because it's very fast and my legs are very small and slow. But soon I will be swift. Soon I will be tall and swift. Soon I will be fast enough to catch the sun. Soon I will. Soon I will. Yes I will."

Brian turned to me in astonishment and I could only toss it back to him. "It's happening, man. It's happening for real." In these days just before Be-ins and the Haight-Ashbury scene to be, a gathering of this size made up almost entirely of ecstatic, painted, long-haired, bearded, beaded, mad-eyed, strangely-dressed, obvious acid-eaters was mind staggering. "This is really it," I thought, resigned to the fact that sooner or later it had to happen, "This is the end of the straight-world. The searching people have been gathered together from the far comers of the earth to witness the end."

Strobe-light. Legendary Neal Cassady in the center ring, surrounded by worshipers as he dances with a fluorescent skeleton, holding it in front of his fly, asking it riddles that he answers in the same breath, pantomiming all-life with his eighteen-year-old body and thousand-year-old mind. Insane—true—impossible—unquestionably happening right there in the center ring under the flash-flash-flash of strobe-light. "That's Cassady! That's Kerouac's holy Cassady!" I say to Rob, unable to believe that I'm really seeing the immortal super-hero, raving-mad and in the living flesh and blood and sweat and action.

"Yes," says Rob. "Yes, they're all here. They're here."

Then five strangest of freaks were on the raised platform at one end of the huge room making thunderous gut-rocking sounds with their electric instruments, moving lights and bodies with their driving sound.

Behind the organ, a massive organist. Shoulder-length black hair, a bandito mustache draped over the comers of his mouth, leather vest over striped T-shirt, a bullwhip coiled on his right shoulder, "I'm gonna WAIT till the STARS come out . . . Till your LOVE comes tumblin down," he howled, the organ squealing under his thick, fast fingers. An eerie graveyard outerspace wail. Have mercy! Have mercy on the poor keys and on our poor souls. And no mercy is to be had, because there's more to say and we all gotta hear it.

Behind the guitar, a sound-god guitarist. Spanish hair, wild and snarled, red-white-and-blue-banded shirt, black Levi's, work shoes. He chewed gum while his fingers—his whole body—tormented, then caressed, then threatened to kill, than made love to the lightning-powered strings, pushing the sounds they made through the music of the souls behind him, driving his pleading-coaxing-wailing-laughing-sobbing-demanding guitar-screams and moans over the intricate patterns of All-sound which He commanded. Winding through it, under it, around it—picking up all the separate sounds and molding them into a sun, then dropping the sun with an explosion of discord made harmonious by the suspension of time, soaring above the scattered music and swoop ing down to pull it all together again in the nick of time and space to save the world.

Behind the bass, a tall, flame-headed bass-man—confident—in love with his sound. He is the deep, eternal, reassuring vibration of the Source. He tells us that we are already there . . . already there. Just listen. It's over long ago and happening now.

A rhythm-guitar driven by a crystal-eyed pilot who validates and proclaims the truth and purity and unshakable foundation of even the most incredible prophecies made by the leader. He knows where it's all going. He's got the pattern and he's got the power.

A drummer who controls the heart-beat of the universe they have created to work with in order and disorder to produce SOUND.

"They're the *Grateful Dead,*" said Brian reverently, getting the information from a small, lost, painted chick swaying in front of him.

"Yes!" A whisper. But a whisper with an exclamation point. True on so many levels. It wasn't until much later that I realized that it was actually the group's name—the Grateful Dead.

The walls change color with the music. Liquid-light projections dance and tremble to the sound. A strobe jerks the environment into ragged film action. The Grateful Dead lead the lost souls through purgatory and hell and to the gates of heaven in search of salvation, pointing out the torments and joys and wonders that we pass. Grateful to be dead—grateful to have been shown the truth of the void. "In the Land of the Dark the Ship of the Sun shall be driven by The Grateful Dead." These are the Grateful Dead. *The Grateful Dead.*

I took the cap of acid from my shirt pocket and swallowed it, surrendering myself to the coming of The Final Truth. All possible variables lined up. Nothing left to do. This is it.

We slip into the Now of Then

The Dead end their sound universe with a multi-nova. House-lights turn the scene to day. Freaks begin to move aimlessly—a twisting mass of painted faces, knowing eyes. With a start, I notice that some are not freaks. I see two straight-looking young chicks walking arm in arm across the floor, gritting their teeth and recoiling from the bodies that whirl past them. There's a man in faded coveralls who looks like a patient old farmer. Leaning against a stair-railing is a gangster in anti-sun glasses and a black business suit—digging the action from behind a toothpick wedged between his front teeth. How did *he* get here? And the farmer and the young straight-chicks? They must have accidentally stumbled across the reality-warp. (Ah, how selfish not to mention foolish, Abel, to imagine that only flesh-obvious freaks may participate in the Final Flash) But still, I wonder if it's strange for them to find themselves among mad freaks? (Not if they've seen the Truth.)

Ben Morgan strides into the room followed by streams of rainbow light. His face is painted in patterns. He's dressed in a white clown's costume. There's a diamond tear, playing catch and toss with the light, defiant and sad and brave on one cheek. The cheek of a big man who doesn't have to display it. Stern, then suffering eyes touch everyone within their range, and he shows us that we are all sorrowful clowns. Morgan is the clown at midnight.

"Back to work, children! Back to work!" he shouts, and bodies follow him to another part of the house—another room of the rambling, endless lodge—a room with crawling walls of liquid color. My own body is among those that follow him, so all this is revealed to me. A smiling witch in a black, spider-webbed cape, her face a lacework of blue-green veins, operates a machine that controls the dripping walls. But a smiling witch! Oh thank all gods, a smiling witch in control of the walls. "Did I frighten you?" she asks Gina, who voiced a tiny gasp upon turning to see the witch behind her magic machine.

"Oh no. Only startled me" smiles Gina, and the witch nods kindly, doing the walls a special pattern just for Gina.

Ben Morgan and a blonde android play electronic strings with their tongues. Morgan sucks the electricity directly into his brain, then feeds it back to the strings. *Fonggg*. "Can you feel the sounds at the very bottom of your *gut*? You got to let it work its way *right in there, people*! You got to feel it right down there in the deepest part of your *gut*! Can you *feel it?* Can you *feel it,* people?"

"Oh Lord!" cries bearded Negro in native loincloth, dancing on bare pink soles and in bare ebony soul much purer than passerby whites, "Oh Lord God O Lord!" and the salt-water that runs from the tiny holes in the comers of his brown eyes leaves long paths of ancient jungle visions on his burnt cheekbones.

The midget, his top hat in his hands, bald head decorated with a single sunburst, walks beside the gangster, saying, "How long?"

"Not long," says the gangster.

"But when?"

"Soon."

"But how soon?"

"Very soon."

The gangster removes his anti-sun-glasses and he has no eyes. The midget cackles, replaces his top hat and walks away dragging his cape.

A skull face, teeth painted over lips, floats by with its body in a shroud, hands twisting a carpenter's drill. "Fill your teeth? Fill your teeth? Fill your teeth?" it sing-songs.

"What ever happened to world war three?" asks a hollow, electrically amplified voice. "World war three it came an done went and we all missed the flash. Back to work, children! Back to work!" and it's Morgan, ushering souls into another room.

Baxtor stands frozen, hands pushed into the pockets of his army jacket, head twisted to one side. I can see that he's gone again, but it's all right because now the end's coming and there'll be a place for him. I hold Gina's hand as we sway with the powerful current.

"WAIT till the STARS come OUT. Thaswen your LOVE comes tumblin down . . ." Neal Cassady, unable to wait, writhing on the floor with lips drawn over clenched teeth, sweating and thrusting his pelvis at the sky, at the stars, at God. "The midnight hour! Oh the MID-night hour!"

Somehow outside to face the ocean—the endless ocean where creatures evolving from the sunless depths in a last-ditch attempt to reach the final flash lie dead or dying, gulping and gasping on the mud-sand beach. It's the end. Soon Morgan will announce the dawn of the Final Reality and we'll all know what to do. "Love," breathes Gina, gazing past the stars. "Love," I reply, thinking that perhaps it is, and we walk back into the dancing-moving-merging energy of the Final Meeting House to face the climax.

"When theresno'body else aroun . . . oh the midnight hour! Yes the midnight hour! I'm gonna WAIT!! . . ."

Light-show—sound—color—people—moving—yelling—swirling-changing—for years, for hours, for life-times, all night . . . it's only for a night

By four o'clock, the climax is yet to come and I begin to doubt that this is the true and final end. Only another acid trip—more people, more equipment, much more acid—but only another acid trip. No conclusion. No meeting of all minds. No permanent break-through.

I'm coming down.

Gina reminds me that she has to go home and I realize that we can leave the gathering at any time. It's only a house full of freaks—only an acid test organized by Ben Morgan, an artist who takes psychedelic drugs.

Find Rob and say, "We gotta go home."

"Take the car," handing me the keys.

"How'll you get home?"

"I'll get a ride. I'm not sure I'm ever coming back. Just leave the car in . . . uh, the driveway."

Search for and find Brian. "We're gonna make it, man. Wanna go?"

"Can we?"

"No reason why not." I'm bluffing—not sure.

Brian looks around in search of a sign. No sign. The way appears to be clear. "We can try it."

"Are you still high?"

"Fooh. You best believe it But half-way down from where I was."

Move through five crooked doors, up a spiral staircase, through a wavering dimension-rip, down into a well where nobody lives all alone, back to point oh and three steps over to Baxtor, still frozen exactly where we saw him first and last. Another cat with a beard like Baxtor's and hair like Baxtor's and an army jacket like Baxtor's stands carved in stone beside him.

"We're leavin now, wanna come?" I ask the real Baxtor.

He says nothing.

I try, "Wanna go home?"

Baxtor says nothing, but when we head for the exit he follows us with wooden steps.

Dan Farnele, a quiet friend of Rob's, also from San Jose, needs a ride home and comes with us.

To the Then of Now in Double Retrospect

The car filled up, I closed the door, turned the key, worked the pedals, steered the wheel and started off down the winding dirt road. A space ship. Flash Gordon at the controls. The inside of the ship bathed in eerie blue light from the fantastic instrument panel. Meteor-moths bang against the view-plates, but we're protected by our humming force-field. Check the leegatron for stress, Zarkoff. Dale! Stay down, darling. Ah, Mongo dead ahead. Have we fuel enough to make it, Zarkoff?

Light-years later, a voice said, "Lemme out."

I looked in the rearview mirror and discovered that there were two Baxtors on Farnele's right. "Lemme *out*!" said one of them, "Stop the car. Sto-op the car!" I recognized him. He was the freak who was a reflection of iced-over Baxtor miles ago at the acid test. I stopped the car and Brian opened the door for him.

"Let's *all* get out," he commanded as though he'd caught us in his Elmer Fudd carrot patch, holding the door open and motioning everybody out. Baxtor followed him immediately. Somehow it didn't seem right.

"Baxtor, get back in the car," said Brian, validating my suspicions.

Baxtor climbed in. The Baxtor reproduction climbed in. I started the car and asked the stranger, "Do you need a ride somewhere?"

"No. I want out of the car. Stop the car!"

I stopped the car.

"Ev-ree body *out*!"

Baxtor obeyed without a moment's hesitation. He looked at the unknown freak. The unknown freak looked at him. Two beards, two army jackets, two identical non-hair-cuts, two equally blown minds. Not a word was said, but the two of them turned as one and started off down the road. Goodbye, Baxtor. Luck on the road of your karma. We shall all soon follow in your wise footsteps.

"Well don't just let poor Frank wander away like that!" said Gina, snapping me back to the land of the reallies.

"Baxtor, please get back in the car!" I called after him. Behind the fading but not entirely faded acid, the situation was getting tense. I didn't want to hassle anyone. If Baxtor wanted to wander off into the dawn, I figured we should let him. But he spun on his heel and returned to the car. His new appendage did the same.

"Just Baxtor," I said apologetically.

"Everybody out of the car!" insisted the stranger.

Baxtor lunged for the door, but Farnele grabbed his arm. It took awhile, but working together we eventually separated Baxtor and the almost-Baxtor, driving away at last with Baxtor in and other out, seen jogging along in the rear window for a stretch, calling. "Out of the car! Ev-ree body out!"

The Other, we learned at a second organized acid test a month later, was a burned-out head named Gordo who, after we left him that morning, wandered around till he came upon a house, walked in the front door, opened the refrigerator and ate everything he found inside. The owner of the house heard him in the kitchen, saw the light blazing away, tip-toed down stairs and saw Gordo chomping his food and drinking his wine and smiling away, and the owner called the cops who arrived to haul this poor mindless cat off to the can.

When we heard all this, we felt bad about leaving him on the road, but at the time we were only relieved to be rid of him and anyway he was actually lucky to have been left behind, because crossing over the Bay Bridge Baxtor screamed when a lightning-bolt split the top of his skull into two smoking, ragged-edged halves. None of us saw it, but Baxtor undeniably felt it. He collapsed, then went totally rigid and began to vomit with horrible retching death-sickness sounds—a soul in utter agony—battle-field-torn-intestine dying. The rest of us shuddering and wincing and wondering what to do and nothin we *can* do but hand Baxtor Kleenex from Gina's purse which he ignores in his blind spasms.

On the freeway he tried to jump out of the car. "Hang on, man. Take it easy," we chorused in standard, trying-not-to-sound-worried, worried voices. Baxtor naturally saw through them and us and it and himself and groaned as he pawed at the door handle. Farnele held his arm, saying, "Easy man . . . just relax," and Baxtor calmed down long enough for us to drop our guard, then pushed the door open. Brakes on hard and car skidding and Baxter's feet hitting the pavement before we'd completely stopped, carrying him down an off-ramp past a red sign that said "GO BACK. YOU ARE GOING THE WRONG WAY" and into a deserted gas-station.

A grotesque, pitiful scene. Baxtor retching and shivering in the sick pale night of the yellowish-white peeling-paint empty broken-windowed station, while Brian and I walked toward him cautiously—like madhouse attendants cornering a hopeless patient. Bad enough for us—Baxtor-eyes probably seeing it much worse—"Come on, Frank. We're going to take you home, man. Everything's cool. Everything's okay, man." Sad lies, but say them just the same. "You'll be home in a minute. Come on man. It's all right."

He stared at us from behind a wax mask, his head still twisted to just above one shoulder, vomit covering his jacket and shirt-front and little specks of it clinging to his beard. Ah Baxtor, how do you get to wherever you get to? How can it be so unfathomably bad?

"Hey man, you know us. We're your friends . . . right? Cumon and get in the car. We're taking you home."

He shuddered once from way down inside, pinched his eyes tight-shut, opened them and nothing had changed, said, "Uunnh!" to mean, "Oh God get me out of this," and let us put him in the back-seat of the engine-idling car.

Brian was sweating and shaking his head, "Man, he's in bad shape, Abel. I don't know. I really don't know."

"Shhhh! He'll be all right," said Gina, worried because she liked Baxtor, trying to comfort him with, "You'll be home in half a second, Frank," smiling with an effort.

Can you hear it if I say that it hurt me to look at Baxtor? Physical pain. Brilliant Baxtor, covered with vomit and insanity, his eyes all suffering and fear and no hope. What does he see that's so bad it shatters his mind and leaves him a terrified robot and yet calls him back for another look?

We took him to the house in Saratoga and he ran down the path. We drove away and rode home in silence after dropping off Farnele and then Gina, "Frank'll be fine in the morning."—"Sure Gina. He just had a little freak-out's all," and, back at my apartment, a joint to slow us down and it fails miserably, only wiring us up, making sleep impossible, so Brian and I sit on the floor trying to straighten things out.

"That was truly one hell of an acid test," says Brian, running his finger through a pool of early morning sunlight that snuck through the drapes onto the rug.

"Do you realize that the magazines define a 'freak-out' as 'acid-heads enjoying themselves freely and having a good time'?"

"I'm hip," says Brian, "And this morning I'm not sure that's such a good place to be. I'd rather be un-hip and digging the acid-freaks from some nice, safe, magazine reality."

It seemed like years had passed since we'd driven into the lodge's parking-lot at far away Muir Beach, where Morgan's thing was possibly still happening. I was convinced that I'd seen the answer and lost it in the confusion of the come-down. Lost it again. Right in my hand and I dropped it again. "Maybe we should have stayed at the lodge and offered our heads to Morgan or something. Those people might really be into something important."

Still fascinated by the pool of yellow sunlight, Brian asked without looking up, "Like what?"

No answer. Many answers, and so . . . no answer. "Ah, there or here, here or there. Same thing. Same illusion. It goes on."

"Look, man," Brian's face down on the floor, inches from the spot of sun, "You can actually see it *move* across the rug. You can see it move."

CHAPTER EIGHTEEN – IT'S JUST ONE *GUY*

Words are such nearly useless little symbols. How can I possibly tuck feeling and friends and fear and hope and intricate flashes of life into words and expect to project and share an experience? These typed words aren't even pretty to look at. Anyone who digs on beauty would rather look at a mandala or a new green leaf or a colorwheel or a friend's face or simply the world first hand. The world first hand—that's where the beauty is—that's the one important flash of the whole illusion . . . and it's not coming across.

"Look at those clouds over the ocean, Abel. Wow! That's too much, man. It's just like a picture!"

Just like a *picture?* Holy smokes, people! That ain't "just like a picture!" That's the *real thing.* That's what a picture's trying to get and not making it. That's the real thing and nobody's interested.

I'm printing these words as carefully as possible, with hope for only a few, without entertaining any mad fantasies of building something beautiful or real from the words themselves. The words are supposed to help you hold special visions. More than pictures. Special personal pictures. Pictures of things that you might not have been around to see. Pictures that I want you to see. Pictures twice removed from what's happening. You can't write about what's happening because it's gone by the time you get it straight in your head and set it down. You gotta write about what *has* happened. That's all that's left. The things I write about once happened. Indian told me to, "Tell it like it is." I try. I tell it like I thought it was. That's the best I can do.

Forgive me, those of you who know that words are meaningless vibrations in the perfect vacuum. I give *you* the number 11 and the number 24 and the numbers 6 and 16.

But share this picture. It's all gone. It's all past. It's already over. These are words about the early morning witnessed by some people who came to be known as "hippies." It's a collection of words written in acid. It isn't a "hip" collection of words. There are no "hip" collections of words. All word-collections are only words. The wisest collections (among them the Christian Bible, beyond all its padding and bullshit) tell us that once there *were* no words, the time will come when there *will be* no words, and in actuality there *are* no words.

And it could stop here, but I keep writing words—asking you to see, among other things, that after the Ben Morgan acid test, Baxtor didn't leave his bed for six days. For five days and nights he didn't eat or sleep or close his eyes, but lay on his back watching the paisley ceiling without saying a word, even to his worried, uncomprehending mother who told me, "He came home pale as a sheet, shivering all over. I put him to bed and he hasn't moved from it since." She moved her head from side to side slowly and stared into the fireplace. "He's killing himself. I don't know why, but he's trying hard to kill himself."

He surely is trying, I thought but certainly didn't say to Mrs. Baxtor. He's trying just like the rest of us to kill that greedy old Self. I even considered telling Mrs. Baxtor about the Void and the world of illusion and the problems caused by getting hungup in various bardos when your ego's too fat to squeeze through. But ego-death sounds just like body-suicide to most straight people, so I said instead, "I hope Frank feels better. He's probably got the flu or something," and split for Oakland where Beau was holding some Mescaline for me.

When Baxtor finally did crawl out of bed, he went to live with a good little chick named Judy who had a cabin near Big Basin where he stopped taking acid, saying, "It almost got me. Next time I *know* it'll get me. It has my cellular diagram in its totality now and the next time I stand anywhere *near* the hole it'll suck me in. The cosmos is on to me. It knows I'm holding everything back."

And I couldn't help saying, "Well Baxtor, you stupid bastard, if you *are* what's holding everything back, would you please have the decency to *let* go."

"Game's over when I do."

"Exactly, man."

"If I could convince myself that it's the right thing to do . . . I would. I'd let go."

"It's the right thing! How the hell can you convince your *self* that it's the right thing to do, when it's your *self*—your *ego* that has to go? It'll come back, man! Unless it's your *time* and you do it one hundred percent right and shoot on over and *stay* . . . and then that's great! You'd be out of the illusion, man! You'd have made it! Otherwise you come back, Baxtor. Honest you do. What have you got to lose, man? It's the right thing to do."

Shifting uneasily in his chair and lighting a cigarette, "Abe . . . don't run that shit on me. What else can an agent of the void say?"

In front of Kaleidoscope Book Store I ran into Larry who, since last our paths crossed, had been through a heavy crystal thing, a heavy smack thing (ugly sickness, blown yellow tubes and all), a long fast to clean out the robot, a short macrobiotic rest period, was now back to heavy acid consumption and had figured it all out. "I figured it all out," he said.

"That's great, man. I mean . . . to have figured it all out."

"Oh yeah. It took me time, dad. It surely did, but I figured it all out."

He figured it all out.

'There's nothing but confusion," said Larry, "Right? And no communication—I mean, flat *no* communication. Alienation on all levels, each man an island, right? And you know that just over the edge, right there on the other side, there's unity . . . right? And everybody wants to get there, right? Only it's hard. It's dead-ass *hard*! Cuz there's something hanging up the break-through, right? You get right up to the edge—*right* up to the *edge* an then something hangs you up, right?"

"Right," I said, because it's the correct answer and also because it's what I've got to say because the rhythm is hard to break.

"Right," said Larry, "And the reason is . . . there's one guy somewhere who won't let go."

"Yeah?" mentally listing the people I'll ask to form the torch-light parade to force Baxtor to let loose.

"Sure. Sure and true. Man you've felt that, haven't you? There's *one* hold-out somewhere. One cat who's hanging us all up by refusing to let go and shoot through to unity and the big ah hah."

Preston will want to bring the tar, Beau can get the feathers, Lyla'll wanna come, after that thing at Marion's . . . but, "how'd you know it's not a whole buncha people?"

"No, man," groaned Larry, exasperated at my ignorance. "It's just *one* guy. I figured it all out."

That settled it. But just to make sure, "who's this one guy?"

Larry pulled a joint from his cig-pack, stuck it in his mouth, looked down his nose at it, saw that it was weed, whipped it out of his mouth and tucked it into his shirt, selected a straight-cig, lit it with a cowboy stick-match, blew smoke into the smog, spit a little piece of tobacco, flicked the non-existent ash from the cigarette and said, "I don't know man. That's the hang. There's always a hang and that's this particular problem's hang. It could be anyone. It could be you, or it could be me. It isn't . . . but it could be. There's no way of telling."

Standing under the eye of the bookstore with its thousand shelves (well, *hundred* shelves) of books on philosophy, religion, politics and poetry, I had my satori of the day. I knew that Larry was absolutely right in saying that one guy was holding us all back from the perfection of the void. It isn't Baxtor—except in Baxtor's case. It's me. It's all the separate me-existences in the cosmos. It's us.

CHAPTER NINETEEN—THE SHATTERED LAMP

A crowded, headaching bus-ride up to Oakland where I try to hitch-hike but end up walking to the College of Fine Arts to wait for Beau's class to let out, sitting under trees lazy-half-working at putting the make on a doll-like Japanese chick who tells me, "You look like a hermit."

"I am a hermit. Will you come live with me in my cave?" Little smile—almond eyes sideways quick and then back to sketch-book where fingers smudge and rebuild charcoal patterns, "Too cold in the winter."

"Not *my* cave. Mine's warm all year round."

Hiding a beautiful oriental giggle behind her hand, lifting my shirt-tail, "Ah. You see? You aren't a hermit. You don't have a rope belt. All hermits have rope belts."

"I'm a special breed of leather-belt hermit. Will you come live with me?"

"No," fingers and eyes busy again in the sketch-book.

"I'll go back to my cave and starve to death and it'll be on your conscience for the rest of your days."

"You don't really live in a cave."

"I'll find one. I'll even let you pick it out."

"I have a boy friend."

"Ah, but he can't love you as much as I do. Would he starve himself to death in cave for you?" and much more with no results and no real hope of any results, till Beau's class is over and, after goodbye to the lovely chick, we walk down College Avenue to his new apartment and, once inside, he turns me on to freon gas which is three minutes of heavy strange high from an innocent looking little can. "Wow. Where do you get this stuff?"

"Any liquor store, man," says Beau, filling the balloon for another hit, "It's for icing glasses. Buck-fifty a can."

Inhale on the balloon—a clown sings happy birthday on its side—pass it on—Beau also inhale—hold it—feel the pressure between the ears—exhale together—inhale again and that's the one that does the deed. Oxygen plus freon equals six-thousand Quasimodo cathedral bells at war with every buzz of twentieth century radio static that was or is or is to be, while the see-set crumbles and then resorts itself into magic Indian energy beadwork from life to death in three minutes clock-time, and you're back again.

"Whoau! It won't be on the market for long." (And wasn't, because only six months later the high-school crowd began tripping with it—spraying it directly into one another's and baby sister's mouth—freezing their lungs solid for undoubtedly radical trips that ended in awed death, and a month later it was off the market.)

Two quick joints and a bennie apiece to fix a warm, energetic, good-time feeling as we drive to Telegraph in Beau's twenty-mile-an-hour Simca, out on the street to merge with the hordes, and everyone you pass is equally high on something or other—all good vibes, as we drop bean after bean into early evening and Beau says, "Oh yes and you have to dig this cat I ran across."

"Whose thing is . . . ?"

"He thinks he's an orange, man. I mean he really thinks he's a round, lumpy-skinned, navel orange."

So, bzazz across town to an ancient, crumbling, once-brown boarding-house where the Orange lives with his also ruined acidhead room-mate.

The place is a shambles. *Great Expectations* revisited, but painted orange since last there. Empty orange-juice bottles and cartons and cans piled everywhere—the human orange sits on a high stool in the kitchen, dressed in a pair of yellowed boxer shorts. "That's the Orange," says Beau, ignoring the body in the other room.

I greet the Orange politely, "H'lo Orange."

"Bahnihm," says the Orange.

"Watch," says Beau, moving forward menacingly, his hands opening and closing on the air, "It's orange-juice time," he hisses.

"Tree-Sweet needs more oranges."

"Squeezers! Squeezers!" shrieks the Orange.

"They wone squeeze ya," says the body from the other room. The body is the Orange's room-mate. He sprawls in the apartment's only chair, next to an eight millimeter movie projector that's throwing a Flash Gordon serial on the wall. On his lap is a bowl of powder into which he dips a licked finger from time to time, then puts the finger in his mouth. "Got the acid yet?" he asks Beau without taking his eyes from the flickering square of light on the wall.

"Not in yet," says Beau. "How's Flash doing?"

"Still in the valley of the stone men," lick-dip-pop.

"That's healthy," says Beau, motioning me out the door with a twitch of his head.

Outside I say, "Those dudes are in a weird place."

"Too much acid, ole pal. The Orange was a big dealer when I first moved up here."

"What's that other cat's trip?"

Starting the car and slowly reaching the twenty-mile-an-hour top speed, "He sells enough acid to pay for his own and sits around watching that Flash Gordon serial while he eats it."

"All the time?"

"All the time, man."

"Hmm. I was just thinking about Flash Gordon a few weeks ago."

"A bad sign, Abel. A very bad sign," as we swing back to Telegraph and pick up two not-quite-ugly-but-pretty-close hippie chicks, take them to Beau's apartment, smoke more weed and make love until the chicks fall asleep.

Still wired and restless at six a.m., I said goodbye to Beau, after pocketing a complimentary lid, and trudged to the bus station for a ride back to San Jose, where I waited around until I knew that Brian would be awake, then phoned and bribed him with ten bennies into picking me up.

"Wanna go visit Baxtor?" he asked, popping two of the beans into his mouth and washing them down with a coke from the bus-station vending machine.

"I met a guy who thinks he's an orange," I confided as we swung through town in the Packard.

"Well *now* we're going to see a guy who thinks he's Frank Baxtor, which is much weirder."

Baxtor was still hiding-resting in the mountains at patient Judy's cabin, trying to get his mind back. He heard the car drive up and met us at the door. "Aha. Cosmic agents from the occupied city."

Up the wooden steps two at a time, "Yah! We got an acid gun loaded with four thousand mics!"

Baxtor jumped back into the cabin and made a dive for the bed, yelling, "Keep away!" as he tunneled under the covers.

"You look like a giant mole." Brian closed the door and we sat on the hard little willow chairs, rapping to and at one another non-stop from behind the speed while Baxtor peeked out at us from under a blanket.

" . . . and the *East*! I mean like New York east—godonlyknows what those people are up to. It's all outta control."

"Paul came back from New York with those stories of smack trends and freaks in XKEs and everything moving hard and fast into some kind of weird commercial survival tactics. Is it all getting lost and smothered in confusion?"

By early afternoon the radio was going strong, playing familiar electronic mind-rock, Brian and I shouting over it, when Baxtor suddenly grabbed the set and spun the dial, saying, "I'm sick of rock and roll! I want to hear something *soft* for a change!"

The dial stopped at a more powerful station so that with ear-splitting volume the radio said, "You're *sick,* Fred, but you're really sick of your *self*!" causing Baxtor to do a complete backflip onto the bed as though he'd received a million-volt electrical jolt, while Brian and I (after recovering from the initial shock of the words) fell to the floor clutching our sides and howling as the radio went on to sing about some cat named Fred who was undergoing Freudian analysis. Baxtor lay limp on the bed, mumbling, "Bowsha bowsha," pulling his mustache and wondering why it was against the rules to dislike rock and roll and how the cosmos had got wind of his rebellion so fast. It could only have happened to Baxtor. The Control Powers harassed him unmercifully with coincidences and inexplicable happenings designed to keep him ever aware of the cosmic plot against his perpetuation. Not a day went by that evil spirits didn't take time out to pick on his head.

On a clear, bright morning, after Judy had gone to work leaving Baxter alone in the cabin, I clomped up the deadleaf path and saw pieces of Judy's big purple-glass globe lamp scattered all over the front yard. Baxter heard my footsteps and opened the door—an old, weathered mountain man by this time—hollowcheeked, a pair of faded blue work pants hanging on his bony frame from a single suspender, barefoot and dusty.

"What happened to the lamp?"

"I broke it last night," said Baxter with his thumbs hooked in his pockets.

"Why?"

Baxter motioned me inside. "Part of the plot. I lost my head. What little head remains, that is."

"How so?"

We sat down and he stirred the fire with a coat hanger. "Last night, Jerry—Judy's old boyfriend—came over to visit her. Of course *he* said 'us.'"

"You hit him with the lamp?"

"Hah! Other way around. He gave Judy that twice cursed lamp you know—about a year ago—and last night, out of the clear blue—hah!—for no apparent reason—hah!—he showed up at the door. And just at the right-wrong time, because for two weeks I've been feeling inadequate in the sex department and all of a sudden—*him*. So I knew that he was to be my replacement."

Crack! went the wood fire, shooting a spark that landed on Baxter's forearm. He accepted it without flinching. "I beg your pardon," to the fire, and then to me, "All the time he was here, I sat off to one side trying to build the biggest erection I'd ever had, so that I could prove myself to Judy when he left, in hopes of a second chance. And it was working. I got a *huge* rod. Magnificent! The biggest and best I'd managed in about a year. I fed it erotic thoughts and promises until Jerry left, then I said, in my lowest animal voice,

'Come, Judy,' and I pulled off my pants revealing my masterpiece."

Snap! went the fire, shooting another spark to land between Baxter's toes. He gritted his teeth, closed his eyes and said, "Forgive me," then continued on bravely, "Judy smiled and undressed and I prepared for the finest piece of mortal ass imaginable. She asked me to turn out the light and I saw how significant the gesture would be, so I reached up, grabbed the chain, pulled and the whole lamp came out of the ceiling and fell with a crash on my forehead directly on the frontal lobe which caused me to *lose* the greatest hardon I ever had, and, temporarily sane, I jumped up, took the lamp by its chain and ran outside naked and proceeded to smash Jerry's goddam lamp-trap into a thousand pieces while calling curses upon his name and his treachery—for which I shall pay many times over." Pop! went the fire, shooting two more sparks riding smoke trails to fall on Baxter's lap, one merely a decoy to distract him from the other, which burned a little black hole in his right leg. "Yes," said Baxter, slapping the leg-fire, "I haven't been able to get an erection since, and I (sigh) probably never will."

"Poor Baxter," I said to myself, remembering how quick his brain had been only a short time ago, seeing him mindless and freaked, no longer interested in Nirvana, longing now for a simple hardon, "What did you do to yourself? What are *we* doing to ourselves?"

I stuck my eyes in the fire and let them tumble on the glowing ember jewels, digging the amazing magic of flame. Sitting smoky and close to a camp-fire in Big Sur, Preston once told me that all of man's troubles began when the first hairy-ape-human blew it and failed to instantly piss on a fire he found. The first foolish step out of line.

"What are we doing? Becoming Buddhas," I reminded my wandering intentions, "and it's a long, hard climb. First you have to let yourself drop all the way to the bottom before you can start climbing for the top—before you can understand that there is no top and no bottom. Hard, anti-life-going all the way, but, unlike all the other paths, it takes you to the end."

CHAPTER TWENTY – AFTER THE RAIN

It rained for five days solid—coming down sideways—driven by the wind. Great. The drops made a steady *shhhhhhhhh* night and day, telling me that all was quiet and cool and the rain had come to clean up the whole set. The rain sound, the rain smell, the rain damp and rain-water-color sky—beautiful. Enchanted rain. It wears away rock, and yet you can walk in it unharmed. Rain only makes you wet. And wet is the way you come into this life. You'll go out dry.

Drifting, falling crystal beads and prisms. Rain. I watched it from my apartment, squished along the shiny streets in it, stood looking up blinking and dripping into endless gray and let it wash my mind as it washed the buildings and city pavement. But as the caked-on layers of accumulated time-thought dissolved and slid down the gutters, I relived other times that I'd watched the rain. Better times it seemed. Clearer days and cleaner times seen through unclouded eyes and an uncluttered brain. Remember how the rain looked and sounded and smelled and felt when you were ten years old? Not the same any more. Not the same for a long time. So after the rain drizzled itself into wispy clouds, I found myself in a mild state of sad. A sad that a half-cap of acid and the better part of a lid only enhanced. Too much nostalgia from watching the lines come out of fat black-gray infinity—puddles everywhere, shivering in the doorways of warm houses. Too much thinking back to other winters, and about the strange trap of time, with so many years and memories all become just a flash in the void, and so many years to come, which in retrospect will also be just a faint flash—are now just a fading spark—so much pent-up feeling released by the rain, that on Monday I'm spent and dreamy and mild-sad.

In early morning cold I pulled on boots and coat and walked

to the San Jose State campus to sit in the cafeteria drinking hot chocolate, watching bundled-up college girls giggle by as I read the newspaper that some extra-early person had left behind. Newspaper morning reality. Grim. Even the "Funnies" hungup and grim and anything but funny. Dick Tracy bullets wiggling their way out of murderer's skull. Orphan Annie with her arm around Sandy as Daddy gets blown to atoms. Terry and the nonexistent pirates involved in complicated counter-plots with insidious Asiatic enemies. Mary Worth's friends fighting out a tragic divorce. Gordo's spider trying to be hip and missing it by ten years. Rex Morgan in the hands of an evil woman who is probably a blackmailer by next issue. Fearless Fozdick too real to laugh at. Pogo locked in some political satire.

Dagwood and a passing bank-robber were being chased by the cops when David Anderly in his fringed buck-skin jacket arrived to say, "Egregore! What gets you up so early?"

"Haven't been to bed."

Finishing my lukewarm chocolate—"You're leading a loose life, Abe. Next thing you know, you'll be turning to drugs . . . which is exactly what *I'm* about to do. Wanna come to the house?"

"It can only be better than here. Let's go."

"I'm gonna drop acid. You wanna come along?"

Quick calculation. "No. It's not getting me there anymore. I gotta wait a few days. Anything happening I oughta know about?" as we stride out the swinging doors, cutting across campus toward the old green house David shared with three other college heads.

Lighting a cigarette and handing me one, "Uh . . . lessee . . . oh, LaMer's reading some of his stuff at about twelve. We could . . . should make it to that."

At David's place we smoked weed and listened to the stereo amid piles of sound equipment—amps, mikes and guitars—until it was time for LaMer to read.

David glanced at his watch. "I'm gonna drop that acid before I go."

"Have a good thing, man."

When we reached the campus there was already a big crowd in front of the cafeteria. Andre LaMer, paying no attention to the cold, clad in a T-shirt, his long black hair flying all over the place as he shook his head and jumped around doing this funny nervous dance, was warming the listeners up with things like, "I'm only a mirror, brothers an sisters. I just reflect what's in *each* an *every* one of *you.* I have had *visions*! Yes, visions that I gotta share with you, an *that's* why I'm here today! Heh, yes. Now some a you are gonna get pissed off cuz I say fuck an shit an other kindsa dirty words, but jus this once try to listen to them words as no more'n *words*! They're only words, brothers an sisters. God knows that. An He knows I gotta use them words to explain things. Well . . . even if I don't *gotta*, I *do.* He knows that too, an it's allllll *right*! I know He knows an I know it's alright, cuz I talked to Him jus last night an He said, 'Andre,' he sez, 'Andre, boy . . . you was screwed-up for most of your *life,* but now you're on the *right track*! You're doin the right thing. Now get out there an do it with a liddle more *soul*!' Yeah, He said that." On and on, yelling it, screaming it, dancing on one foot and then the other, hunching his shoulders, dipping his head, smiling and grinning and moving and talking without so much as a breath in between.

David and I sat on the grass with Ted and Rusty who were passing a fat yellow joint that was so obviously a joint it prompted me to say, "Hey man, is that a good idea?" indicating the mob of not necessarily sympathetic spectators.

Ted considered this as if for the first time, then shrugged. "No call for paranoia." And he passed the joint to David.

LaMer was yelling out one of his early-angry poems so fast that the words were a machinegun-burst-blur of sound . . . "an-the-cops-shouldbe-madeta-sitt-in cells-withpaisley-walls while million watt amplifiers-play-hardacid-San-Fran-rock-soul-music-an six-fan-tastical light-shows drive thewalls-symotaniously budeye wonnerifeven-t/wt'd-do-anygood-cuz-copsiz-shiddy . . . copsiz fuk'dup . . . they-holleratya-fer not-waitin-on-the-yellow'n-the-yellow-takesolong-when-yer-goinasee-a-friend they-make-ugly n'pullgunswhenya-tellemya-lovem . . ." and then Lamer goes into " . . . on cold nights when there's no warm woman sweet-smell soft-body next to me an I got too much love to hold, I ain't ashamed to admit that I beat my meat over a mental pitchera Brigitte Bardot."

A fratman walking by yelled, "Nice talk, faggot!"

"Yessir!" LaMer shouted back without breaking stride. "That ole mirror gets painful-bright at times, don't it brother? But really now, man, I'm one-hunner'd percent all American red-blooded furry-assed boy, an mind-fuckin Brigitte Bardot ain't *no* kinda faggotry!"

The crowd—mostly straight college types—was beginning to warm up to Andre. His stark-raving insanity in the form of crude honesty was growing on them. They'd come to see a crazy hippie poet and Andre played the part for them like a champ. He's got it down pat. He tells them what they want to hear, then throws in a little more when they least expect it.

"My nex poem's one I wrote on peyote in Berkeley after I accidently threw up on this chick I was ballin. It was like kind of a humbling experience for both a us an I tried to put it all down in words but while I was writin I seen that it was a sign meant to say that there was too much to do an I should be out doin an sayin what I gotta say insteada ballin in an apartment in Berkeley, so I left the chick an the poem unfinished an went out to tell people an here it is . . . heh, yes . . . Masturbatin on the toilet seat at two ae em with diamoneedles in both eyes an a yet to get rattle-snake fix on my glass-mad mind . . ." and much more, designed to make straight-people shudder and maybe fall out of their tight iron cages for a fraction of a flash—to make his friends laugh inside.

LaMer danced and sang to the crowd, banging their ears with his interpretation of "The New Madness," and I saw that above and beyond his huge ego and crazy power-games, he had honestly seen the Big Eternity. ("That's it," Baxtor is saying somewhere, "use a sufficient number of meaningless generalizations like 'Eternity' for effect." But just the same . . .) Go Andre. Do it to em. Let em know that there's nothing to be afraid of anymore.

After the reading, Andre strutted over to our group with his hand-written, scrawled, half-printed, crossed-out and re-scribbled poems clutched in his construction-worker hands. "I really *got* to em today!" he bellowed, then laughed his Snidely Whiplash, "Heh heh heh heh."

I told him that I thought it was a good reading and he said,

"Man, I really been writin more *great* stuff lately! I'm writin a whole epic poem that I'm gonna put in a book . . . like Beowulf . . . only *better*! Heh, *aw-right*!"

A stick-thin kid with a giant dandelion for hair who was a follower-worshipper of LaMer's pushed his way through the milling bodies and announced that Andre had only ten minutes to make it to a panel discussion on psychedelic drugs that was being held at a local school.

"Ah wow yes!" said Andre. "They *need* me at that thing!" And we're all invited to come along.

Into Ted's VW bus where Andre smoked a pipe of hash to prepare for the event as we chugged along. We arrived stumbling and bumping into one another, had to be guided to the auditorium by an excited kid who asked us if we'd sell him a lid. A confused, noisy jam-up at what turned out to be the wrong entrance, where we were confronted by the school's principal who had to think it over a long while before agreeing to let us in. "I'm one a the *speakers.* I'm Andre LaMer!"

"Mm," said the principal, frowning, consulting a clipboard. "Oh yes . . . the *poet.* Uh, but these others . . .

"They're my managers. I take em everywhere."

"Well . . . The entire auditorium was neck-craning to see what was going on. A scene was in the making and the program was late, so he waved us in against his better judgment. "Please take seats, uh, gentlemen."

The panel consisted of a cop, a social worker, two converted junkies and LaMer. The cop spoke first:

"There is no doubt in my mind—and I'm in a position to know—that there is undeniably a direct correlation between the use of marijuana, or *pot* as it's called by addicts, and crimes of violence."

"Bull!" said LaMer.

The principal (now the em cee) said, "I must ask Mister LaMer to wait his turn, and remind him that this is a high-school auditorium."

"Heh, right," said Andre, looking serious until the principal turned his back, then smiling and giving the audience the weed sign which causes waves of laughter and a round of applause, and the principal thought everyone was applauding him for putting Andre in his place.

The cop continued:

"Regardless of statements made by a few supposedly *learned men,* marijuana is the first step down the long, degrading road to narcotics addiction. Marijuana destroys the user's morals, his reason, his sense of right and wrong, his ability to . . ." and a lengthy description of the effects of alcohol followed, with some of the aspects of heroin addiction added for good measure. The cop had obviously never smoked weed, but he knew all about it.

The social worker wasn't quite so heavy—even had a few good points—but she pulled all of her knowledge from experiences with down-and-out Mexican kids and street gangs. Upper-middle-class and college educated weed-freaks were beyond her. She mentioned them only once, saying, "In recent months, there has been some experimentation with drugs among the intellectuals in college. It's a form of rebellion."

The converted junkies were the high-light of the show. One was a twenty-seven-year-old, pock-marked hard-guy hep-cat from the old school who told how he started on "reefers when I was a smart little punk, dropped out of high-school at fifteen," then went almost immediately to smack, got a righteous habit going, robbed a liquor store, went to jail, got out and jumped right back into his habit, knocked over another liquor store, this time with a gun, went back to jail, barfed all over the place from smack-withdrawal, repented and finally got paroled on the condition that he would set himself up as an example of a reformed junkie and "Tell it like it is, baby," for the establishment.

The other was a fairly nice looking thirty-year-old bleached-blond chick who had pretty much the same story, but didn't try to come on like the last word in cool. She frankly admitted that she knew nothing about LSD (hard-guy hep-cat said that it was "Ten times worse than heroin, baby,") then recapped by saying that drugs had nearly ruined her life, and sat down.

Andre skyrocketed to his feet and danced to the center of the stage. "Now you're gonna hear the *reallies*!" he said. "And the reallies start with this poem."

He recited his "Smoke more weed, take more acid" chant, glided into "Hare Rama Krishna" and wrapped it up with the full-minute-Om for which he was locally famous.

The principal glanced at his watch and shifted uncomfortably in his chair.

Andre told the audience that they could dismiss the statements made by the cop and the social worker because they only knew what they'd read from nineteen-thirty's propaganda pamphlets. "And these poor people," he said, waving his arm at the ex-junkies, "They ain't any kinda representatives of the psychedelic revolution! They're like alcoholics, only they got hooked on junk insteada booze! Nobody oughta take *junk* except for medicinal reasons. The psychedelics ain't *junk*. The psychedelics are holy *sacraments*! Everybody should take acid at least once to straighten-out their heads! Now when people tell you that . . ."

The principal announced that the discussion was over and would everybody please fold-up their chairs as they left?

Andre got in a big verbal battle with the hard-guy hep-cat who said, "Listen, baby, I was in the action . . .

"Don't give me none a that old-time junkie noise! How many times've you dropped acid?"

"Look, baby . . .

"You're the *worst* kinda cop-out. You coulda been lookin for *God* when all you was doin was lookin for *kicks*!"

"Would you please fold your chairs as you leave the auditorium?" said the principal.

"You gotta do it with a little more *soul?'* yelled Andre into the dead mike, "Here's a poem I wrote while I was a Marine trainin to kill-off babies!"

LaMer's dandelion-headed disciple was standing on his chair, clapping his hands and saying, "Tell em, Andre! Read em the one about instructions for the eleventh hour news!"

The hard-guy ex-junkie was working up to punching LaMer in the mouth and the cop was five seconds away from acting in an official capacity, so Ted and I coaxed LaMer from the stage and hustled him out the door without giving the principal a chance to say thank you or come again.

"You were *great,* Andre! Wow! You were *great*!" enthused Dandelion-head as we climbed into the bus. I figured Andre'd single-handedly canceled any slim chance that might have existed of acid-freaks being accepted by the straight world. But I held my peace while David held his head, moaning, "Shah. Never again. Never *again,*" and Ted held the wheel, saying, "We're runnin for the hills," and Andre held his pipe of hash, smiling, "Yeah! I really *got* to em!" and similar statements of satisfaction all the way to the Santa Cruz mountain cabin that Jean (Ted's new chick) had rented, where we piled out, stoned out of our heads by this time, and stumbled inside to huddle around the fireplace, shake our heads and giggle.

CHAPTER TWENTY ONE – THE ELECTRIC CHAIR

"I'm by far *the* greatest poet in the world today!" proclaimed LaMer, bouncing from fireplace to kitchen to chair and back to fireplace, pulling on hash-pipe then joint then hash again. "McClure is good, Ginsberg's great an so's Corso, yeh he's one a the best, an so's Kerouac . . . no, he ain't really a poet . . . *yeh* he is . . . maybe better'n em all . . . except me! I'm the greatest in the world today. *Yesterday* too!" Tongue in cheek only if you look real close—and even then, chances are he's merely removing a speck of weed from one of his molars. Andre's confident. It's a fact. Dispute it and he'll challenge you to a debate that he'll either win or stick with till you're hoarse, confused, exasperated and too tired to stay awake any longer.

"Listen to *this,*" he insisted. "I just wrote it." And everyone had to listen while Andre recited his latest fifteen-minute poem dealing with his reaching for the generator of all life and knowledge, almost making it, but burning his head out at the last second to fall back to earth and ignorance once more.

Jean nodded and said, "That was beautiful, Andre. That was one of your best," when LaMer was finally silent.

"I got *better* ones!" roared LaMer, launching into an even madder glory-chant—"Harry Krishners take more acid keep on pushin turn em on for the ole alma mater rainbow raga fox trot, an this is how it goes!"—His loudest, opening with a thirty second solid wall of sound, interrupted for a breath, resumed for another thirty seconds till it crumbles into a series of, "Hooh! Hooh! Hooh!" followed by suggestions toward building a better life through chemistry.

"No one can read a poem as loud as you, LaMer."

"Heh, yes! Lissen ta this one. It shows my religious background: 'Babylon! You whore! Eater of unborn babies! De-baller of holy black-men! Defiler of . . .'"

Al Vaughn arrived in his beat-up Falcon. Al Vaughn who will soon—not tonight, but soon—drop one cap too much acid in San Jose, freak-out while listening to the news on the radio, realizing suddenly that the motivation for all of America and possibly all the world is hate and fear, realizing that he is part of America and part of the world and therefore bound by this heritage, at which point he will grab a brass candle-holder and run into the street to tell everyone and stop a car with a frightened old grumpy man in it and pound on the poor cat's chrome with the candle-holder, screaming, "Open your eyes! Get those stupid blind eyes open! Don't you see what's happening?!" until the cops come and drag him off to jail for assault with a deadly weapon, disturbing the peace, malicious mischief and possession of a dangerous drug (which, when tested in the super cop-lab, proved to be an aspirin given to Al by the college health clinic earlier in the day).

Now Al was wired tight on speed, flapping his arms and running all over the cabin on destinationless crystal impulses, finally getting into a long, loud, sputter-worded argument with LaMer just for something to do.

"We're all Communists," Andre insisted. "We don't like to admit it, but we've all become hopeful Utopian Communists!"

"A triple ton of bullshit!" said Al, unbuttoning the high collar of his electric-blue Chinese shirt. "I'm not a Communist! I'm an anarchist. Communism is a form of government and I don't believe in or want *any* form of government! Down with all control!"

"*All* control?"

"Give control back to the individual!"

"Pure communism ain't no form of government!"

"You can say *that* again!"

"Aw, Al! Holy smokes! Don't play those games with me. You know what I *mean.* Now if we wanna *get* somewhere we gotta be *honest* an argue honestly an make it *easy* for the other guy! Now, when I say . . ." for hours, while the rest of us smoked hash and tried to listen to records. Soon, Andre craftily worked the conversation back to his favorite subject and said, "I'm definitely the greatest poet in the world today! Who's better?"

"Maybe no one," agreed Ted. "But poets play with words and all words are meaningless." Just to bug Andre, and of course it works because Andre, above all else, loves Andre's words.

"Well okay, but you gotta do *somethin*! An playin with words—tryin to *say* somethin—is a good game to play. An I play it better'n anybody. I'm tryin to tell it like it is!"

From my place on the floor I said, "Andre, you *can't* tell it like it is, cuz by the time you get the words out it *isn't* anymore. Can you hear that?"

"I surely can, Abel. I surely can. But I gotta pretend I don't, cuz it means there's nothin for me to do, an right now my karma's *doin*! Can you dig it?"

"Yup. Can't buck your karma. That's a fact." And then I can't resist asking, "What's the moment of truth like on acid for you?"

"Ego death?"

"The same. How's that huge ego of yours die?"

"Hard!"

"Like how?"

"Like a guy goin to the electric chair!" LaMer leapt to the center of the room and began to act out a little play for us, taking all the parts as only fast-moving Andre could.

"All the way, condemned me's screamin no! no! I wanna live!" Andre was struggling with imaginary guards as they drug him down the last mile.

Andre as Guard—"Take it easy now, son. Take it easy."

Andre as Condemned Andre's Ego—"I don't wanna die! I wanna keep on doin! Please don't make me die! I'll be good! I'll do anything! I wanna keep on goin!"

Andre as Another Guard—"Come on you chicken-shit little bastard. Take it like a man!"

A as C.A.E.—"No! I wanna live! Lemme go!"

A as The Priest—"Do you repent your sins my son?"

A as C.A.E.—"Yeah! Anything! I don't wanna die! Lemme go!"

A as A.G.—"You admit you're a nuthin, no-talent, goldbrickin, miserable, worthless excuse for a man?"

A as C.A.E.—"Yeah! YEAH! Don't make me die! Tell me what I gotta say! Tell me what I gotta do! Don't make me die!"

A as G.—(Kindly) "Do you admit that you are ignorant, unworthy, contemptible and a charlatan?"

A as C.A.E.—"Wait a second . . .

A as G.—(More firmly) "Now, son . . . admit it. It can hardly matter at this moment."

A as C.A.E.—"I admit it! I'm ignorant. I'm unworthy. I'm a fake! I'm an out an out charlatan! Now lemme go!"

A as Pr.—"You are going to God, my son. Soon you will enter His Kingdom . . .

A as C.A.E.—"I will *not* you dumb-ass wafer-pusher! I'll be *dead*! *I* won't be goin *anywhere*! Turn me loose you mutherfukkers! I ain't ready to stop bein!"

Andre was strapped into the electric chair—struggling horribly—his face red and sweating—teeth clenched—it's too real.

"Now I'm tryin to die an cop-out before the current hits me . . . but I can't. I tell myself how much I wanna, but I can't pull it off! I keep hopin for an out. Then the juice hits!" Andre writhed in convincing pain, arching his back. "An for a long, hard flash I hang on even though it's the worst pain an bumness I ever felt an I can't stand it! An then I see clear as daylight that soon as I turn loose an die everything'll be awright, but still I hang on to the very last possible second, hopin there's some other kinda out, an a course there ain't, an then I'm dead." Andre twitched once—his muscles relaxed—his head fell back against the chair. The dead Hamlet. Goodnight, sweet Prince. Andre has gone to the other side. The room was silent. Time ticked by. Then, says Andre, "An it's *great*! It's alllll *right*!I come back slow—ego real small an humble an just glad to be back. Then it looks aroun an nuthin's gonna happen to it anymore so it gets a little bigger, an says, hey . . . I ain't *really* ignorant! Then says, I'm pretty damn good to make it through that an still snap *back*! Then pretty soon I'm all the way down an back to me again an I know that I'm the greatest poet in the world today . . . an *brave,* too! Heh, yeah!"

"Right back to where you started, man."

"Yup. But after what I just been through . . . that's *great I* An now I can appreciate just *how* great!" and he giggled into his LaMer dance, reaching for the hash-pipe.

Watching Andre jump around and laugh—glad to be alive and anxious to turn everyone on to life—I realized how much I liked him. He's the rubber-band motor behind our little shingle paddle-boat. He knows the end—he's seen it and accepted its finality—but he keeps on moving just the same. Good or bad? I don't know.

I do know that Andre was high on acid in Berkeley once, singing to a Howlin Wolf record at a semi-FSM party, when an old Spade, drunk on wine, put his arm around his shoulders and said, "You godda do't wif a lil moe *soul,* brutha."

Andre started to cry. "Beautiful," he sobbed, burying his wet eyes in the old philosopher-Spade's raggy coat, "That's really *it*!"Now Andre said, "You gotta do it with a little more *soul,* brothers!" all the time. No matter what was happening—tight-times or loose-times—"You gotta do it with a little more *soul*!"

Fraternity boys pushing their stalled car, drunk and late one night. LaMer, walking home stoned and full of Jesus, jumped over to help them. "You gotta do it with a little more *soul,* brothers!" he advised them.

They heard it wrong, of course—thought he was making fun of them—didn't take to being called, "Brother," by a long-hair creep. "Fuck you," said the Frats, and Andre took down his pants right there in the middle of the San Jose street.

"Okay, but do it with a little more *soul,* brothers!" he pleaded, bending over and turning his back to them.

"Get the hell outta here, faggot." "Let's kick his ass!" "Cumon. Let's Ar-ef'im good!" "We're gonna pound your butt, queer!" And LaMer beat it on home, fast and sad, muttering over and over again clear into the next day, "They missed the point. They missed the whole *point.* They always miss the *point*!"But by the next sunrise, Andre was back in form, telling the story as though it were a wise Zen teaching. And whenever one of *us* would get the miserables and talk about copping out of the non-movement, he would shake his head and say solemnly, "Don't do it, man. Don't cop-out. We all gotta keep on *doin*! We gotta keep on doin with a little more *soul.*"

During the first three years that I knew him, Andre spent a lot of his time naked or getting naked. When the impulse hit him, he simply took off his clothes. At his poetry readings he took off his clothes in what many thought to be a tribute to Allen Ginsberg, but it was really just Andre. He took off his clothes at The College of Fine Art in Oakland and chased a nude model across the campus. He took off his clothes in front of the fountain at San Jose State College and was chased across campus by security police. He took off his clothes at Cal Berkeley and persuaded twelve others to join him. He took off his clothes at the first Be-in in San Francisco and nobody even noticed. I took him to meet a little sophomore chick I'd found who was just starting to turn on, and when she didn't come up with the answers Andre expected, he took off his clothes, ending my relationship with the chick there and then.

"Why'd you haveta do *that,* man?"

"To make her *see.*"

"Make her see *what?* Your magnificent tool?"

"Nope. Just a body without no clothes on."

Andre took off his clothes when he was happy and just wanted to be naked, he took off his clothes when he was confused and all else failed, he took off his clothes when people were acting pompous or when he felt that they were taking themselves too seriously or not seriously enough. Andre took off his clothes in public because, "Man, there's a *law* against bein naked! That's insane! Everybody's naked unnerneath their *clothes*! How can you forbid people to be naked? It just ain't *healthy*!"

On this particular night, following the one-man ego-death play, Andre took off his clothes. The kid with the dandelion hair (whose name, I learned, was Rube Clemin) stripped down immediately and sat beside his ideal, smiling and listening for wise words and smoking hash when it came his way. Ted had crashed in front of the fireplace, sound asleep with tight-closed eyes behind his crooked glasses. David was so high, sailing on the weed and hash-fed tail-end of the morning's acid, that never-before-played far-eastern music drifted out of his guitar in an uninterrupted rippling stream as his fingers touched the strings and he himself stared at something deep inside the dying fire. Rusty slumped against a wall, listening to David's music or, perhaps, his own. Jean nodded and hummed to herself, curled-up warm and soft in a big leather chair, refusing the pipe that Andre offered her, quiet and beautiful in the rose-glow of the fire. Al split for LA., tight and fast.

A ghost-shaft of moonlight on smoke anchored itself on the wood floor and pointed through the window into the sky. Outside, a white full moon turned half the leaves of every tree in the forest silver. Crickets beeped their sad nighttime-insect-songs to David's guitar and it was so peaceful and good and—no matter how tired it sounds—holy and holy and truly holy that I couldn't bear it. I got to my feet, took off my shirt and boots and walked out into the yard.

The night so perfect. Guitar music from inside the cabin exactly in tune with cricket music and wind music brushing the half silver, half midnight trees. The sky, with immense white moon and ice crystal stars, so absolutely endless and clearly infinite that I felt helpless tears screaming to get out and I wanted to cry with all my soul but had been conditioned against it for so long that I couldn't—could only throw my arms up, reaching into the space between the stars, head back, moaning, "Oooooohhhhhh!" while all around me the night so perfect.

I prayed aloud, "O God this is all so big and real . . . O God I'm lonely and I don't know what to do . . . God I'm . . ." but my words in the quiet forest—my selfish word-prayers against the harmony of the infinite night—were so out of place, so ugly and pretentious, that I felt ashamed and then foolish and I dropped my arms to my side and dropped my eyes to the ground. What's wrong, man? What's really wrong?

Andre and Rube came out of the cabin, banging the screen-door behind them. "Ah *yeah*! Aw *right*!" shouted Andre, dancing and spinning in the moonlight.

"Wow," said Rube, doing the same.

Naked and free, they made me feel ridiculous hiding in my canvas pants. Andre jumped up and down in the dust, saying, "Hoo hoo! Heh heh, *yes*!" while Rube did his best to imitate the dance.

I pulled off my Levi's and threw them into the air, then stepped out of my shorts and kicked them aside. The night wind felt good on my legs—an Indian, noble and free and at peace with all the gods of tire new world. "What's that moon sayin to you, Andre?"

"It's sayin, 'Be glad, lunatics!' It's sayin that everything's gonna be allll *right,* cuz people're doin it with a little more *soul*!"

"More soul!" says Rube, running in crazy circles, kicking dust until he stubs his toe on a tree root and has to hop around on one foot, going, "Ow ow ow ow," under his breath.

Andre yelled, "Waaaaahhhh!" and suddenly sprinted down the dirt path that led into the forest. I followed him just as glad but not as fast on feet less tough and legs not as Marine-trained and baseball-trained for running, bash! right into an unseen bush—Andre laughing at my white behind sticking up in the moonlight, and me also laughing as I try to untangle myself from the branches, hoping it isn't poison oak and amazed at the fact that you don't get any more hurt naked than you do all covered with white-man's clothes.

"Ah, this is great," I say, sitting on cool, damp, crumbly leaves, hugging my knees. "We should do this all the time. The Indians were on to this trip. They knew how great it all is."

"People gotta get naked more!" asserts Andre, chewing on a twig. "It's simple as that. People gotta stop bein afraid of naked!"

I raced Andre back to the cabin and of course lost, padding in on tender feet to find Rube and Andre squatting in the yard, talking to Jean who sat on the steps, smoking a cigarette, her feet tucked under her blue and gold Sari, saying, "Mhm . . . oh I know . . . mhm," to Andre's dissertation on the purity of nakedness and why didn't she get undressed and make love to him?

While they were talking I picked up my Levi's and put them on, forgetting my shorts which were lost anyway, and walked back along the forest path all the way to the creek where I sat on a stump, tossing pebbles into the dark, hearing, *ploop,* when I hit the water and nothing when I missed it.

Ploop. What's wrong, Abel? *Ploop.* Ten minutes ago I was glad. Why not now? *Ploop.* Because now I'm thinking. Thinking's the cause of it. *Ploop.* When I'm not thinking, I'm happy. Happy and naked in the woods. Is it really just food and being naked and free and sex to insure its perpetuation? Is that really *it? Ploop.* Could be. *Ploop.* Maybe so. *Ploop.* How do you stop thinking?

In the dark silence, with only the hushed murmur of the little creek in my ears, the pieces began to fall into place. When first the fluttering moth of truth drew close, I moved quickly to touch it and it darted away. I sat still and tried to empty all greed from my mind. The water that I had clouded with my movement began to clear again. I caught a glimpse of a tiny fish. So hard to keep from moving my eyes to see it better. I waited in patient silence as the murmur of the creek grew to a roar, as the moonlight began to turn to daylight, as the tiny fish—breathtakingly beautiful in its simplicity—swam closer . . . closer . . . closer . . .

"You've found my meditation spot."

I almost fell into the creek as my mind fell into Abel and I turned to face Jean, standing only a few feet away, a slender woodland phantom, holding her Sari in one hand.

"Oh, I'm sorry. I really walked in on something."

"No. I was just throwing rocks in the creek."

She sat next to me on the mossy stump and offered me a cigarette. "You got dressed again."

"Mm. It's gettin kinda cold."

"It's warmer here than it is by the cabin. The trees hold the heat."

"It is warmer here," I said, and took off my pants.

When Jean and I got back to the cabin everyone but David and Andre were asleep. The fire had burned down to orange coals and there was no wood left to feed it. David was still playing his guitar, but not nearly so high—not nearly as much magic.

Jean went into the bathroom and Andre said, "You an her?"

I rolled a joint from Ted's weed and put on my shirt.

Andre pounded his knee with his fist and said, "You know, I figured out why I can't make it with the chicks I wanna make it with."

"Why's that, man?"

"It's cuz I'm ugly."

"You're not any uglier than anybody else."

"In the mornin's I am! When I get up an look in the mirror I say, Holy smokes! That's ugly!"

"Everybody's ugly in the morning, man."

"It's morning now," says David.

An hour before sun-up Jean turned on the radio and a dead voice said that more men were going to be drafted, the City Council had decided against a new recreation center and two of our friends, Pete Winters and his chick Nadien Hiler, had been busted for possession of weed the night before.

Ted woke up long enough to say, "Nazi Germany," removed his glasses, rubbed his nose, put his glasses back on and went to sleep again.

We all got quiet and David played soft pieces on his twelve-string until the sun came up. We kicked Rusty and Rube awake, took Ted's car-keys out of his pocket and stumbled to the VW bus, red-eyed and wasted, for the drive into San Jose on the cold cement freeway.

I saw all the citizens going to work, looking relatively secure and content and well-fed, and I tried to read their minds as they whizzed past us, teeth set and angry at the traffic. Do they wonder about the purpose behind the last time they woke up? Do they think about and try hard to believe in some kind of God? Do they see how infinitely small they are in this infinitely vast cosmos? Do they wish for knowledge or at least peace? Do they wonder about time and the reason for wonder?

But when we'd passed the Campbell exits I'd realized that none of these people had time for such foolishness. They were busy men and women—their thoughts consisting of finite, workable plans—heads full of day-by-day undertakings. They had a great deal to think about; their work, the passing of hours, bills, payments, elections, clubs, income tax, and the task of keeping the flood from engulfing them at the end of each month.

The bus stopped in front of my apartment and I crawled out.

"Keep on keepin on," Andre reminded me. "We'll turn the world on yet! It's jus gonna take a liddle more *soul*!"

"Right, man," I called after the bus as it clattered away.

Homer, is it really only squeaking little misty souls drifting down to Hades after the death blow? Is this vision *right here* really the final important *IT?*

It seems to me . . .

It seems to me I ought to remember that nothing is what it seems. And that means that everything could be *exactly* what it seems.

CHAPTER TWENTY TWO – HUNG RIGHT SMACK IN THE MIDDLE

New acid hit the street. Little caps of white powder guaranteed by various sources to be, "Owsley's finest effort to date. Handle with care, man. They're White-lightnin's."

I bought twenty of the new caps from Tilding and dissolved ten of them in a milk-bottle full of water, locked the apartment, closed the curtains, shut the world off and began drinking LSD and H2O while meditating—trying to meditate—on the void.

For the first few days I made elaborate plans for gauging the amount of acid I consumed, marking the water-level on the side of the bottle with a crayon, drinking exactly the right arbitrary amount every eight hours by the clock, playing the microgram game as though it were important, until I'd completely lost the beginning—crawled out to the end of the silk time-continuum thread and, without thinking, let go and drifted around. When I looked for it again, it was gone. Don't panic. Nothing to do. No reason to find it. Wander for a while and perhaps it will turn up. Drink from the enchanted milk-bottle.

The clock ran down and it didn't matter because numbers mean nothing. I fasted without realizing that I was fasting. I prayed for a definitive vision. I finished the liquid in the holy vessel, filled it with water once more, dropped white insect eggs—one for each finger of my left hand—into the water and sat on the floor which soon fell away and I saw that I was levitating. Ignore it. It's a by-product sent to tempt you. Only a shabby toy compared to what is to come.

I looked at the infinity of space and let my soul drift as it would. Carnivals were staged between the stars, but I noticed them only in passing. I was searching for council.

Always awake or always asleep. There was no difference. I'd accidentally seen that it made no difference and so . . . there was no difference.

Drift—drift nowhere and everywhere through the always Now—in search of council.

Magnificent galaxies tempted me with their majestic silence and staggering beauty, but I drifted on—resolute. The sirens of space whispered and begged, low-moaned and murmured in my mind, but I drifted past them. Lace and gossamer veils of pure liquid-light encircled my arms and legs, stroking me like warm thoughts—like warm winds—dissolving into cool vapor, swirling and eddying away, forming whirlpools of colorless color revolving faster and faster, becoming pin-points of white-light, exploding in a shower of bright kaleidoscope-sparks—each spark an entire galaxy—each galaxy containing an infinite number of sparks. I drifted on . . . searching, without trying to search. Difficult because it's so easy—bullshit because it's so true.

All and everything, waves of changing, neutral, trying to be charged energy, and no way to describe it. Much later, I structured it in celluloid, cow's tongue and geraniums as follows:

Balanced on a network of unblinking suns, a tiny, cream-colored cottage swung gracefully with the universe. A thin curl of cotton smoke from the red-brick chimney. Warm yellow glow from the white-lace curtained windows. The mailbox said, HIM, in old-fashioned gold script. I followed a cobblestone path to the open door and stepped inside without knocking.

The inside of the tiny cottage was the enclosure of all that existed outside. Sitting on a three-legged stool beside a pleasantly radiating Franklin stove was Krishna's, Buddha's, Christ's, earth's and our Father. He held a dying sun in His gentle hands, speaking softly to it and stroking it with His thumb. The sun flared with pleasure, shortening its life span by eons.

"God," I whispered.

God looked up from His dawning nova and smiled in a way that would have utterly disgusted Michelangelo. A benevolent grandpa smile. "Ah," he said, and motioned for me to be seated. "You're God," I breathed in awe, settling on a tassled hassock. He chuckled and shrugged His holy right shoulder. "Only a portion," He said, "but I go by that name. Makes it easier for certain factions, you know."

"You're exactly as I once expected You to be," I marveled. "Of course," He replied matter-of-factly.

The nova burned itself out with a tiny gasp. God deposited its ashes in a brass ashtray.

"Help me," I said, getting right to the point.

"Certainly," said God agreeably. "What can I do for you?"

"Show me the right path. Tell me what to do."

"The right path to where? And what would you *like* to do?" I hesitated, wondering why He didn't already know . . . being *Him* and all.

"I do," He said as the thought winked in my mind, "Do you?"

"The path to Truth," I said with certainty.

God shook His head gently from side to side. "Ah, Abel, you've come so far. You feel that you've searched and suffered for a terrible length of time, don't you?"

I nodded sincerely.

"You've come so far," He continued, "and yet . . ." He got to His feet and sighed. The universe echoed the sound. "Let me show you something," He said, pulling a large ring that hung from the invisible distant ceiling, close to one recently materialized wall.

I looked at a huge graph. God opened the top of my skull and pasted the graph onto my exposed brain. The lights went out as though a master-switch had been thrown and I saw only the graph and heard only The Voice of God. A God that I myself had created, but, having been created by God myself, a God none-the-less. God the narrator.

"This graph," said God, "represents your progress toward Truth . . . toward enlightenment or illumination, if you will. Yes. Little lines . . . dots . . . um, etcetera, yes. The goal, you will notice, is not represented on the graph. I hope this doesn't disappoint you."

A rubber-tipped pointer appeared and tapped a small black dot. "This," said God, "is you four years ago, and this . . ." the pointer moved up several hard-won inches, "is you today, (actually tomorrow, but we needn't go into that)."

A second graph superimposed itself over the first.

"*This* graph," continued God, "represents your proximity to, ah, the state of enlightenment two days after your most recent birth, when you were . . ." the pointer touched another tiny black dot, "here." The two-days-after-birth dot was noticeably nearer the unrepresented goal. A wave of dismay swept over me. I fought down the dawning light and studied the graphs more closely. Always check the small print. I'd been to college. I knew the ropes. There's always an out if you look close enough.

"Hey," I protested, "the second graph is upside down!"

"So it is," said God kindly. He spun both graphs round and round like a wheel of fortune. "It makes no difference, Abel. The beginning and the end are the same. At birth you were close. At death you will once again be close. Right now, you're hung right smack in the middle."

The graphs revolved while I sought refuge in a four-day fantasy diversion. When I had exhausted myself, God peeled the graphs from my brain and the house-lights leapt to life. I stared at a point just below God's eye and He smiled sad at me. "It's hard, I know," He said softly.

"What can I do?"

"What do you *want* to do?"

"I want to know the Truth. I want to *be* the Truth. I'm tired of all the illusions. I want to see the Final Reality."

Without speaking, God asked, "Why, Abel?"

I slumped in the chair. "I don't know. I just have to. I have to see it. Once you've decided that It exists, you have to try for it. Nothing else comes close. I don't know why. I want to know why."

"That is perhaps the only answer that a man bound to life and the earth can give," said God, "But don't you *see,* Abel? You say '*I*' want to know the Truth, '*I*' want to be the Truth, '*I*' have to see it. Don't you understand that when you *do* see the final reality, when you *do* see through the illusions, you will see through the illusion of your *self* as well? And, in the Final Reality, *you* do not exist. There are no 'I's or 'you's or 'them's in the Final Reality. There is only the All . . . which is exactly the same as the nothing-at-all. The knowledge would, therefore, do *you* absolutely no good. You wouldn't be there to savor it. Do you understand?"

I nodded slowly. "What can I do?"

Impatient with my stolid refusal to see, God sighed, then said, "Well . . . you may either return and enjoy the beautiful illusions (which I think are quite good, Myself), or . . ."

"Why did You make them in the first place?" I interrupted. God laughed like thunder. "I didn't make them, Abel! You did. They're *your* constructions. Don't you see?"

Once again I nodded, and this time fought back tears.

"All right, then. Now . . . where was I? Ah! You may enjoy the illusions, live with them and make your stay on earth as pleasant and comfortable as possible, or . . ." He paused for emphasis, "Or . . . you may strive for the Truth which means that eventually you must forsake the world of illusion, embrace enlightenment . . . and cease to exist. Realize now that I don't simply mean that your *body* will cease to exist. I mean that *you* will cease to exist. No more Abel. No more Abel or rebirth of Abel or Abel's earth. Instead . . . everything . . . and nothing at all. Total enlightenment."

As He spoke, He fashioned the void in His palm and held it out to me. I looked into its endless depth and felt the powerful pull of eternity. God's voice droned in my mind, "Total enlightenment . . . the Final Reality . . . the void."

I drew closer and the pull became stronger still. My pitiful, laughable life not even a faint flicker in the perfect vacuum. All life only an illusion of vapor. I watched from a great distance as my body began to shift and fade.

"Enlightenment . . . final peace . . . illumination."

The pull was now irresistible and I felt my Self falling into an eternal sleep.

"Death."

Now hold on . . . death? . . . discorporation is a bit much to ask.

The void beckoned with fingers of soft mist. Death's only a word. Leave the realm of word-symbols.

"Your illusions . . . shut them off," whispered The Voice.

Layer after layer of illusion dropped away and crumbled into nothing. The Final Reality began to dawn.

"Here, there is no suffering, no struggle, no fear, no death, no life . . ."

"No life?" the tiny dying I whimpered with growing understanding.

"No life . . . All Life . . . accept it. It's the meaningless price of enlightenment. No pain, and no pleasure . . . no struggle, and no success . . . no hate, and no love . . ."

"But," said the rapidly disappearing, frightened I, "no love? How can that be?"

"No love as you selfishly know it, because there is no you." And the Final Reality grew clearer as the All of the Nothing Void began to wrap itself around the expiring I. It was good. It was peace. It was the end.

"No!" I shrieked, ripping my Self from the embrace of the void and gaining substance and strength. I ran madly out of the cottage and across galaxies and over time-warps and through the seas of space, searching frantically for the green planet earth among the infinite suns. I searched forever and gave up and began again after another forever of doing nothing behind a blue star, finally spying the earth nestled between Mars and Venus.

"Thank God!" I cried, rushing toward it.

"Not at all," said God. "Do come again sometime. Any time."

On Earth, I ran past the androids, bumping against a plastic arm, stumbling over a hard-rubber foot, levitating to my mumbling apartment where I pulled a bread knife from the wall and removed the memory of the Final Reality from my spongy brain in seven swift strokes, leaving only a microscopic speck stuck to the side of my skull.

Immediately after the operation, I collapsed on my pulsating bed. "I came very close," I thought, when thinking was nearly possible. "I know that I almost made it. Next time . . . next time . . ."

- a gray fade-out -

time must pretend to pass

i must pretend to believe in the passage of time
and the validity of the world around me
i must pretend to ingest the remainder of
the second bottle of lsd and H_20 in hopes
of a revelation
- a gray fade-in -

The wheezing, belching, howling, grinding machinery is hidden (none too carefully) behind a smoke-cloud of yellowish ash, hanging motionless in the dead, burnt air. Smoke. Smoke and ash—ash and smoke. Smoke veils and dirties the suffocating, crawling city. I watch its life being pumped away, while it squirms and quivers in blind asphalt agony.

The police-siren-wails snake their way across the pitted pavement and rear up into the dry, brittle air to entwine themselves with the frail tentacles of the human-howls. I wonder fleetingly where these tortured souls are being kept. I've seen no human life in weeks. Only the mock-life of the mind-vampires and the electronically controlled, captured corpses, those sad rotting carcasses that plod the scorched streets at certain ordered hours.

If only it weren't for the dense gray smoke. If only I could see a bit more clearly. But perhaps it's better that I can't. The flash-by moments of absolute clarity are appalling.

The smell of ozone and burning cells is everywhere. My eyes smart and water, cloud over and I must blink rapidly to clear them. Stifling one moment, sweating a thin oil that smells of mold, and then suddenly shivering uncontrollably the next moment as I pass through a heavy pocket of icy air that clings to my body, sucking the heat. I walk stiffly and haltingly to an alley I glimpsed through a brief parting of the smoke. Direction shifts three times and I freeze motionless—fighting down panic—waiting to reclaim my bearings.

The alley appears—disappears—forms itself again, and I leap for it. Safe. I recognize this alley. Is it a clue? Is it a clew? Is it a cluu? Is it a klu? A Cloo? Is it important? I've been here before. No, I am here now . . . yes, but I will be here again or have been here . . . no, I am here now and it is possible that this means that I have caught up to my time and my mind and the beginning which it (time) has been holding, fulfilling my obligation to the future, thereby leaving my original arrival in the past.

No. No, that's projecting far too much structured hope. Carefully step from the entangling, clinging concept. Try not to disturb its framework, risking a re-activation before it has safely and completely disintegrated.

What the hell's happening? Think this over. There's a way out. There's a way back. There's a back to get back to. At least there always has been . . . hasn't there?

Wails and moans all around me. Across the street, several of the decaying automatons walk stiffly by. A mind-vampire is hiding, pretending not to be, watching the street with sharp bright eyes. Everything's in shades of gray, some rust oranges, dusty blacks, a sick yellowish tinge around the edges. Foul air. Chemicals or electric spark.

My apartment! I've got an apartment! I left my apartment to . . .

Wait-wait-wait. *Where* do I have an apartment? Try to remember. Can't remember. The harder I try, the harder it gets. Yes, something's definitely wrong. I've forgotten . . . I've forgotten what I've forgotten. For gotten. Strange. Hold on. Grab hold of a concept . . . any concept.

I'm missing something. There's something happening that I'm not in on. It's probably something simple, but I'm missing it.

Crawl deep inside where an idea is painfully pulling itself together. It all gets . . . down . . . to . . .

No. Drop that one fast. That's too utterly ugly and finally bum. I've been up against it before and it goes nowhere . . . by the longest and slowest route.

On the other hand—on the brighter side—we have . . . love. *That's it*! Good ole love! Yessir, love. I can be anywhere I want. In the coolest of fine happy places. It's all in your mind.

In a burst of joyous relief, I ease into a perfect Alpine mountain set. The air is so clear, so *clear*, and like ice, but I'm warm inside a glow produced by good thoughts and love. Green trees with white powder snow on their branches. A stream makes tumbling, gurgling water-noises over the frost silence of the cold mountain-side. Plenty *nice*. I'm strong and new again and there's no such thing as dark soul-fear and confusion. It's all love and beauty.

And I can't hold it.

Without a transition, I'm suddenly into the nasty countervision, watching a life-picture of myself murmuring, "It's all love . . . it's love . . . love . . ." groveling in a filthy gutter on Main Street, deluded into thinking it's a beautiful snow-covered peak.

"He's mad," whispers an on-looker to his horrified girl-friend. I can see the fear and repulsion in their eyes.

"Love . . . nice . . . ooohhhh, luhhhhve."

A cop is elbowing his way through the crowd, trying to reach the hopeless geek who's disrupting the organized flow of the city. With tangled, matted hair, with drool soaking my greasy beard, I crouch in the gutter eating a cigar butt. I've lost all control over my bowels and the stench is sickening. Middle-aged woman in mink claps a hand over her mouth and is led away by her shaken husband. A vacant, idiot's smile dangles under my dripping nose—twitching lips babble, "Love . . . uhhhh, love," as I rip off my soiled, ragged clothing and lie naked in the street. The cop covers me with a blanket as he and another uniform shove me into a black van under flashing red and yellow lights. "Love . . . beautiful . . . buuuuuh-uhhh, love," as the paddy-wagon wails off toward the madhouse.

I chop off the vision hurriedly although the quick rip costs at least a thousand brain cells. Maintain, boy. Brace up. Pull it all together. Get the ole head straight. Mm-hm. Breathe deep. In, out, in, out. Not too fast. Slow an easy. All's cool. A little freaked, but all's cool. Things are falling into place. Let em come. Easy. This is a wall—the wall of a building—and I'm on a street and, by God and thank de Lord, I recognize the street I'm on. Close to LaMer's house, so I hurry in that direction saying, "Phew . . . wow . . . big . . . strange . . . phew." A long list of memories tied up in half-dreams and phantoms, and too soon to sort any of it out. Go to LaMer's place. Andre'll talk me down.

From the street, I can see a light in Andre's room. I walk in little circles and stare at the glowing yellow square of window wondering what to do.

A long time. Many little circles.

Many thoughts whizz past or float by between the basic wonder of what to do, which is presently structured as whether or not to climb the creaking stairs, go down the dark hall-way and up to Andre's door. Then I'm at the door without a transition, reading the hand-painted APT. $ 5 sign and the penciled *If You Are A Nark, Go Away* beneath it, knocking quietly, hearing rat-grumbles and footfalls. The door opens a three-fingernail-crack and, not Andre, but a cheap wax reproduction of Andre peers out at me with blue-circled, glass-eyes. Don't look at them straight on—they may be lasers.

"Egregore! Holy smokes, you *really* look stoned," says the wax figure in very close to Andre's voice.

"I been, uh, alone, y'know . . . walking."

"Acid?"

"Uh, yeah, but . . . y'know . . ."

"When'dya drop?"

"Mmm . . ."

"Well hey, come in," opening the door wider, sucking me inside with a whoosh, "Man I just got back from The City," closing the door and double-locking it—click-clank—ominous, but then again, safe, "An man, things is *still* spinnin. Hoooeee! You know that farout dude, Mark? The one'at plays that weird box thing with all them strings an stuff? Yeah well he give me this cap an says, 'Take it, man. It's very very super-good shit.' So a course I take it, an then, after it's down, he tells me, 'You jus dropped two thousand mics, ole pal, cuz I think you deserve it,' an he quick-hustles me out into his Renault an we zoom up to Haight where this acid starts to really come on! I mean holy fires an *smokes*!"

I sit back and listen to Andre's somehow reassuring rap. Good old Andre. It *is* Andre, even though he looks like he's made out of soft wax. It's still Andre. He's saying, "Man, so *heavy*! There wasn't nuthin I could do. The whole *sky* was one big generator sayin, 'Come on, Andre . . . come to the source . . . come back to the generator of it all,' an I'm just wide-eyed an in it, y'know . . . stoned so bad in this place where it's all really *happenin* an I can't unnerstan any of this shit that's goin on. I ask Mark, 'Hey man, what's happenin? Is all this really goin on, or is it jus me?' An Mark sez, "You know it's for real, LaMer. You know that ole generator wants you back,' cuz I already tole him about my poem, *Generator*, a couple days before. An then we end up at this party by the Fillmore an there's too much goin on there—radio's makin fun of me, people pointin an laughin at everythin I say . . . even when it ain't atal funny. I don'know. Man, I jus don'know."

Something *is* wrong. There's a heavy tight something in the room. Can't put my finger on it yet, but it's there.

From Andre—"I go into the john to take a piss an can't, so I come back out an everybody in the room's naked. Everybody but *me* . . . naked. I real quick start to unbutton my shirt, but this dude comes up to me an sez, 'It's too late, LaMer. It's *too* late,' and everybody goes, 'HAH!' an starts gettin dressed again, an I figure I've blown it as bad as it can be blown an I'm willin to do anything to get back to even the bottom again instead a wherever I'm at. Then this chick I met in Oakland comes over an starts me thinkin maybe I can ball out, so I take her into the bedroom, but Mark pokes his head in the door and sez, 'Andre, don't you know that when you screw a chick you're really only screwin yourself? When're you gonna *learn?*' An here I am on top a this chick an everything starts goin faster an faster an I'm hearin all these voices laughin at me an I'm tryin a hole on to somethin an gettin more an more fogged out, an then I can't take it no more, an I jump up an say, 'Goddam it I'm *sorry*!' an run into the other room with jus my unnershirt an a paira socks on, an I slip on the floor an ka-whamo into this wall an forget to hold onto my bladder, so I'm pissin all over myself an the floor an this guy an his chick who're sittin on a straw mat, an I'm yellin, 'Tell me what I gotta do! I'm sorry I don't know! I confess! I don't know where it's at! Tell me what I gotta do!' An Mark come up to me with this big joint an sticks it in my mouth an says, 'You just did it, Andre. Yessir, you juuuhst *did* it.'"

Throughout this whole monologue, I've been nodding and yes-ing and right with Andre—seeing it with his eyes—empathy lying in puddles, gasping on the floor. The break comes with no warning. There's a howling silence in the room when Andre stops making words. Then, "Wow . . . so what happened, man?"

Sitting in a chair, moving no more than a normal person would—one of the few times I've seen him this way—Andre says, "Whadya mean, 'What happened'? That was it. That was like the climax. I jus stood in the middle of the room in my own piss, tryin to work it all out an not bein able to, except in these little Zen flashes, an then after awhile Mark took me back to his place an sat aroun playin his box-thing an I sat there wonderin what I was gonna do now that there wasn't nuthin left to do, an this morning Nick'n JoAnn gave me a ride back here, an here I am . . . still there. I been through some big ones, but that was the biggest yet. I burned up all my poems an it still didn't do no good. I looked out the window today an found out that while I was gone they sucked all the tree-spirit outta the trees. There's still trees out there, but they ain't *real* trees. Jus trees on the outside. Nuthin on the inside."

Andre doesn't smoke tobacco, so there aren't any cigarettes in the house. I have none of my own, and right now I'd give anything for a legal drug to hide behind. I can feel, and almost see from the corners of my eyes, stealthy worry-demons inching out of the shadows. In the silence I begin to sink deeper into the final bog of walking-death all-stop. Talk to keep things going. Words from the top of my mind. "We oughta . . . we oughta get a car an go over to the ocean. Or maybe go see Ted . . . or something."

Andre responds to the sound of the words, but none of them register—or perhaps he realizes where and why they were born and simply ignores their meaningless meaning. He leans forward in his chair, growing waxier by the second. "Do you think we're doin the right thing, man? I mean, we been bums—jus wanderin aroun, doin really nuthin accordin to a lotta people—for three or four years now. Do you think we oughta do somethin else? My head feels like it's been through sixty kindsa meat-grinders an I'm still not close to anything. Are you, man? Are we goin anywhere? I mean, are we really *goin* anywhere?"

Strange words from Andre's lips. Could be merely an echo in my own mind—a projection. But then tilings click into place and I realize why Andre looks like a wax figure. He *is* a wax figure.

They sent a robot down in his place after they captured him in The City. Or maybe he defected. Or maybe it wasn't and isn't a case of defecting, but of seeing the truth and accepting it.

Been through all this before. Without a word I get up, unlock the double-locked door, and leave with quick footsteps, heading for my apartment. When I reach the street, the light in Andre's window is out.

Andre gone. Now they've got everyone but me. The last hold-out. Everyone else copped-out? Or has everyone else broken through?

At home, I count my acid-caps—one, two, three, four, five—only five left—how many did I have to begin with? Ah, what an absolutely insignificant thing to hang up on. How could it possibly matter? Take two. Break through.

Before moving on, I had to relive the some-number of weeks just passed in order to work it out of my system—out of my head—in order to understand how unimportant all of my conclusions to date were. That taken care of, I relived my life from birth to, "Andre gone. Now they've got everyone but me," over and over again until I was finally forced to accept the fact that there is no conspiracy. I was happy with this realization and, had I been content to stop prying at this point, would probably have enjoyed the remainder of the trip and perhaps even several life-times to come, traveling behind pleasant, low-level, humble ignorance and well-being. But, with the conspiracy smashed, I felt the need for a new explanation—a new direction—a new plan. Fool that I was (and am), I demanded to know what was happening. I let down my guard and looked.

CHAPTER TWENTY THREE

In the beginning there was nothing. Nothing. So much all-cool nothing that it was everything. Nothing. Perfect Nothing. Why should anything else exist? Perhaps it was and is because the All or the Nothing was and is so immense (infinite and eternal to be exact) that hand-in-hand with each why (or with the only Why) walks an equally valid why-not.

The perfect All of Nothing hummed on forever with no time and no structure to hang it up. Then It said, "Let there be a game." Why? Why not? "I will take part of me (since there's nothing else to work with) and set it apart from the rest by giving it conscious ego-existence. Then I'll hide the knowledge of the deed from that part of Me and pretend not to see it. That accomplished, the rest of Me can sit back and watch and wait to see how long it takes Me to figure it all out and remember *what is happening*. It should prove interesting. It will be a trip. The game will grow more difficult as the flash created by the realization of a seemingly separate existence begins to fade and the concept of the ultimate struggle and its goal become evident. (Cosmic chuckle) As the poor part of Me locked in the contest draws nearer to the goal of knowing what has happened and what is happening, it will begin to painfully realize that when it *does* find out, it will no longer have the contest—the game will be won—it will be forced to stop playing and, therefore, cease to exist as a seemingly separate entity. This will make the last few steps the hardest of all."

And from the Eternal Nothing came an illusion of a separate something faced with a task. A quest, the beginning and end of which are exactly the same.

There's nothing to say—it's been said and it meant nothing. There's nothing to do—it's been done and it meant nothing. There is nothing. Nothing.

But some of me can't help asking, "How can that be? How can that be when I see a whole world of people and vast oceans complete with changing tides, forests made up of millions of trees with leaves that move in the wind and magically change color with the seasons and fall one upon the other to hide velvet moss holding perfect spheres of diamond water drops to make other living, growing things come to life and reach for the sun before my eyes? How can there be nothing when I see and feel the joy and ecstasy and pain of the entire world?"

There is nothing. Only the illusion which you yourself have constructed.

Then there's at least *me,* if I constructed the illusion.

There is you. A nebulous little will-o'-the-wisp of a lonely small part of the All and Nothing, clutching desperately at ego-existence, manufacturing illusions to keep you company in your self-imposed exile.

Then why are my illusions tarnished with pain and hate and sadness and strife and frustration and fear? If I create them, why don't I create them perfectly?

Because you aren't perfect. You aren't complete. If you were . . . the illusion wouldn't exist. Nor would you.

But I exist! The world—the illusion exists. The universe and all its intricate beauty exists! It's too complex to be nothing. It exists!

The Void exists. The nothing of the Void embraces and cancels all other existences. Hold your world—your universe—with all its intricacies, up to the Void. What do you see?

Only the Void. Nothing. Only the Void. The universe—the illusion of the universe and the illusion of my Self watching the universe are nothing. But how do I stop the illusion? How do I stop my Self? I keep coming back.

You know how to stop it. It's easy. It's the simplest path, although also the most elusive.

I can't hold it. I've tried.

You can't try. Stop trying. Let go.

I can't. I don't know how.

You do know how. It's easy. You don't *want* to let go.

I only want peace.

True peace exists only in the Void. No conflict. No confusion. The beginning and the end together—at once—as one—the same—everything—nothing.

How does one live *life* in peace?

Patiently. Living is conflict. Life is suffering. Life is confusion, suffering and conflict. That's what life *is* to anyone who thinks long enough on it.

Life is all I have.

Life *is* all that *you* have. You . . . the ego-you can never enter the Void. Life is all it has.

Why can't I just go on living life?

You can. You can go on. And on and on and on and on . . .

It's true. I know it's true. I'm sorry. I'm sorry I'm me.

Then let go.

I can't. I'm sorry, but I can't. I'm sorry that I can't.

Aren't you tired? Aren't you tired of playing the game? Don't you want to see the end? Don't you want to be the end and the beginning and nothing and everything without the sad drag of identity?

Yes!

Discorporate.

I'm afraid to.

Let go.

I can't.

silence for seven heart-beats
silence for seven life-times

Then you'll have to go back. Wade through the next ten units of hallucination and then think it over.

CHAPTER TWENTY FOUR – THE SOFT TIME

Hank Mortimer. You gotta hear about Hank Mortimer with his bunched-up tight little iron-hard muscles and his always bloodshot beady eyes behind light green script shades and his arms like big city rail-road yards from four years of crink and his head going so fast and so messed up and somewhere else that he'd only connect with *this* zone maybe once every three months long enough to peek around with his ruined little eyes and say, "Shit man, this is flat insane," then gas-up one of his six-hundred fits and shoot into a scab without waiting to register (all of his ropes so blown and low that they usually wouldn't anyway) and flash out the door not to be seen again until the next time—whenever that might happen to be. Hank Mortimer who geezed a shot-glass full of crink on a dare from some New York speed-freak, split for LA. at seven that evening and was back by eight the next morning, shooting crink in Lyla's kitchen. Hank Mortimer who mixed himself up an utterly mad concoction of brown Mexican smack, cocaine, crink, acid and lemon juice, shot it right into the eye of his coiled snake tattoo while everyone sat watching him with open mouths waiting for him to die, said, "Ho, mm-*mm*!" turned on the television, watched *The Creature Walks Among Us,* stood up to sing the *Star-Spangled Banner* with the TV as jets streaked across the screen, soldiers, sailors and marines saluted Old Glory and the station ended its broadcasting day with a hymn. He rolled two joints, lit one and stuck the other behind his ear, adjusted his shades, said, "Ahhh well, ah well," and walked out the door into the cold March early morning leaving his blue nylon jacket hanging forgotten on the back of a chair, leaving his borrowed-from-someone '58 Ford parked in the street to be towed away a week later, leaving a room full of awed people to wonder many wonders. Hank Mortimer who filled his pockets with lead tire-weights, walked into the ocean near Davenport (Davenport haunted by the spirits of cruelly murdered whales) on a Wednesday night, breathed water instead of air until his lungs remembered the womb and quit creating vacuums, and he settled to the bottom thinking final thoughts that, like all his previous thoughts, no one ever knew, and he washed up on the beach that following Friday without his pale green script shades, all dead-white and crab-chewed, (not a single Catholic crab content to eat fish on that particular Friday, or perhaps that's being too hard on them and they merely mistook Hank Mortimer for some kind of fish) where he was found by an early angler out after Jack smelt who said, "Das da tord one I fine. Das no shid. Das da tord one I fine. Das tree drowded people I fine. I fine one las year oh up by Half Moon an I fine another one down to over by Moss Laning tree year ago. You know, both time I'm out after jacks too. An dis time I'm out for jacks agin an I fine another one. Das tree drowded people I fine. Das da tord one I fine."

When Hank Mortimer walked into the ocean he had forty-one dollars in his wallet, but by the time he reached the morgue he had one dollar-bill. Neptune or the fisherman, forty dollars richer.

But Hank Mortimer drowned himself without my consent and without my even knowing about it. While he was breathing cold Davenport ocean-water I was mourning in big cold tears, wallowing in all kinds of self-pity, feeling that I was now forever hung in a sadder-by-the-second illusion due to my selfish refusal to accept discorporation and the final truth of the void. With rain falling again outside, hearing in it all of humanity crying along with me, I was drenched by waves of humiliation and unbearable regret, remembering all the times I'd been cruel to other poor bungling beings, all the times I'd failed people, failed myself, failed to understand or try to understand. I saw every microinstant of my past as a hazy, gray dream with me stumbling through it in a half-sleep—never fully awake—never truly aware. The white light of the void had burned a pin-point hole in my retina into which all the world and everything I could conceive of continually poured and was lost—then reborn again to torture me with its breathtaking beauty and detailed craftsmanship. Beauty and craftsmanship that I could only *now* appreciate in the light of the knowledge that it was merely a tiny, insignificant illusion.

Nothing to eat in the apartment and no reason to take food. I lay on my bed and looked at nothing—eyes on infinity—trying to decide what to do—always returning to the realization that there is nothing to do—there's nothing.

Intense sensations weaving and crawling through my body. Electricity crackling over the network of veins, sudden surges of raw power from the center of my stomach, internal organs ever changing shape and location, body boundaries nebulous and flowing. Sometimes I'm a tiny ball six inches above the robot's groin, sometimes I'm the entire apartment and the walls pulsate with my life, sometimes I'm the unseen young Negro who moved in next door, and he and I clomp around changing records, fixing breakfast, humming James Brown songs and getting ready for work. When I'm in my body—when I'm inside Abel's body it's just that and nothing more. I'm inside a plastic doll that can feel very little external stimulae. Hot or cold—impossible to identify—just part of the swirling collage of sensation. I failed to notice that the sickness I'd been coming down with had taken this opportunity to install itself in a position of power. The sore throat and kidney pains that had made themselves known some forgotten time ago were lost in the deluge of flowing energy.

Days passed. I watched the burlap curtain go from light to dark to light to dark without changing my position on the bed.

Let it go. Let it flicker out slowly . . . like a candle. There's really nothing to hold onto. Let it whisper itself out.

Somewhere, time was passing.

An idea came and got in the way and hung me up and wouldn't die, so I stood up. My legs wouldn't support my weight. I was on the floor without experiencing the fall. I lay face down on the rug. The idea returned and I crawled into the kitchen, opened the refrigerator, took the remaining caps of acid from the bottom shelf, crawled back to the bed, lost the idea, waited on my hands and knees until it swam into focus once more, put the little white caps into my mouth, let them dissolve under my tongue and the idea passed away.

glory that which lies beyond the veil
let it come
this time accept it

Noise. Bam bam bam bam. Noise. Bam bam. A familiar sound. It means something. Listen. The sound is gone.

Time passed.

The sound came again. That sound means . . . that sound means . . . it means that someone is outside hitting the door with a hand. Holy the person outside my door. I was satisfied, but the sound came again. Then I realized that the person outside my door wanted to be inside my apartment and I could help them. How? I slipped off the bed, watched my body perform, got to my feet, nearly fell, steadied myself, tried to make my body go forward and, in doing so, suddenly felt confused and lost and things got that special uh-oh weird. The sound came again. I remembered the person outside, moved in underwater slow-motion to the door, pulled back the curtain, peered out into rain-fall computer beadwork, focused with an effort and saw a pale little female phantom Edgar Allan Poe creation. Recognition sailed in from a zone six billion light-years away. *Adriel.* Adriel framed in the black sky of the open doorway. Adriel—sent to entice me back from the gates of Eternity.

She came into the room all covered with night-time rain-smell. "Hi! You didn't come to see me, so I decided to come see you." She took off her coat and scarf, shook her hair free and surveyed the apartment. "Mmmmm. Definitely a bachelor's dwelling." Tiny mist-drops of water fell on the swirl-patterned carpet. I watched them shrink and disappear. Adriel turned and said, " 'S cold in here. How've you . . . Abel? What's the matter?"

I tried to look at her face but couldn't get past the eyes.

Like looking at twin novas. All that mind-essence pouring out. I began to feel my body again—weak and neglected, gone sick and sulking. A mistake to crawl back into it, but once there the webs grab hold. "Nothing," I croaked. It sounded horrible. I couldn't swallow.

Tight throat. Machinery all rusted out.

Adriel came closer. Too close. I could feel the electro-magnetic bio-chemical force-field. "Are you sick?" she asked.

It was supposed to sum it all up when I said, "If you miss, you always have to settle for less."

"What?"—reminding me of the inadequacy of word-communication.

"If you . . ." I lost the thought. "I can't talk."

"Are you on something?"

Oh yes, they always want a rational explanation. Cause and effect. "Nothing."

"And how long have you been on nothing?" enunciating carefully, as if to a retarded child.

The effort of relating to another person, of relating to the Earth-set, brought on a new wave of low-level hallucination. Situationally parallel transparent overlays basically of a paranoid nature. I saw doctors studying me with interest, scribbling observations on their note-pads, whispering to one another and forming learned opinions. "Shock-treatment."—"I agree."—"Prepare the machine, nurse."—"Burn him back into line." Turbine-whine electric spark-crackle ozone.

Not terribly heavy, but I just wasn't up to it. "Get me outta here."

Nurse, looking concerned, said, "Are you on acid?"

Too smart for that one. State- and mind-police hovered behind the white-uniformed doctors, waiting for my reply. I've sat through forevers. I can outwait them all. Refuse to answer.

"Babe, you are really gone," said the nurse, preparing a hypo, pretending it's a cigarette.

Time to speak up. "I don't need that." Why'd all this have to happen? What'd I do to call all this confusion and bullshit down on my head? Everything was going along fine—I was almost there—almost through—and now . . .

The nurse chewed her lower lip, dismissed the anxious doctors and skulking police with a secret command, replaced the disguised spike in her black bag, and folded her face until it was Adriel's. "Would you like to come home with me? Is that all right?"

I nodded because it was easy to do. I felt utterly defeated—knew I'd blown my chances for the umpteenth time. Rebellion had broken out among various factions of Self once more, and now not enough of me was into merging. Stuck again. And the return trip's as grueling as the voyage out.

Adriel-turned-nurse-turned-Adriel dressed me in a heavy coat, guided me into night and put me in a machine that was waiting for us—all set for the get-away.

Somehow up a flight of stairs and into an apartment other than mine and into a strange bed. A series of reality-spins and I fell into a period of average perception which would have been comfortable if it hadn't been marred by dull body-pain. With the exception of phosphenes, flashes, and a kind of light mist, my eye-vision was clearer than it'd been for days (weeks? some time, anyway).

Adriel put her hand on my forehead, then put her cheek against mine. "You've got a fever. Do you have a sore throat?" She disappeared to clink bottles in the bathroom, returning with a bottle of cough medicine and a huge silver spoon from the kitchen. She undressed beside the bed and slipped in next to me, warm satin against my body, giving me cherry-flavored medicine with the big spoon, spilling a crimson drop on the sheet where it spattered and spread into patterns while Dylan sang the appropriate words of *Baby Blue*—from a phonograph playing low in a comer of the room. Adriel looked at me and laughed in soft delight, hearing (as she always did and, hopefully, always will) the same thing that I was hearing even out of all the countless variables. "How beautiful," she said.

And it was beautiful. Suddenly, it was all soft and quietly beautiful.

That night I lay close to Adriel, my eyes moving slowly about the room, resting on Adriel's paintings that hung on the wall or sat unfinished on easels and the floor—sketches tacked here and there, or crumpled in the wastebasket. All life in microcosm symbols. If only I didn't know the Truth.

Soft finger-tips light and cool on my cheek. Adriel whispered, "Sleep now, baby. Try to sleep."

I knew I'd never sleep again. No such thing as sleep. But I closed my eyes to please her. Go with the flow. Follow the path of least resistance.

Gray dawn through the blue-curtained window. Adriel asleep and breathing softly with her lips slightly parted, a wind-tossed and tangled cloud of storm-black hair surrounding her face on the white pillow. My eyes traced the line of her nose, the blue ghost-paths of veins under her nearly transparent eyelids with their dark lashes that trembled from time to time in quiet dreams. I listened to the peaceful life-sound of her breath and felt tight steel cables snap, even heard them twang, as my head settled on the cool linen pillow and I drifted into a calm state of almost non-think.

From aum abruptly to an angry alarm that wrenched my eyes open and threw my mind into the first available gear. I caught a glimpse of a departing figure in a flowing white robe. An angel? My judgment come and gone? Without turning my head I rolled my eyes as far as they'd go to one side, trying to see what was going on. I got a cramp in my left eyeball.

I'd studied every inch of the cryptic ceiling and was about to try moving my hands, when the white-robed figure returned to stand far above me. I recognized Adriel in the misty distance.

"Good morning," she said, offering me some kind of magic orange potion. "How do you feel? Can you drink this?" kneeling beside the bed.

I could and I did. It tasted like thousands of busy sparks. Adriel smiled her approval, took the glass from my hand, touched my forehead and said, "I have to go to work in an hour. Will you be all right while I'm gone?"

I said, "Of course," wondering why she was treating me like a sick three-year-old (but kind of digging it).

She rose to her feet, drifted around the room, opened drawers and closets, And then, suddenly older, dressed and lipsticked and ready for work, she bent over me, brushed my lips with her own (strange taste—nice, but strange) and pulled the sheet up to my chest. "Bye now. Try to keep warm."

A split second after the front door clicked shut behind Adriel, the walls began to smoke. I paid no attention. The ceiling fragmented and the fragments evaporated leaving a big square hole full of gray half-light. I let it happen. Time passed. Minor hallucinations flared and faded, carrying me in slow wobbly circles.

Somewhere, a public clock said *pong* twelve times. I knew that it was noon, but it sounded like midnight. The set rearranged itself to validate the impression. A breathless, expectant feeling—waiting for . . . something.

What? Waiting for what?

Ahhhh . . . waiting for me. Waiting for my decision.

I grew restless. The restlessness became painful. I kicked the blankets off my body and flexed my arms. My eyes fogged, cleared, fogged and cleared. I crawled off the bed and stood up.

Tree fingers seeking refuge from the wind clawed at window glass as I explored the Abbey of Theleme. On a table under a single black candle was a leather-bound copy of *White Stains* and a volume of *The Book of The Law* opened to page sixty-six.

A musty smell and the sound of muffled footsteps announced the arrival of the Abbey's master. He paused halfway down the circular stairway and regarded me from the cold shadows, saying, "Welcome, Abel. Here at last, eh?"

"Rabelais?"

Footsteps again—carrying the man down the last thirteen steps of the stairway, out onto the marble floor where he paused once more and said, "I should be insulted, I suppose. But then . . . ah so many years. What does it matter? I ask you . . . what does it matter?"

"It doesn't," I replied.

"You're wrong," smiled the man, stepping into the candlelight, "You're quite wrong." He snuffed-out the candle with his thumb, gestured, and a pale blue luminescence filled the room. "It matters," said the master of the Abbey. He brushed damp earth from his coat-sleeves. "I'm Crowley. Aleister Crowley. You've heard of me?"

"Yes. Would you be here if I hadn't?"

"No," admitted Crowley, "I would not. Shall I proceed?"

"Shall *I* proceed?"

"Exactly. Attend, Abel. Mankind has been and, to a certain

extent, *is* aware of the struggle between Light and The Absence of Light. They structure it as 'Good versus Evil' which is, of course, ludicrous on any scale other than man's. But, as I was saying, they are aware of the contest. They have been duped into believing that Light or 'Good' or 'God', if you must, will ultimately triumph. They're wrong, of course. If there is a contest then it stands to reason that there exists a chance for either contestant to emerge victorious. In truth, Abel, the contest *has* been won. The game is over."

"And?"

"Sell out, Abel."

"The earth's overrun by those who have. What've they got?"

"Ah!" a derisive grunt. "Those poor puppets are still uncertain of their choice. They still fear punishment. They sell out to minor powers, to small beings, and, therefore, reap small rewards. Go beyond the flea-people, Abel. Skip the insignificant lesser steps. Sell out to the ruler of life! Sell out to *The Power*!"

Fog in fast—gray to white to bright. I was standing near the window in Adriel's bedroom, looking down on rain-shiny San Jose streets. My neck twitched. I turned from the window, walked three steps in a perfectly straight line which brought me to the exact center of the room where I sat down, crossed my legs, and watched a tiny red scratch on my right wrist heal itself.

Gods and goddesses, earth and air spirits, benevolent and wrathful, great and small, hovered and sailed and stood and shimmered close, speaking to me and to one another, individually and in awesome beyond-musical choruses that surged to holy crescendos of sound and then receded to equally holy silence. A tinkle flash-past almost invisible speck of spirit darted above my head chasing sun-lit dust particles, driving them into merry-go-round dances.

Thighbone trumpets heralded the arrival of a nameless Eastern Deity who was terrible to look at but a pleasant conversationalist. He asked me important riddles and helped me with the answers as the sun reached the end of its arc.

It was dark when Adriel came home. She touched a spot on the wall and light-brighter-than-day instantly filled the room. Electric light. The whole concept blew my head. I stared at the glowing bulb, saying, "Wow. That's incredible. That's just too farout."

Adriel was mad because I was sitting on the floor naked. She made me get back into bed, brought me more orange elixir, said some words that I've forgotten, made the record-player do some music, walked around, rattled things in other rooms, ran water, appeared in a towel and extinguished the light.

I said, "Hey!" suddenly afraid.

"What's the matter, Abel?"

"The light's gone."

Adriel sighed and moved toward me. She sat on the bed and pushed hair from my eyes. "Come down, baby. Try to get straight. I only turned out the light so we can go to sleep." She left the bed, then returned with two little yellow pills. "Take these. They'll make you sleep."

I swallowed the pills, saying, "They won't make me sleep." Sliding into bed, Adriel whispered, "They'll *help* you sleep."

"Nope. Nope, there's too much to lose. There's all this. All *this.*"

Adriel put her arm around me and spoke close to my ear. "Abel, please try to sleep. Try to get some rest. You've got some kind of bug and you're not going to get rid of it unless you start taking care of yourself."

In the warm dark I put up a hard fight against the drug, refusing to let it put me into unconsciousness where I had no defenses and no control. It was a hard fight that I soon lost sight of and then lost altogether.

When I awoke, it was afternoon. I knew it was afternoon because it smelled, felt and sounded like afternoon. Street noises outside—hurrying traffic sounds—a jet booming overhead—kids laughing and goofing on their way home from school . . . afternoon for sure. Four walls around me, a window and a door. Adriel's apartment. Afternoon.

There was a note on the pillow next to my head. Printed in Adriel's lacy, fairy-tale handwriting, it read:

abel—

must leave you alone till five
o'clock—orange juice in the
refrig—drink some!!—i've decided
that you will be well in one week
because that's when we're taking
my sisters to the zoo—
—adriel.

I got up, went into the kitchen, and the sun had taken over the entire room. "A new day," I said in hushed reverence (although the day had actually come and nearly gone). I walked through the apartment touching, seeing, digging everything. So long since straight that down's high. Head all amazed and happy to be at the wheel again. On each wall, Adriel'd pinned sketches she'd done, poems and little sayings she'd written or found, pictures and photos from magazines or friends' cameras. I dug them all, studying each one carefully, taking maybe fifteen minutes to absorb each detail, flashing on like one word or one small kid's eye in a group photo, pulling it all together with an "ahhhh wow," then moving on to the next multi-satori for a gasp at some before unseen simple truth, almost crying over discoveries of subtle loneliness or more sophisticated truth. So much truth and beauty in the world, and everyone so pitifully blind to it . . . especially me.

I was sitting on the couch reading a book of Haiku, when Adriel came home in her Nun-like dental nurse's uniform with packages from the market in both hands and just enough face peeking over the top to kiss me lightly and say, "You look a little more back to earth," and, after my positive reaction, "Oh what a day," with a sigh, going into the kitchen to set packages down and call, "Did you eat something today, baby?" seeming so suddenly natural and sort of half-remembered from a nearly perfect television life-time of nice middle-class-dream-of-perfection that I dropped into this fine, warm straight scene and saw with absolute clarity that the straight life was comfortable, mercifully unparanoid (except on what now could be viewed only as the lowest of gone-in-the-morning levels), relatively simple to maintain and, in fact, the best of all possible existences available to those sentenced to life, and I realized that I was oh yes for sure shit-canning my all-too-short life by running around in a furry Halloween disguise, taking drugs that left me dazzled and spaced and unproductive for months at a time—maybe forever burned-out and bent—searching for a nebulous enlightenment and an unsound, naive concept of peace. I vowed then and there to cop-out without another second's hesitation, drop back into TV control, grab off a nice, fat-city job after finishing college, and perhaps change my name while trying to live down the last few confused and misguided years. I was about to pick up the phone and call the White House to let The Man know I'd seen the light so he could inform the FBI, CIA and SS that I was no longer a threat to The Great Society, when Adriel returned from the bedroom wearing jeans and a sweater, bare feet and a heavy gold cross on a chain around her neck, no make-up and big, sad, pretty eyes that hurled me right back into an all-too-natural, wild and satisfying, defiantly brave psychedelic religious pioneer existence, backed by smiling Buddhas and holy Christian martyrs all giving me the nod and the go-ahead, and I tasted shame for contemplating surrender and I quickly revowed to hang on as long as I could and never cop-out and never sell out to compromise until things and time fall into line again and the Bodhisattvas are rewarded for their unfailing patience.

Never cop-out. There have to be some who never cop-out. There must be those who show the limits.

"How do you feel?" Adriel sitting on the couch next to me, her bare feet curled under her bottom.

"Good. How long has it been?"

"How long since what?"

"Since . . . uh, since I got here."

"Second day. Did you eat? You haven't answered me that yet."

"I drank some orange juice. Man, it's good to talk."

"How's your fever?" touching my cheek, kissing me on the nose.

"It's good. Everything's good."

"Everything's better, but you're still a little hot. I brought you some pills. They're supposed to cure anything."

"Wonder-drugs. What've I got?"

"Flu, I think . . . on top of a bad case of starvation. What were you trying to do to yourself, Abel?"

"Break through."

"Isn't there an easier way?"

"Is there?"

We ate a just-married-young-couple-still-in-love kind of dinner in the bright little kitchen. Great. Everything clean and comfortable and great I started to help Adriel wash the dishes when we'd finished, but got in the way so much that she finally took the dish-towel from me, grabbed my hand and led me into the living room where I was deposited in front of the TV with, "I'll be done in a minute, love."

The shadow-puppets performed meaningless dramas behind the glass screen while night fell soft and slow. Adriel yawned in my arms and stretched like a cat, then climbed from the chair, "Come to bed pretty soon, baby," stood in the long hallway, "Also, take your pills," and disappeared into the bedroom.

The puppets are in a fox-hole—dirty faces—white eyeballs in the night—mortars going POOM POM BOW in the distance—"Medic! Medic!" down the line—cut to mean, sneaky figures creeping through the jungle—cut back to dirty but honest American faces in nighttime fox-hole and an ominous silence—"Sure is quiet out there, Sarge."—Sarge spits tobacco, *spwick*, and says, "That's when ya start sweatin, Richards. Fix bayonets . . ."—and click, chunk, click down the line, as knives snap into place on rifles—cut to a parking lot full of cars and honest Sam is saying, "Your credit is good at A-OK Executive Car-City, friends. Let us put *you* behind the wheel of this nineteen-sixty-two four-door beauty for only two-ninety-nine down! That's two-ninety-nine, friends. You heard it right. How can we do it? You think we're crazy? Well maybe we *are,* friends, because during our A-OK Executive Car-City Bonanza Gala Once-a-year Sale we're practically *giving* fine automobiles away. We pass our savings on to you. Want a late-model top-quality second car for the wife to do her shopping in? We got em, friends! Come on in and check our million-dollar inventory. Here's a little gem that I know you're . . .

"It's after two," said Adriel, sleepy-eyed and wearing nothing but a tight little frown, taking me by the arm and leading me into bed after reducing honest Sam to a single star in the center of the glass screen—a star that blinked out as I watched. "I wish you'd learn to take care of yourself."

"When it's quiet, that's when you start sweating."

"What!?"

"That's what the Sarge said."

"The Sarge is a very paranoid individual. Get into bed."

Pulling off my shirt—"Adriel, you're beautiful." It meant a considerable bit more than it appears to when re-said in twenty letters here.

"You too," she smiled, turning back the covers. And, in awhile, we made love for the first time.

Later, cradled between Adriel's strong teenager legs, her breath warm on my shoulder, I moved my hand across the cool flesh of her breast and told myself that all this was real and had some meaning and a direction.

Four more rocket-by days of pulling things together, working out kinks, just getting straight enough to make it on the street again, then it's up to the Zoo all wrapped in San Fran fog with Adriel and her two little half-sisters. Sticky pink-brick popcorn and walk along kicking paper cups, looking at yawning animals. "I hate to see them in cages. Don't you?" says Adriel, trying to hold hands with a monkey through the iron bars which are probably steel.

"Yeah, I hate to see em in cages," says I, seeing them all in cages, which is exactly what we came to the Zoo to do.

Dark-haired, quiet, four year old Bobbie and blonde, jumping-bean, three year old Diane ignored panthers and exotic beasties, but were fascinated by an everyday brown squirrel who was free to eat candied popcorn right out of their hands.

"Oh Bobbie, look at the lions. See the lions, Diane?"

"Yeah," after a quick, uninterested glance, "Ooooh, lookit the pigeons!" and they take off like leaves in the wind to scatter the birds.

With an arm around Adriel, Bobby warming her nose in my coat, Diane's little sticky hand in mine, I felt proud of my family-for-the-day. Father-pride for my two little sunshine daughters and husband-pride for my beautiful young wife.

That night, Bobbie and Diane stayed with Adriel and me at the apartment in San Jose. Both of them so tired from the long ride up to The City, a whole day of pigeon and squirrel chasing and then the long ride back, that they have to be carried into the bedroom, undressed like limp rag-dolls and tucked into bed without opening their eyes. Adriel and I laid blankets on the living-room floor and talked and loved in a square pool of moonlight until someone started to cry in the bedroom. Adriel in quick, a few minutes gone with crying stopped and muffled voices, then back again, "Bobbie was afraid of the dark coming through the door. Did that used to scare you when you were little?"

"Damn right. It still does. There's nothing worse than all that black dark creeping in around the door. Is she asleep now?"

"Yes. I told her we'd keep an eye on the dark for her."

"That's a big job."

"We'll take turns."

A street-sweeper went by, polishing up the city for another day. Lonely kind of sound—good kind of lonely kind of sound. "Adriel . . . let's make a baby."

"Mmmmmm—no, sweetheart," pretend-serious, "I think I'd like to be married when I have my babies. You know . . . please their grandparents and all."

"We'll get married, then."

Adriel turned over and put her chin on her hands. I saw her eyes close in the moonlight. "You don't want to be married to me, Abel."

Street-sweeper going *burrrrshhhhhhhhh* as it rounds the corner. Fat white moon through the window. An over-anxious bird announcing dawn prematurely. Adriel all soft and fine beside me. *Married.*

One more attachment, one more set of life-cords that'll have to be ripped painfully loose before I can enter the Void. But holy God, do I have to give up *everything?*

I do.

But hell's bells, it's too much to ask, and anyhow . . . I'm not sure. Adriel so soft and fine beside me—beside *me*—and if *I'm* not, then neither is that, and it's too much to ask.

"Adriel, I think I'd like to be married to you."

"Abel," she said quietly, " 'I think' isn't good enough." And, as she leaned toward me, I prepared for a kiss, but instead she spit a small girl-spit right into my open mouth, which sounds absolutely revolting but was actually sweet and funny and beautiful because it was done by Adriel who I was very much in love with, and because it was followed by an Adriel giggle that lit up the whole room, and an Adriel kiss and Adriel love that nearly convinced me that the Void was a cold, lifeless, poor substitute for what I had going for me in the warm illusion.

In two weeks' time my body, which I'd neglected to feed or maintain for months, began to get what could pass for healthy again. Adriel saw that I ate and slept, slept and ate, until the section of my mind that had forgotten the routine pattern of day-to-day life-renewal remembered it once more, reprogrammed itself and switched to semi-Automatic. The dance of life was so fascinating, the pull of personality—of identity—so powerful, that it rapidly drew me back to the robot's hallucinatory controls. Back in the driver's seat. I repressed the realization of the life-illusion, hiding it away in one of the countless seldom-entered closets of the brain where I wouldn't constantly stumble over it and be reminded of the futility of the perpetuation of separate existence. Of course a trace remained, leaking into my conscious mind during unguarded moments of thought-wander and daydream, but the reality, the sheer existence-blocking truth of the lead curtain final realization was gone—hidden once again—covered up, pretended lost, and I surely wasn't about to search for and find it again. Not just yet. I decided that the essence of the experience I'd weathered was a lesson. A lesson which had been sent to teach me humility, to show me how significantly insignificant and utterly tiny I am—how tiny we all are. No need to compete with, to fight, to drag down other small conscious beings. In the face of the unbelievable magnitude of the Whole Show, in the face of *Eternity,* we should all be continually, every second of the incredible day and night, humbly, reverently awed and thankful for the miracle of our impossible existence. No reason to boggle your head with schemes and plans for amassing stock-piles of material junk. No *reason* to bring other equally lost and wondering people down.

Echoes and visions of LaMer—LaMer, now vanished to some say The City—LaMer naked and red-faced and bellowing like Doc Faith the snake-oil dealer, like Laz'rus back from the dead, like Mordic Sal driven completely sane by an accidental glimpse of Christ while he pissed in an alley, but more like Andre LaMer the once-upon-a-time hardguy-boxer-Marine-racist-beer-drinker who had a vision and took off his clothes on street-corners to shout at snickering, disgusted or outraged crowds, "An that's how it *is,* brothers an sisters! An if it sounds like somethin you heard before, it's cuz it is somethin you heard before an you didn't lissen *that* time round either, but it's *still true*!"

We have to jump off the hate-go-round. We gotta stick our fingers in the spokes of the bullshit wheel . . . even if we lose a few fingers. We gotta stop it because it's only noise and suffering and movement that goes nowhere in the most uncomfortable fashion imaginable. We all gotta open up and help every other man and woman along the road—even if it's just a matter of staying out of their way.

Ah, but it's hard. There're so many people all squashed up together. There're conflicting ideas and ideals and visions and rules backed by laws and jails and hate and intolerance and just plain ignorance. So many people, and it's hard to love them all. Even the best intentions warp under time and bad weather.

Out and around again, visiting people, seeing friends, I realized that the scene had changed for sure. The Jesus trip had taken it in the shorts.

Beau, Todd Bailey, Ted and I sat with Carl in front of his fireplace discussing the riots past and the riots to come. "I'm sick'n'tired of being called a fuckin pacifist creep," fumed Carl. "No more of this pacifist crap. We tried it and it didn't work. Nobody can say we didn't give it a hell of a good try. I went to *jail* for it twice. It just doesn't work. Pacifist is a dirty word in this society. Now we've gotta start playing the game on *their* terms. The Bloods're hip to it. They were pacifists for centuries and it didn't get em jackshit. They didn't move forward one lousy inch. *Now* they're goin somewhere! *Now* the society is listening to them. You bet your ass it is! Because it's *scared* of em! *Fear* makes the United States go round."

"It's all gonna come down around the bigot, plastic-pushers' ears," predicted Todd who was out of the love-bag and back into the leftist-bag from which he'd come. "The whole thing's so top-heavy it's all gonna come crashing down once a keystone gets pulled. It's really happening."

Carl, who no longer took acid, smoked weed seldom, drank wine alot, said, "You're damn right it's happening! I give the system three more years at best. At *best,* man! Three more years of rioting in every city across the nation. This is just the beginning! That war in Vietnam is gonna end because they're gonna have to pull all the troops back *here* to hold the country in line. We've got to arm ourselves. We're in for some tight, tough times. It's only just beginning."

Talk of revolution everywhere. Not just the Bloods, but whites as well. Not a peaceful revolution of love and understanding anymore, but a fire and gunpowder revolution. I met old friends who'd painted *love* on their foreheads a year ago, who'd let themselves be insulted and beat and jailed for their belief in peace, and who were now buying ammunition at the sportstore. I saw unbelievable arsenals in ex-acid-and love-freaks' basements—M.1.s, .45 automatics, little cheap throw-away revolvers, even Thompson submachine-guns, crates of dynamite. In Oakland, a guy showed me a .50 caliber air-cooled tripod-mounted machine-gun complete with three-thousand rounds.

"Not this summer, man. This summer's for the Spades. Next summer's ours. Get em before they get us."

Timid families of macrobiotic sun-lovers hiding in the mountains armed with pitiful little single-shot .22s. "I don't want any trouble, man, but there's 'spose to be concentration camps all over California. Nobody's hauling me an mine off to no concentration camp."

In Berkeley, Johnny Calpert, a Blood who'd eaten my food and smoked my weed on several occasions, told me, "You best paint *Soul Brother* on everythin you want saved, Abel. Then you jus hope for the best. Cuz we're burnin this fuckin country to the *ground,* baby."

Everyone but the authorities seemed to accept the fact that it was going to be a very hot summer.

At night I'd go home to Adriel, watch her work on her paintings, watch her move gracefully about the room doing sweet woman-things. After a particularly heavy week of war stories and paranoia from friends and newspapers, I said, "There's a revolution coming, Adriel."

She was making curtains for the kitchen and didn't look up, but smiled and said, "There always is, babe."

"I mean it, Adriel. It's different this time."

"It's always different. And it's always the same. I think Bobbie and Diane are going to stay with us this week-end. Would you like to take them to Santa Cruz Saturday?"

"Whatever you wanna do."

There *have* been revolutions, I told myself. It really *can* happen. Changes *have* been made by the people.

Searching for an argument to break into Adriel's exasperating indifference, I thought about the French revolution and the Russian revolution and then the American revolution of 1776, and there wasn't any argument. Always different and always the same. The power simply changes hands. Nothing *really* changes. Chances are, it gets worse.

"Adriel, it's an unchangeably sad world. It truly is."

Cleaning her brushes, a finger-smudge of white zinc on her cheek, hair tied away from her face and her work by a strip of leather, kitchen curtains unfinished and forgotten on the floor, a new canvas waiting to be sealed, she paused long enough to say, "No, it's only a sad Abel looking at the world. When are you going to stop being so gloomy? I think I liked you better when you were mindless. You were nice and wide-eyed and . . . *amazed* then. What's making you so unhappy?"

"The world. No . . . all the angry people on it trying to make me see things their way."

Adriel dropped the brushes in the sink and washed her hands. "Well *you're* not all the angry people," drying her hands on the gold smiling sun-face towel. "Don't pay any attention to them."

I followed her into the bedroom, saying, "But I *am* all the people. We all are!" as she shrugged out of her painting smock. "We're *The People.* How can I just turn my back on it?"

"Like this." And Adriel turned her back on me while she untied the leather thong that held her hair. She shook her head and ran her fingers up and through the long black snakes, letting them fall over her bare shoulders and down her pale back. *Adriel the Gorgon. If she turns around, I'm stoned for good.* A brush through her hair once, and the snakes are gone, so it's safe to look when she faces me and says, "I wish you wouldn't feel obligated to save the world. One person can't do it. It's only making you unhappy, and when *you're* unhappy, I'm unhappy, and I promised myself in grammar school that I'd never be unhappy." She sighed and put her fists on her hips. So cute standing there in her bra and panties, with the white paint spot on her cheek and her hair all long and straight and free.

I wanted to say something important, something beautiful and pure to her. All I could think of was, "Let's go to bed."

I woke up the next day and found one of her poem-notes tacked to the kitchen door. Under the morning sun, everything looked considerably more innocent and peaceful, and with no gun-fire in the street, no buildings sending oily smoke into the sky, a revolution seemed awfully distant and hard to believe in.

Drinking a glass of milk, I thought again of LaMer and said aloud, "You just gotta keep doin your thing with a little more *soul,* brother." But LaMer's down. He's down somewhere in the City and no one knows where or how or what he's into. But rumor has it, LaMer's down.

CHAPTER TWENTY FIVE – ODYSSEUS OR BUDDHA?

Well into November, Adriel's drunken, garlic-breathed landlord began to stumble out of his wine-stupor more and more often to give us considerable gas about my presence "in a young lady's rooms," so I moved back to my apartment where my own landlord informed me that he was glad to see me because the rent was past due. A Thanksgiving Day visit to my parents, several sad hints to my sainted father, and I appeased the landlord for another month.

Good times with Adriel, doing all the standard things—things that aren't in the least standard when they're happening to you—special standard things that're terribly important and memorable and personal and poignant, but not very interesting to read about

Christmas came and went. The American City Christmas was responsible for my thoughts the following day, which were of money. Although I'd received seasonal gifts of silver from relatives—gifts that would help me frighten off starvation for some months—I began to have cold suspicions that, with no means of support, money might become somewhat of a problem for me. I took one of the dollar bills I owned, put it on the bed and stared at it for a solid hour, trying to make it multiply. George scowled back at me and dollar-bill-flatly refused to co-operate. The more I studied the bill, with its funny small numbers and signatures, its elaborate bordering and reassuring, printed notices attesting to its legality, the more unreal it looked. How could I take a pocket-sized rectangle of greenish-gray scrap paper signed by some unknown cat named Henry very seriously? I put the dollar-paper back with its six identical buddies and hoped that they would mate or something. I figured that if I really needed money, it would come. It always had. America's full of money. You can find it on the street, in phone-booths—people will give you money for empty bottles or for mowing their lawn. Besides, as the shady underworld teevee characters always say, "If you want it bad enough, there are waaaays of making big money."

One whole day of thinking about money . . . then I smoked a joint and forgot about it . . . for a while.

In Berkeley, Preston was taking insane piles of speed so he could stay awake for weeks at a time doing incredibly complicated math problems, getting locked in crystal psychosis, wasted and thin and black-hollow-eyed and oily looking, accusing everyone of being secret cops or of making time with Sharon behind his back or both . . . or of worse. Standing in a white sea of discarded scratch-paper with both sides of each individual sheet completely covered by tight columns of cramped figures, he threw down his pencil and faced Beau and I, saying, "I've got to take acid—quick! I've gotta clean my fucking *head* out. This is getting not only *hideous,* but also *ridiculous.* Seemingly more hideous than ridiculous, however. Agh . . . a giant bummer."

We smoked opium cross-legged on the floor, roasting the black dot on a piece of tinfoil, inhaling the thin ghost of smoke through a ballpoint-pen casing. A nostalgically euphoric high. "Meditate on love," I advised. "Love'll pull you through."

Preston did a slow, disgusted double-take. "It seems to me I've *heard* that somewhere before," he said, lighting a match that burned his fingers. "Isn't that the *Hippie Creed* or something equally nauseating?" He struck another match and held it under the opium. "I certainly wish someone would come up with a few new slogans. I'm getting awfully fucking tired of the old ones."

Later that same day, when a female beggar wearing a pendant that said ALL YOU NEED IS LOVE stopped Preston on Ashbury, asked him for fifty cents and called him a "mutherfukkin capitalist pig" when he refused to give it to her, I said, "I'll admit that I'm beginning to have doubts about the purity of the hippie movement. Have you been noticing more an more unloving hippies, man?"

"What's a *hippie?*" snarled Preston. "I don't know any *hippies.* Are hippies those mindless, incense-burning, money-hustling, bead-wearing fuck-heads that infest the streets these days? If so, I can't imagine why I would *want* to know any."

I wandered around San Jose, avoiding the coffee-shop hangouts with their crowds suddenly too young and nervous and loud, wondering what I was supposed to be doing, wondering how I was going to expose the plastic-time-monopoly to the world and make everything all right, wondering how I was going to pull off a successful drop-out. I mean, you can't just say, "Well man, I quit. I'm out of the game." It's a good start, but saying it doesn't make it true. How do you eat without money? Money printed and controlled by the society. Beg? That's a cop-out. You pay homage to the society by begging it for food. Where do you live? All the land is owned—owned by someone or something. All the soil bought and sold before I was born. When we set up little camps on open land, we were thrown off. What do you do for clothing? You need money to buy clothing or cloth to make clothing. You could hunt like the Indians and make clothing from animal hides, but you have to have a license to hunt and a license costs money. You could make clothing from plant fibers, but to grow plants you need land and land costs money because *all the land is owned.*

On a Saturday morning Beau picked me up at Adriel's and drove me up to The City, telling me that there'd been a flash-powder blast of Negro rioting the night before and more action rumored on the way. "It's starting to go," he said. "It is, man. How come you're still in school, Beau?"

"Because I don't want to get a job and earn an *honest* living, for kristsakes, and it's either college or work, and besides . . . I dig playing with clay and making pots an jugs an things. I mean, it's not really as though I were going to *school.* Just arts an laughs, man."

"But don't you feel like you're wasting *time?*"

"How can you waste *time?* Man, that's ridiculous. Whatta you suggest I do with the days?"

We pulled into the Haight-Ashbury where Beau was to pick up a key. I waited in the car while he made contact, watching the street and thinking how much the scene had changed. Everything was sagging under the weight of the fringe element. Heavy crystal consumption had turned the vibrations jagged. Guided bus-tours chugged along full of camera-clicking pointing tourists. *Get a shot of that one, Harry. The folks back home'll never believe this.* Weekend hippies in a day's growth of beard and carefully tattered "psychedelic" outfits told hungry reporters what "The Love Generation" was all about. "It's groovie, man. We're all like one, man. LSD is a real trip, man. It's better'n sex, man. Hippies are in, man. We're takin over the world an if the straights don't like it that's tough shit, man." High school kids, lured by full-color magazine stories promising an all-free happening in psychedelic San Francisco, crowded the streets dressed in hippie uniforms, wearing five-dollar rose-colored shades, high on acid for the first time. Yessir, it's *in.* Then, busted and sick, picked over and head-ruined by the circling vultures, they're home again on probation to tell mom an dad and the local newspaper all the inside scoop on the evils of hippie-life.

Beau returned with the key, tossed it in the back seat, and we shot over to Oakland, dropped the dope off at his place, then cruised through Berkeley, ate dexies, parked the car and walked along digging chicks and talking. On The Avenue Beau was hailed by one of his partners who opened with, "We got the cop!"

"Jerome the Gnome?" yelled Beau, causing heads to turn.

"The same," affirmed Beau's partner.

Into a Doggie Diner, and Clyne (Beau's partner) bought a chili-dog before saying, "Fucked im over but good, man. You 'member he asked Howie to get im a brick?" Chomp on the chili-dog and some chewing took place. Then, "Same game he run on Morris 'n Patty in Monterey. So Howie tells me about it an I say, the time is *now,* man. We set it all up. Tell im we got sixty-dollar keys lined up for im from the biggest man in the city. Ole Gnome's mouth is really waterin." Nuther chomp on the chili-dog. "Then we go to Howie's place an get his big vet setta works—the one he keeps aroun for a joke, with the number double oh blunt point on it—an we gas it up with two thousand mics of righteous fine acid . . .

Beau was completely into the story—pounding the table with his fists, saying, "Oh wow! Ah beautiful . . . wow perfect."

"Yeah, can you dig it, man?" says Clyne. "Then we go pick up the Gnome, and he's just jumpin up an down thinkin about how he's gonna make at least Captain an all kindsa good shit when he pulls off this colossal bust—nailin the biggest Man in the city an all. So we drive im through all these back-streets an all over town an up an down an round an round, an he keeps sayin, 'Where *is* this connection?' an, 'How much *farther* to pick-up?' throwin in all this extra super-cool dope-talk, an Howie tells im, 'Look man, we just don't wanna take any *chances,* cuz this is a very big thing.' If he only *knew*! If ole Gnomie only knew-hoo-hoo. So anyway we finally take im down to the Panhandle an Howie pulls over an turns to the Gnome an says, 'Hey . . . the hell with the weed, man. How'd you like some acid?' An the Gnome says no, he wants the weed but maybe later on the acid. An Howie says, 'No, man, cuz right now it's free,' an right then I grab im aroun the neck from the back seat an Howie whips out the super-fit an rams it into the Gnome's ass an loads im up *none* too gently. An you gotta picture the Gnome screamin an kickin while Howie reaches over an opens the door, boots im out an says, 'Think it over, *cop.* Think about all the good people you busted, mutherfukker,' an we slam the door an split!"

"God!" roars Beau. "The Gnome on two-thousand mics! Imagine what his poor little cop-brain went through!"

"I'm hip," says Clyne. "Dig this . . . he's in the hospital. No more busts for Jerome the Gnome. He's seen the *light*!"Back at Beau's apartment, I said, "It's not what we started out to do, man." I couldn't seem to get behind the idea of acid as a weapon—as revenge.

Beau was still smiling about the burnt cop as he matted one of his watercolors. "Whataya mean?"

"I mean all this negativity. Acid to get even. I thought it was gonna be different. I actually thought we were the people who were gonna put an end to all that."

Beau looked up from his painting and gave me a fatherly smile. "Egregore, old friend, for your own good I tell you, man . . . you have been taking too much acid yourself. The love-thing is dead. That's cold fact, Abel. What's it gonna take to convince you? It's dead. Let the teenie-boppers play the game if they want to. It's a stage you've gotta go through. But face it, man—we've got to stay alive. And the only way we can stay alive and keep doing our chosen thing is to fight back. Aren't both your cheeks sore yet? We *lost* ground trying to love em to death."

I was laid out on the afternoon grass at Williams Street Park, just watching the clouds roll, when a face leaned over me and said, "Ah. Ahhhh. Ah-hah!"

I'd never seen the dude before in my life. He was wearing a BSA T-shirt and he was obviously ripped on something powerful. I said, "Ah-hah what?"

He giggled, held up his forefinger, reached into his pants pocket, fumbled around for a second and handed me a little orange tab. "STP. It'll set you free. He he he." Without another word, he wandered off in the direction of the creek.

I went home to my apartment, put some records on the player, broke the tab in half, put one half in a pill bottle and the other half in my mouth. When the cosmos sends you a sign like that, you can't just ignore it.

An hour later I was into a heavy case of formless fear. I fought with it until the sun was long gone, until the clock jammed at two minutes to eleven, until *make it to Adriel* was the only thought I could hold. Forgotten conclusions were pulling themselves into unmistakable patterns as I slid out the door into a turned-cold and dead February night. Dogs barked, mistaking me for Hecate, warning their masters of my approach. Lights and city-sound. Lost for centuries. Have to hide in a bush that might not even be there as a prowl-car snarls by sniffing me out. Street after street after alien street, and then there's Adriel's door at the end of a long tunnel. Pray that it's open. Is open! And I'm inside and can hear her moving in the bedroom. I was trembling under the crackling power of unknown-origin psychedelic when Adriel appeared sleepy-eyed and still in the half-sleep she clung to for long minutes after being awakened. Using her special nighttime radar, she floated over with her eyes closed, put her arms around me, felt the surging waves of raw energy, locked her eyes on mine with a snap of spark and said, "You're all vibrating inside."

It was a brain-rending effort to drag words out of my

four-thousand-mile-per-second mind. "I'm really stoned. I mean, I'm totally out of my head . . . you know? I mean, I want you to know that. I want you to know because I'm utterly out of my skull and I'd appreciate it if you'd do something." I hoped it was enough. When you're there, it's hard to talk about it. The terror's too big and too fast and far, far too complicated . . . or maybe far too basic.

Adriel put eye-scan on my face, trying to gauge just how serious the situation was. She evidently decided that it wasn't too terribly, and said, "Can't you slow down a little? For *me* if not for yourself? You've got a nice mind. Why do you want to burn it out?"

I didn't answer because, although burning out my mind wasn't exactly the way I saw my plan, I didn't feel like arguing . . . or explaining. I wanted down. And I wanted Adriel to give me a few hints as to the best way to go about it.

"How heavy?" she asked.

"Heavy. Better now."

Light scolding—"You're using a beautiful, delicate computer to play checkers. Mental tic-tac-toe with unimaginable billions of volts of power behind it!"

A much better concept than the one I'd been traveling behind—not nearly as grotesque. It made simple little cartoons in my brain that I could play with and laugh at, so I dug it and started to grab firmer footing as Adriel led me, with head shakes and soft grumblings, into the dim, familiar bedroom decorated with memories of comfortable good times and safety.

"Sometimes you make me doubt your intelligence," she sighed, helping me undress.

I sat foot-dangle on the bed, letting the world shift itself into Place, feeling muscles relax, feeling brain whizz back to near normal as vision clears. "But I stupidly love you anyhow," Adriel concluded when I was under the covers. Getting in beside me—"Even if you are a big baby and not too awfully bright."

Adriel slept, curled up fine against my body, and I spent the night sexless, high and content, fantasizing vast science-fiction computers engaged in complex chess games upon the outcome of which depended first my fate, then Adriel's fate, then the world's, then the universe's, and then . . . my fate, which was actually the fate of us all and it all.

I finally admitted to myself that Adriel, for the time being, had won out over the Void. Once, I'd thought I might like to marry her. Now I was sure of it. This is the turning point, I thought, feeling hopeful and glad. One third of a lifetime spent walking in someone else's grooves, then running in circles just to be running because I felt the need to run, then climbing for a promised something that's probably (and it sure seems to be) nothing, and now . . . now maybe it levels out and takes shape. Maybe this is when it all starts to mean something. Adriel. And children by Adriel—children built from Adriel and I. A home and a place and a purpose and Adriel. It all begins to fit. Waiting and searching for the end-all final answer, for the ultimate final flash, means that your entire life will consist of nothing *but* waiting and searching—until the end. An entire lifetime of suffering and unfulfilled longing for The Answer, and when it comes . . . that's it. Flash! . . . and that's all, man.

Settle down with Adriel. Start living every day of life. That's the trip. That's what it's all about.

Hailey was staying at my apartment. I told him about my new direction. "I'm thinking in terms of something permanent, man. No, I'm serious. Adriel's the finest thing I can touch."

"Yeah, she's a good little chick," he agreed.

"She's the *greatest* of chicks. She's everything a chick should be. She's everything," I insisted, and probably shouldn't have—because, following a strange blue week, far too intricate, warped and interrelated to fully explain, I discovered that Hailey had taken it upon himself to sample the sweet sex of my very personal darling Adriel. A cold shot, a cruel blow, an unwashed and treacherous foot grinding grit and gravel into the tenderest section of my unguarded gray matter. And, to make it all the colder and crueler, it was a good friend Hailey himself who made me a gift of the information while we smoked a good-natured joint of my weed in my apartment—telling me not only when and where and how done, but also how many times and what a great fine soul flash it'd been. "You don't mind, do you, man? I mean, it just sort of happened, you know."

What could I say? What I *thought* was, "Goddam it, Hailey, *why?* Why Adriel? What evil mean thing could I've possibly done to make you wanna jump up and down on my favorite sand castle?"

The whole thing strained my relationship with Hailey a considerable bit. It strained my relationship with Adriel a much larger considerable bit. As a matter of fact, it offended the selfish, sin-conscious, possessive puritan that'd crept back into my cells so much that, after a very cold confrontation, without really saying goodbye or even trying to hear her side of it, I stopped seeing her. Sad that Hailey would lay a chick he knew I felt for. But sadder still to think that Adriel would let him. Sad, hurt and downright pissed off, disillusioned and betrayed.

Take it like a man, Abel. It's almost a clichÃ©. How can you let such a low-level bummer hang you up, man? You're supposed to be hip. Free love and all that. This is the sexual revolution! Kick free of those Victorian snags. Accept it as a lesson. You were getting hungup in a very worn pattern. Friend Hailey actually did you a favor.

Yes. Mmm-hm.

Up to The City, down to Big Sur, to gatherings and coffeeshops with anything that was around—wandering in alone, head all muddled and thick, taking yellows and reds and rainbows to slow my brain down as far as it would go, sleeping fourteen or fifteen hours a day when no one came over to wake me up. Blue Jello city, and it's an easy place to live.

Two nights in a row I heard Adriel's footsteps outside my apartment, recognized her shadow on the curtain. I didn't answer the door. Nobody home, baby. Go find Hailey.

A little smack from an old Night Rider buddy—just a taste. Well hell yes, buy a balloon just to have it around, man. Beware the snares of straight-city with its fat cows who fear life in heaven. It's cooler still on the dark side of the moon.

"You're ruining your head," said Ted.

"It's my head, Ted," I said, laying on the bed all underfed and eyes mud-red and feet like lead.

"Well . . . I'm not your father."

"Very true. My father wouldn't be caught dead in those owl-glasses or that somekinda page-boy."

"Are you going to make it down to Monterey for the folk thing with us?"

"I'm makin it nowhere. I'm makin it right here till kingdom come, an it mighta already come."

"Man, you're in a strange place lately."

"Hmp," I replied, meaning that I had every right to be in any kind of strange place I felt like getting into, meaning that Ted had no real grasp of the situation, meaning, now that I think about it, "Hmp."

Out on the street for a rare daytime appearance, I put in some loitering time in front of The Weightless Albatross after hazy hellos to the good people who ran it (who are such good people they catch my low brain-waves and run no games—just let me alone to stand with folded arms watching bodies move past the front of their shop). Very green shades, so my eyes can do anything they want—even close. The sun's out, but it's far away and weak—just light—no heat, and I'm nodding, unbugged and unhung, focusing and unfocusing on the little pile of mashed cig-butts I'm building, when scuffed, open-toed shoes with red, pinched knobs of flesh sticking out of them, push their way into my field of vision. The shoes are attached to scaly, unshaven legs that run into a baggy, faded garment that's trying to cover a pudgy, middle-aged lady who says, "Aren't you ashamed? Aren't you *ashamed?* It's disgusting, that's what it is, it's disgusting! If you were a son of mine—if you were a son of mine, I'd be ashamed! I would be *ashamed*! Aren't you ashamed!?"

Out of nowhere—out of a quiet contemplation of a pile of cig-butts and a low mind-hum, there's suddenly a saggy blob of moist pink dumping noise on my head. I regard the blob from behind my green screens, watch the slash-wound full of liver squirm and bubble until it's more than I can take, and I say, "Fuck you, stupid fat bitch. Go away or I'll piss all over your scaly legs," validating her impressions of Hippies and probably making her day. But it sinks mine into embarrassment, and I walk home wishing I'd kept my mouth shut. Ashamed—just like the lady said. She got the reaction she expected—the one she was looking for.

The smack-balloon was empty—inside-out with the last dusting of white powder licked from it, and I'd like a little more, but not bad enough to go out looking for it, which is disappointing, because I'd figured that, by this time, I would be hopelessly addicted and, therefore, more to be pitied than censured—safe behind a legitimate excuse for being a lump—but instead, here I am still an excuseless lump. I filled the balloon with air, pinched the valve between my fingers, held it at arms length, opened my fingers and it jetted around the room, giving me the razz-berry.

No longer pretending to be a shut-down junkie, I wound up at Beau's place one night after a day of fruitless searching for lost LaMer with Ted and David.

"The FBI got him," Ted assured us. "He's in a federal prison for deserters."

"Not what I heard," argued David. "Nickie saw him in Oakland and said he's totally blown—so mindless that his chick has to feed him an take him to the john."

Beau's door was unlocked, so I stepped in, followed the light into the bedroom-kitchen, and, with a mental Donald Duck "Wak!" came face to face with Adriel. It was one of those truly gummy scenes that are movie-done by splicing together a long series of emotional, revealing close-ups, while crisis-music howls in the background. Doing it live, however, I had to stand behind my amateur eyeball-camera, unable to cut, splice or edit for artistic effect, while hurt feelings dripped all over the room, making it so damp, slimy and uncomfortable that I turned and, with not a word said by anyone involved, walked out the door feeling seven levels under down.

"And it's all the fault of selfish, possessive mock-love," I told myself. "Adriel's in the right. I don't own her. I'm in the wrong. I'm hungup on some greedy possession game. That's what's causing the pain. It's not Adriel. It's me and my selfish hangups." But how do you convince yourself of this? After a life-time of silver-screen validation of the merits of fidelity, virginity and the one-true-love concept, how do you convince yourself that it's all bullshit? I tried—I honestly tried, but no matter how many smoke screens I covered my thoughts with, I still knew that I wanted Adriel, wanted exclusive rights to

Adriel, wanted her to love *me alone,* and I was hot-mad-indignant that she would lay anyone else.

Not ready yet.

Not even sure I want to be ready.

Not even sure there's something to be ready for.

Which shall it be? A man or a Saint? You can't have both. Odysseus or Buddha? Spartacus or Christ? Better decide. Everything's waiting for you. Nothing moves until you work it out.

CHAPTER TWENTY SIX – JUST YOU AND IT.

At Baxter and Judy's cabin I spent a long day reading Baxter's philosophy books and listening to Eastern music while squirrels dashed across the roof and blue-jays chased lesser birds in and out of the redwoods. Then, tired of deciphering print, no longer even aware of the beckoning sitar, I did a hands-in-pockets, head-down, leaf-kicking walk through the woods in a big circle that brought me back to the cabin and, "Baxter . . . is it just me, or is everything getting progressively more screwed up? All these words, man. All these things being said and nothing being said."

Baxter picked up a copy of Hume. "You mean the philosophers you were reading?"

"No, man. I can dig them. A lot of the things they talk about are like mind-games—something to figure out just to see if they can do it and then put it all down in words that follow a logical pattern . . ."

"A 'logical pattern' which they themselves have established, of course."

"Okay, right. But they play pretty good games. They have interesting things to say. It's just that . . . beyond all those games, what's really happening, man?"

Baxter lifted a pot of tea from the wood stove, poured two cups and handed me one. "Tea, Abel. Three sips to peace."

"A lot of time and brain damage to get back to the same old question—'What's Happening?'" I say, sipping tea and burning my tongue.

"I don't think anything is happening, Abel."

"Something is. Something's happening."

"Nothing as important as you and I want it to be."

"Okay," three sips and no peace—one more and, "What've you

seen, Baxtor?"

Pause . . . while Baxtor lets his tea cool, flicks piles of imaginary ashes from an un-lit cigarette and stares out the window at some fascinating nothing hidden in the trees. "I don't think you really want to know, Abe."

"Yeah I do, man. I wanna know."

"Ah look, Abel . . . it's my own sadness. Why should I run it on anyone else?"

-magazine article-

> In recent years there has been more than enough misery forced down our throats in the name of literature. It is high time a new era began. The public wants to see something light—witty social criticism concerning witty and delightfully sophisticated people. It must be vibrant, exciting, but above all . . . hopeful and *affirmative*. Heroes fighting for moral issues. Heroes with *backbone* fighting against heavy odds. That's real life! There has been enough sickness, depravity and negation!

"I still wanna hear it, Baxtor. What've you seen?"

A long pause . . . then, "We're not going to make it, Abel. None of us. Not you or I, not Preston or Levin or Zad, not Faulkner or Kelly—none of us. We're not going to make it to any of the wondrous places we thought we saw. We're not the ones. We've already gone wrong, already copped-out. And now, all the rest will be meaningless games designed to keep ourselves busy—to keep ourselves from having to admit it.

"Acid was a sad mistake, Abel. First it promised us things that we'll never obtain—states of existence that we'll never attain and hold. Then it showed us a glimpse of the end. Now that's a dirty trick. Once you've seen the end, the race *to* the end becomes an out-an-out drag. We're going to grow old and die. That's all. That's all there is. The enlightenment-game is just *that* . . . another game. It's a variation manufactured to occupy the minds of those mortals foolish enough to overindulge in mental exercises directed toward seeing through the illusion. Beyond the illusion there's nothing.

"Now, I know that you maintain that the nothing behind the illusion is *The* Nothing . . . the 'Void' and a perfect state of wise Buddha-being; but Abel, that's only a more sophisticated variation on the old bullshit heaven concept. You've simply eliminated all the things that you can't accept, can't believe in—the harps and streets of gold and winged angels and benevolent old daddy God and all the rest—after which you had nothing, which is uncomfortable, so you ripped-off some validation from the Tibetans and called your nothing 'The Perfect, Empty Void.' But it's nothing, Abel. When you get right down to it, it's nothing. Once you accept that, you can either play the game and try not to think about it, or pretend that it's all somehow worthwhile, or you can follow the example the Yogis set and concentrate all your mental power on a point in the center of your forehead until you have successfully burned-out the brain cells in that area—which is the prefrontal lobe where all human hangups are located—and then you can go around smiling all the time. But Abe, when all is said and done—and it probably already is—at the very bottom of everything there's absolutely nothing. There's no divine plan, no final judgment, no glorious reward, no hellish punishment and no payment due. It isn't a morality play that we're caught in, it isn't a drama, it isn't even a joke . . . there's no punchline. We only expect one and search for one in order to give the show some meaning—in order to give the show a semblance of order. And you see, Abel, it's much easier if you don't *know* that—don't even *think* about it. It's too bad we ever started."

No point in arguing. Baxter knows both sides as well as I do. We could choose either side and debate far into the night for the sake of the game, already knowing the conclusion . . . no conclusion. "Maybe so, Baxtor. I don't know. I don't know anymore. No, that's wrong. I never did and I'm no closer to knowing now."

Watching Baxtor play with his four fur-ball kittens, I put in some heavy brooding over lost time and just being lost. Baxtor says, "We're a cosmic experiment that failed. Freaks. Acid freaks."

"You just said there's no plan behind any of this."

"There isn't. Are you trying to get me to make sense? I'm a

chemically deformed freak. Are you asking me to be logical?"

"No. Forget it man."

"An experiment that failed."

"Okay, but there's probably a lotta good karma in being an experiment that failed. People can learn from it."

"Possibly. I wouldn't bet on it. As your favorite sage says, 'Failure's no suck-cess at all.'"

One of the little fur-balls leapt on my hand, tap-bop with miniature fish-hook mittens soon to be weapons, rolling over on its back after the attack, suddenly springing straight up into the air as though on a string jerked by the puppetmaster, dodging one of the room's countless energy-snakes.

I better get a job and fill my head with good old busy money thoughts and day-to-day and long-term existence thoughts, and forget about enlightenment. "I'm almost ready to quit, Baxter." Something from Baxter that sounds like, "I wish it was that easy." I could ask him to repeat it or explain it, but why? He admits that he's mindless. One of Baxter's favorite expressions is, "The blind leading the blind."

" . . . and if it's a money-thing that's got you hung, man, you should start dealing dope. That's where the money is." Curt and I chug along in a borrowed Ford, heading for Stanley Gramer's place in Felton. Gramer is Curt's friend and The Dealer for most of the area at present. Curt is on pick-up for half a key. I'm along for the ride.

"It's not just the money. It's the whole job-thing, you know? An excuse for existing. So when people ask what I'm doing, I can say, 'Well I got this little job, see . . ."

"Sounds like a cop-out," says Curt.

"It is, but I need the vacation."

"I'm hip. But if you've got the *money* you don't need any other excuse. It's the money that counts. Not working your ass off to get it. It's the *money.*"

A point. Money. It might be nice at that. Buy a Lincoln and drive around invisible to cops, bail your friends out of jail, never fear another parking ticket or jail sentence for being broke and getting a traffic citation. Better still, buy a thousand acres of land and never leave it—let all your people come live on it. Money. "How much does Gramer make on a key?"

"That's thinkin pretty small for Gramer, but probably . . . oh, two-hundred-fifty profit . . . if he busts it into lids. Plus all his own dope free."

"Not bad."

"Not bad at all. Tax-free, Abel. And more customers every day."

Bonga-bonga-clump, over a wooden bridge and up a dirt road. "Over the river an through the woods . . ." sings Curt, pounding out time on the steering wheel, "to Gramer's house we go. If horse is the way you start your day then Gramer's the man to know-oh . . ." and several more verses before we stop in front of a cabin that's actually a good-sized house and the home of Stanley (The Big G) Gramer. A VW in the garage and a blue panel-truck with *Mind Medicines Inc.* printed like a rainbow on it, sitting off to one side. "Big G's delivery truck," Curt informs me.

Gramer himself can be seen behind a screen-door. A huge bar-bell held over his head, naked to the waist exposing a wrestler torso, prescription shades hiding his eyes, Muddy Waters moaning loud on the stereo (on the eight-hundred dollar stereo), sleepy blonde chick peeking around the door-frame to see who's outside, big police-dog going, "Grrrrr," and looking hungry—well-fed but hungry.

Curt identifies himself with, "You got my half key, man?"

No sign of recognition from dog, chick or Gramer, but thud goes King Kong's bar-bells and creak goes the screen-door and I follow Curt inside.

"Who?" grunts Gramer as I squeeze past, his tree-stump arm terminating in an index finger that points directly at my chest.

"Grrrrrr," says the dog, who's being held from my throat by the blonde chick.

"This is Abel Egregore, Gramer," out of Curt.

Tiny smile on Gramer's thin lips. No telling what his eyes are doing behind the shades. "Ah yes. I've heard about Abel Egregore."

I ask, "From who?"

"Mutual friends," says Gramer, moving to get a shirt from the back of a chair. "We have several mutual friends."

The dog says, "Snuff," and drops its chin on the floor. The chick is rolling joints on the sofa, holding them out to Gramer when they're finished. He takes one without looking at her or it and hands it to me. "Gran'ma Gramer's private stock," he bear-chuckles. "It'll ruin your head. Nobody leaves the house of Gramer with an un-ruined head. Business reputation to consider." The first toke eats all the lining from my lungs, but I pinch off the cough in my throat. I can already feel the weed rotting my brain as I pass the joint to Curt who says, "Mother Q. *Fug*!" after his first hit. "What's in this shit, Gramer?" Buttoning his leaf-patterned shirt, Gramer nods and does a funny giggle, "Tsee-tchee-heee. It's just fine weed, man. It's just old-fashioned hemp . . . cured in embalming fluid."

"That's poison!" squeals Curt, regarding the joint in horror. Gramer's dressed for business now. "Only if you drink it, man. Now let's see . . . you purchased one measly half of a key. Correct?" He snaps his fingers and the chick runs into the kitchen, returning with a brick wrapped in blue tissue-paper. "Scale," says Gramer, and the chick darts off again to get an elaborately engraved brass scale.

During the weighing ceremony—Curt watching the process like the proverbial hawk—a car drives into the yard. "Check it," says Gramer to the chick. My eyes zip to the door, then back to Gramer who is now holding a long barreled .22 magnum in his right fist. Headlines flash across my brain-screen . . .

FOUR DOPE-DEALERS
KILLED IN GUN BATTLE
WITH NARCOTIC AGENTS

"It's Marty an those people from Massachusetts."

The gun is magically gone—dematerialized as quickly as it had materialized—and the weighing continues as a kid in his midteens hustles into the room leading two completely straight college types who stare with cartoon-character round eyes at the broken key.

"God! Look at all that *pot*!" exclaims one of the college types, distinguished from the other by a button on his shirtfront that says,

FLOWER POWER.

"That's how much you'll be gettin, man," says the kid, Marty, shifting his weight from foot to foot, fiddling with a coin and bouncing his eyes, obviously wired up tight on speed. "They got the bread, Gramer. Is that one theirs?"

A nod to the kitchen from Gramer, and the chick is already there, returning with another key.

"Jesus Christ!" from Flower Power, fondling the key, holding it out to his smiling friend. "Look at *that*!"

Friend nodding. Friend touching the weed as though it were a holy relic. "Goddam that's a lot of pot. That's a whole kilo, huh?" A Christmas morning present-opening scene. "Is it good stuff?" they've been told to ask.

Not a word from the Big G. Curt's weed is measured and, from the pile remaining, Gramer takes a pinch, powders it between his thumb and forefinger, drops it into a Rizla and hands the finished joint to Flower Power. And three minutes later, when that joint's been done and another's followed it around, it's giggles and, "Wow. No kidding. Wow," then, "Uh . . . it's a hundred and fifty?" Apologetic for bringing up money matters in front of all these California heads who are undoubtedly so far above and beyond such earthly trash.

"That's right," says Gramer. His first words to them.

"Outta *sight*! Wow, I can't believe this deal. Are you sure that's enough?"

"That'll cover it." Not the faintest ghost of an expression on Gramer's face—black polka-dots for eyes. Flower Power hands Gramer a wad of bills which he folds into his fat wallet after a quick trained glance.

"A hundred an a half for one lousy *key?*" I whisper to Curt.

"Out of the kindness of Big G's heart. He's only making maybe eighty bucks off the deal. Where those guys come from they pay thirty bucks a lid."

The Massachusetts people, almost oriental-bowing, back out the door amid sincere, "Thanks a lot, uh, good to have met you, uh, thanks a lot, uh . . . Gramer." Unsure whether or not they should be calling him *Mister* Gramer.

"Give em a button, Marty." Gramer pointing to a pile of small red disks on the coffee table. Marty sprints over, grabs a button from the pile and pins it on Flower Power's friend. The button reads, MIND MEDICINES INC. THE BIG G. STANDS FOR GOODNESS.

"Nice doin business with you," and Gramer turns his back on the trio as they re-mumble thanks and the door bangs shut. An oil-baron smile from Gramer when they've gone. "Interstate commerce is picking up. They come to sunny California, turn on, then cart it back to their underprivileged comrades in the more backward states of the union. Good to see. Very good to see. Shipped twenty keys to Iowa last week. It's very good to see."

Customers come and go, buying two lids or five keys, putting in orders, setting up huge deals that involve hundreds of dollars. Gramer keeps track of it all in a red notebook. High school kids roll up in sports cars, lay down a hundred and sixty bills for two keys that will be broken into thin lids to be sold at a profit to school-mates. No longer room for shifty-eyed gangsters pushing crumpled yellow reefers after school at the hamburger stand. The kids control it themselves now. Sixteen- and seventeen-year-old studs with wallets full of cash, hip to the prices, gauging the weight of keys in one hand, figuring lids and profits with an ease that would boggle the minds of their math teachers, making ten key pick-ups in their mothers' cars, all cool and knowing, reporting busts and burns matter-of-factly to Gramer. I watch them haul away pounds of weed and think back short years ago to running all over the City, talking to shady Mexicans, fronting money and probably never seeing it again, waiting behind bars for hep-cat Spades, nervous and paranoid, all for a single starved joint that might turn out to be tobacco after you paid anything from fifty-cents to a dollar for it.

"I only need a key," says a clean young stud in a high school block-sweater. He counts out eighty-five dollars, tosses the brick in the back seat of his GTO and drives off.

Gramer warms up as the day wears on and he drinks wine from a gallon jug. "Another six months of dealing, then I'm gonna pull outta the scene," he tells me. "Hey, you knew Cage, huh? Cage an I had a beautiful scheme goin for us once. We had this plan for making nine-million dollars selling medical supplies to Cuba. Had a team of burglars to get the stuff, and a plane an a pilot lined up to fly it into Havana—the whole thing down pat. Of course I realized later that as soon as we landed we would've all been shot and the medical supplies confiscated, but at the time it seemed like a pretty good plan."

A car swings into the yard and a guy in his early twenties steps out. Gramer goes cold. "What's happ'nin, man?" says the guy when he reaches the screen-door. But Gramer says nothing. The guy does a couple of head-bobs and, "Can you turn me on to a tin of pot, man?"

"I don't know you," says Gramer behind ice.

"Yeah, man. You met me at Rita's. Remember?"

"I don't know you."

"I'm Steve. You said you'd turn me on to some grass. I'm a friend of John's, man. He said you had some stuff for sale."

"Get outta my sight."

"Ah come on, Stan. You know me. I'm a friend of John's. I know Gene and Garry."

"Get outta my sight, punk."

"Hey look, man. Don't call me punk . . .

"Move, punk!"

"Listen, man, I just came here to score some pot. You can't start . . ."

This time I see where the gun comes from. Gramer keeps it in an end table next to the sofa. Now it's pointed at the stranger in the doorway. "Get outta my sight, punk!"

"Hey, hey, man, that's not cool," stumbling over his feet, trying to keep an eye on the gun, trying to retreat gracefully, trying to smile it all away, blowing all three. "I know Gene! I'm a friend of John's, man. Look now, this isn't cool . . ." Gramer follows him into the yard and stands like an oldtime Western sheriff while the guy jockeys his car around, spins tires and burns off down the road.

Later, en route home with loaded Curt, loaded myself and uncomfortable about all the weed in the car, "A lot of money, but a lot of fear."

"How so, Abel?"

"Whattaya mean, 'how so'? That gun scene, man."

"Aw, Gramer just gets edgy when he's dealing hard. He probably only did it to blow your head a little."

"Yeah. Well it worked. Every dealer I ever met—too much paranoia. I've got enough right now as it is. I'd never be able to deal."

"Somebody has to. Somebody's gotta keep the new religion supplied with sacraments. Better fellow freaks than the Mafia."

"Truth. But not me. It's just not my thing."

"It's not mine either," said Sarah that night, shuffling a deck of Tarot cards. "Did Curt tell you that Gramer pays his lawyer five hundred a month to keep him out of jail for his last bust?"

"No."

"And they busted Lyla, you know."

"No. What on?"

"Dealing speed, but she'll prob'ly get off because she's pregnant."

"Lyla? By who?"

"Oh, that weird burglar from the City. The one that got busted in March. Lyla says it's him."

"Gah. Busts and confusion, confusion and busts. I gotta find my way out of this labyrinth *soon.* Door after door, and nobody we know has opened the one with the clear-light behind it. That tends to dump water on the seeds of doubt, Sarah."

"Very poetic. Would you get me a small glass of wine?"

Naked on the floor, I smoked a joint and watched a moth bang against the window trying to get inside, while Sarah drank red wine with precise little sips and turned over Tarot cards with ominous, fatal snaps. "Hmmm," snap snap—"How bum," snap-snap—snap snap—"God save us all," snap snap-snap—snap—"Ech," snap—

"Sarah, would you cut that out."

"Grouchy, grouchy," snap—snap.

"At least refrain from making comments on them."

"Would you like me to do your destiny?" snap-snap. "Tsk-tsk—grim."

"No!"

Snap—snap and a final slap. "Well, I just did."

At the employment agency—"Mister Egregore, if you're, uh, serious about finding a job, then may I suggest that you remove that beard and get a much-needed hair-cut?"

"It's against my religion."

"As are baths?"

"My body's cleaner than yours."

The chrome stapler went chunk-schick. "I think that will be all, Mister Egregore."

A short, two-day fast and some meditation alone with an incense burner.

what's a head of hair, man?
it's the principle behind it.
what's a head full of principles, man?
it's a head full of hope, can you eat it?
nope.

And I mix and drink a glass of instant breakfast, chocolate flavored. Magic instant breakfast, with all the protein, vitamins and calories necessary to sustain human life—in an envelope—in a box—it says so right on the side and even shows you which direction to stir. Follow the arrow.

A week of male rag-time—tight and nothing makes it. I started a run for Adriel's, then remembered the situation in mid-flight, changed course and ran instead to Sarah's where a light died on my first knock and no one answered. As I left, I noticed a yellow MG in the carport.

Peggy responded to my pounding and appeared at the door in her underwear. "Abel! I was just getting ready for bed."

"Beautiful." I reached into the elastic band of her panties as she closed the door behind me.

She pulled away with a squeak. "Your hands are *freezing*!"

"That's all right."

"For whom?" dancing out of reach.

"Everyone involved. They'll warm with passion."

An explosion of movement—bed-springs and tongues—warm, overjoyed to be free seed, and too fast and gone past before I really even start to get behind it.

"Abel, get off for a minute."

"Go to sleep."

"I have to get up and take my pill, Abel."

"I don't wanna move. Don't bring me down with noise about drugstore seed-killer. I don't wanna move."

"Move, Abel."

"No. I'm sterile, nothing'll happen."

"Are you really?" with womanly feeling.

"Yeah. I fell into a fireplace once." I lack sincerity.

"Hmph. Now cumon, get up for a second."

"Do you think I should cut my hair?"

"No! It's beautiful. Why do you want to cut it?"

"It gets in my eyes all the time . . . and my food."

"I'll cut it for you if you want."

Hah! I'll bet you will. I roll off Peggy and cover my head with the pillow. "Guh unker bil."

"What?"

"Your pill. You better take your pill."

Up to Berkeley on a note found tacked to my door from Preston. The note read:

> berkeley—acid will be taken—the cracks
> grow wider—bear witness—
> —b.p.

But no one answers the door when I finally arrive at his cottage, so it's hitchhike into Oakland where I find Beau clad in his pride-and-joy Confederate Cavalry uniform, preparing to make it into Berkeley. "What for?"

"Music," says Beau. "A new group that you'll surely dig. Wanna split a cap?"

And I do, so we mix it in coffee with cream and sugar, and drink it on the way to our destination, a coffee-house, where we're served more coffee, and I've never been too terribly wild about coffee, so, by the third cup, I've decided that I'd rather be somewhere else, when Country Joe and the Fish assemble slow and easy on stage—a cleared area in the back of the smoky, cramped building. "Dig," says Beau—the music does a sound-bubble—dig I do.

Hang just above drift on the lead guitar, so pure that I've gotta groan with empathy, through four numbers which merely set me up for "Bass Strings" which is one foot into painful with soul-pulling sadness and beauty—the beauty of the void as seen from very close to the edge of the infinite abyss—so unfathomably beautiful, and yet frightening and deep deep blue-sad when viewed from so close, knowing how far you've come, how truly close you are, and how far it is to all the way back, refusing to take a step in either direction, floating just this side of let-go and all-stop. The music is from *there*... and these tight little inadequate word-symbols can't possibly show you where that is. The music is from there and it's the most you can hope to bring back and still *get* back. I'd never heard it said so straight, so simply, so truly, with no riddles or mind-games or trippy little piles of shit—just the best sounds the man can find to say how high he is, how big it is, and how much he wants to stay there. Country Joe moans the song from behind half-closed distant remembering eyes, and from a pinpoint at the exact center of his grown-infinite skull where his soul is wafting lost and dazzled, bathed in cold eternal light. Singing:

Truth lives all around me
But it's just beyond my grasp.

My God yes, as the guitar and ghost-harp lead me further and deeper into windless, silent eternity beyond the siren-call of the beckoning notes. I want to go. I want to blink out and stay forever. But, like Country Joe, when I'm spent and can reach no further—too tired to try—I realize the truth quietly and, "let the wind carry me back." Joe McDonald's voice trails off into totally spaced guitar-talk to fade with a whispered, "Ehhlll . . . ehsssss . . . deeehhhh . . . and in the silence that follows, I know I've heard the purest acid song, and that none more pure will ever be written from or about the powerful catalyst. Joe McDonald cut through all the colored lights and paisleys and borrowed-stolen symbolism and cover-up cheap love messages, to sing about what it feels like to see so *much* with an untainted set of newly aware but long-time hip lenses and *still have to come back.* Surrounded by patterns of sound, he stood with his men, brave and defiant and cool by nature, not design, lost but still pushing, and I wanted to shove through the crowd, face this man, grab his hand and tell him, "Make it. No matter how hard it gets, hang on. Make it," but of course I realized what a bad scene it would be, so I sat quietly in the dark, wishing him well, not even hearing the rest of the set, hearing instead:

> *Just one more trip now*
> *And you know I'll stay high*
> *All the time . . .*

over and again from the base of my mind. "Just one more trip . . ." and one more trip always one more trip away. One more trip . . . but for how long? How many trips now? Count long since lost. Many trips, many tries, and it's still one more away.

"They're gonna be big," from Beau when Country Joe and the Fish amble off the stage.

"They're already big, but if you mean nation-wide . . . AM radio isn't gonna play their stuff."

"Wait and see. It's changing, man. How's the acid?"

"From a strange place. Let's go up in the hills an look at the City."

Until three-thirty in the morning, when we've smoked so much weed that the acid's been defeated and we're both bleary-high and tired. Snail slow to Beau's place barely keeping the car on the road, stumble up stairs into the two-room apartment for a final joint which goes out unnoticed in my hand only half gone. I consider relighting it, but drop it into an ashtray after long moments of deliberation during which I fall asleep twice.

Whattid Preston mean by, "the cracks are widening—bear witness"?

"It's so high this time, that you know . . ." sings Country Joe, bare chested against night-sky, wind-blown on a cliff seven-thousand miles above an angry ocean, goosing the storm with his high-voltage ax, not expecting the cavalry and no cavalry on its way.

Oakland afternoon. I went to the Zoo with Beau and two chicks who were friends of his from the college, and I tried to coax the great Ourangoutang out across the cement moat to run amok among the Zoo people. "Come on, man! Do it! You've taken enough shit from these insects. Break out!" But he turned his huge shaggy red back on me and was having none of my silly games. "Fuck yourself," he said with a black-nailed long leather finger, and he proceeded to demonstrate how this was done to the delight of several high-school girls who shrieked with laughter and ran off to get their friends.

"I wanna be an Ourangoutang next time round," I confided to Beau.

"I'm gonna be a bear," announced Beau. "Nothing has it as good as a bear. God loved bears more than any other animal."

"Fact?"

"Solid truth, man. Think about it."

"Let's go look at the bears."

"What's *that* thing?" asked one of the chicks, pointing into an empty cage. We borrowed a zoo talkbox-key from a kid wandering past, and the magic storybook told us.

Oakland made me dream that a holy wounded Saint with gray eyes and smallpox held a stone tablet against my forehead. Cold stone upon which was written:

THIS IS TRUTH, DON'T TRY TO UNDERSTAND IT.
IT IS BEYOND UNDERSTANDING.
THIS IS THE ONLY TRUTH.
THIS IS TRUTH.

In the morning, I said goodbye to Beau and hitchhiked back to San Jose, getting a ride first with a young GI who was leaving for Vietnam and wanted to know if I could get him weed or speed, then with a nervous Haight Street freak who told me that the Mafia was after him, had killed his buddy, and would soon be bumping off all the independent dope dealers in an effort to re-capture the market. "An the Feds're in it with em. Yah, the Feds an the CIA and the local cops're all in it with the Mafia," he assured me. "It's like big-business corporations, man. It's jus'same's big-business, you know."

I told him about my Oakland dream—the dream that sent me back to San Jose—and he said, "Yah, man. I had that one in December."

"Never take a dream at face value," Sarah cautioned the next day, snapping Tarot cards again, smoking a Salem with short puffs. "They'll fool you every time."

"Every time, eh?"

"Sure . . . because sometimes—sometimes they mean exactly what they seem to mean." She laid cards in neat rows and began to turn them face-up one by one.

"Whatta the cards say?"

"I thought you didn't believe in them."

"I don't. Whatta they say?"

"They say, uh, more of the same."

"For who?"

"No one in particular. What sign were you born under?"

"Uh, Cancer."

"Oh, wow."

"Oh, wow, what?"

"Just oh, wow."

Out of weed and sick of the City, so up to Carl's cabin for clean air and a lid if he has one to sell. His bus is loaded with belongings, Sherry adding a beat old suitcase, when I pull into the yard. "Camping trip?"

"Something like that," says Carl, dragging a duffle-bag from the cabin. "Dig this," handing me an official-looking letter.

The first line tells me all I need to know. It's the dreaded black spot. "Your induction notice."

"Yup. Uncle Sam requires my assistance in killing some of those people who're in grave danger of becoming Communists. Better dead than red."

"You're splitting?"

"Already gone. Gimme a hand with the rest of this junk. No sense leaving it for the vultures."

"But this is your home, man!"

"Not any more."

Following him into the cabin, "Whatta bout all those nights we sat up singing *This Land Is Your Land, This Land Is My Land*? You can't just run out on America the Beautiful. Where's your patriotism?"

"Abel," sitting on a cardboard box full of paperback books, "I've given it considerable thought. If I stay in America, I'll go to jail. There's nothing they can do to make me fight this war, so they'll put me in the can. Jail, man. You know how shitty it is in jail? The America I had hope for isn't happening any more. This is Nazi Germany, man. There are sixteen concentration camps just *waiting* to fill up with 'subversives' and 'potentially dangerous individuals.' Sherry and I aren't going to help fill them."

"Aw cumon. That's just paranoia . . . isn't it?"

"They did it to the Japanese during the last war! The country's getting ready to *explode*! You can *feel* it! The hard years are coming closer, Abel. Watch TV, read the papers—you can see it happening. That's what is truly frightening. You can *see* it happening, and there's not a damn thing you can do about it. Joe citizen is too fuckin fat and drunk and brainwashed to read the writing on the wall."

I remember the book of the hairy nezbet, although I try not to. "Well . . . where you off to?"

"Canada. I'll watch the revolution start from there."

Nothing more to say except goodbye Carl . . . Sherry. Good luck in exile. FBI and CIA and SHIELD agents trace my route home. All the walls are bugged and the radiator is a huge microphone. I turn on the TV, and the President glares out at me, saying that there has been enough dissent and the time has come to *crack down*. The President's act is followed by *Dragnet*—re-runs—twice as scary.

"Ted, when I think about what's happening . . . I mean, it really puts a big gob of clammy fear right in the pit of my stomach. Carl had to leave the *country,* man! Doesn't that sink in, Ted? He hadda *leave* the fuckin *country*! And he's just *people.* He's just people like you an me. None a this can really be happening: Spades with machine-guns, riots, cops shooting kids and kicking the crap outta pacifists, the war eating-up all kindsa people, everybody mad at somebody else, love-freaks turned gun-carrying hardcore dope-dealers, those concentration camp rumors that keep popping up . . . all this *fear,* man! None of this can be happening! It's all too far out."

And Ted says, "I'm hip."

"Yeah. Yeah, but who else is? I mean, people're still behind TV quiz shows, they still believe all the crap the idiot magazines run on em, and think that acid is like booze or smack only bigger, and they still tell their kids that weed causes rape-murder-insanity, and men with long hair don't take baths. I've even talked to voting-age people who think the constitution should be changed so that 'radicals' won't be able to use the press. Some people actually think that Wallace is a good Governor! Television commercials are aimed at *somebody,* man! That means there's people around who *believe* in television-commercial-reality!"

And Ted says, "I'm hip."

"Well *so what?* So fuckin *what?* Everybody keeps tellin me they're hip, and so *fuckin what*! What's it *mean?* You're hip an Beau's hip an Sarah's hip an Carl's hip an all these people are *hip,* but nothing gets done! If everybody's so stinkin *hip,* how come the bullshit factories are still goin night an day?" And Ted says, "Hey, be cool, Abel. There's nothing you can do. Don't let the old paranoia spider get hold of your brain, man. We have to wait awhile. Changes take time. We have to be cool and wait."

—pause—

"It's hard to wait, Ted. When it's happening all around you and you can see it and you know it's totally messed up and in dire need of repair, it's hard to wait."

And Ted says, "I'm hip."

Larry committed suicide on a Tuesday. Shot himself through the right temple with the 9mm Beretta he bought from a guy in Fresno. "Just in case, man. Just in case it actually come to that."

His chick, Donna Garcia, found him and his note on Wednesday afternoon. They were supposed to buy a dog at the city pound. Donna'd already picked up a collar and a box of fleapowder.

After five letters requesting, pleading for, and finally demanding his CO status, Larry'd received his induction notice commanding him to report for service in fourteen days. He'd always insisted that he'd die before serving in the military. No one took him very seriously. Almost everyone had said the same thing at one time or another, but, when the official-actual-signed-sealed-validated papers came, they rationalized, shrugged, said it would only be for two years, and went. Not Larry. I still think there must've been more to it than just the military hassle. Somehow, it didn't seem like enough cause. But Donna told us that Larry's note said:

> I will not be a part of an organization that exists to make war. I will not help a machine kill innocent people at a dictator's request. There will be no more killing only when no more people will kill. I can think of no other way to prove the sincerity of my convictions. Please give this note to the newspapers to explain the reason for my suicide. Bless the holy people who will understand. Peace. Peace. Peace.

But the newspapers didn't print or even receive Larry's explanation because his parents (who flew in from Colorado) had strong feeling about their son "making a spectacle of himself." What would the folks back home think?

"HIPPIE SUICIDE" declared the evening paper. No mention of the induction notice or the note, but they did manage to squeeze in the fact that, "The twenty-one-year-old ex-Cal student was known to have been experimenting with LSD and other drugs . . ."

Larry Anthony, the guy who'd figured it all out, dead as a suicide.

Ted and I prayed for Larry's unfortunate soul, trapped now in purgatory, from the top of Mount Umunhum.

"He shoulda split for Canada like Carl."

"He was more honest and holy than we thought."

"I hope he makes it through all the Bardo hell-worlds and such. Being a suicide, he's gonna have a lot of explaining to do—lotta bullshit to go through. Hope he remembers to drift free."

Smoke a joint for Larry.

"It didn't do a bittagood. Didn't change a thing."

"Have to ask Larry about that, man."

"I mean here . . . in this scene. It didn't change anything at all."

Smoke another joint for Larry.

"Accept the clear-light when y'see it, Larry!" Yelling at the sympathetic sky. "Don't flinch, man! Abide in that state! Make it on through to the void!"

"Don't let em trick ya with that Bodhisattva vow, man! Don't worry about us! Shoot through, Larry!"

We saw his pushing soul in falling stars and blessed it with all the power we knew how to project. Five falling stars—five powerful blessings.

Quiet, warm night. Crickets clicking to one another. A fingernail of moon inching past the stars. Down the mountain at midnight, silent and far inside ourselves. Larry journeying somewhere near the truth. Make it on through, Larry.

Hailey and I received orders to report for pre-induction physical examinations on the same day. Ugly into Oakland together, fortified with uncountable pills. Three days and nights of preparation, so we arrive at the induction-center in beautiful shape as a senile old sun coughs out of the morning fog. A drearier scene can not be had. Pacifist pamphleteers thrust scraps of paper denouncing the war and/or the draft at everyone who steps within range. Seeing Hailey and I as soul brothers, they load us up with double copies of whatever they have to push. "Good luck, man."

"Thanks."

"There's eight good lawyers' phone numbers on that green sheet."

"Oh . . . thanks."

"Hell no, we won't go!"

"Uh, yeah . . . thanks."

A bus pulled up and a guy stumbled out all bloody and hurt, his glasses broken and his shirt tom. A flurry of action, and he was hustled down the street by a group of unidentified samaritans. Word came, "Some jocks beat him up on the bus for handing out anti-war literature." I dumped my handful of incriminating evidence into a trash can and followed Hailey into the induction center where we sat at little school-days desks, filled out forms, listened to a Negro soldier who told us that if we lied we'd go to jail for ever, left him and went into a room where men in white coats took our clothes and lined us naked against a wall with, "All right, gentlemen, bend over and spread those cheeks."

Skinny dude with butter-yellow face and angry tracks up both arms, saying, "I got rats in my gut! Augh! I got rats in my gut! Lemme outta here!"

A uniform said, "Follow the blue line to station three. Follow the blue line to station three."

Urinate in a paper cup, and, "Follow the red line to station five. Follow the red line to station five."

"This," said a uniform, "is an intelligence test. You will have one hour and forty-five minutes in which to complete this intelligence test. If you fail it, you will be given another chance. If you fail it again, you will be given another test. If you fail *this* test, you will be given a test which has *never* been failed . . . by *anyone.* I suggest that you make an effort, gentlemen, if you want to go home to mommy and daddy this month."

> If farmer Brown had six apples and he
> gave three of them to farmer Green,
> how many apples would farmer Brown have?
> 1). eleven. 2). eighty. 3). three.
> Circle only (1) answer.

"Your time is up. Close your booklets and stand beside your desks. Row one, come forward single file, leave your booklets on the right side of my desk, leave your pencils on the left side of my desk. The pencils will be counted. Leave your pencils on the left side of my desk. It is a felony to remove government property from this room. Follow the yellow line to station six. Row two, come forward single file, leave your booklets on the right side of my desk, leave your pencils on the left side of my desk. The pencils will be counted. Leave your pencils on . . .

Blood test—bodies fall to the floor in dead faints. X-ray—bodies fall to the floor in dead faints. Hearing test—bodies fall to the floor in dead faints.

"I got rats in my gut! I got rats in my gut!"

"Follow the yellow line to station nine. Follow the yellow line to . . ."

"Didn't we already follow the yellow line somewheres?" asks the naked body in front of me.

Someone is singing, "Follow the yellow-brick-road! Oh follow the yellow-brick-road! Follow the . . ."

"No talking! No talking!"

"I got rats in my gut! I gots rats in my gut!"

The station that counts belongs to Doctor Fate. He's the man who decides. He's got his own office, an assortment of rubber stamps, and The Power. "Next," calls Doctor Fate, and a body is sucked into his chamber.

"I got rats in my gut!"

The good doctor surveys the material, measures the thread, chooses the correct stamp, and thump, rats and all, this boy is 1-A. "Next."

"I'm a fag," says a dark-haired dude who just might be.

"You're a homosexual?" asks the doctor.

"Yeah, I'm a homosexual," agrees the dark dude.

Thump, and he's now a 1-A homosexual. "Next."

Next is me. I hand Doctor Fate my papers.

"You have nightmares?" asks the doctor, reaffirming the information on his desk.

"You bet."

"What are these nightmares about?"

"Uh . . . different things."

"Give me an example."

"Sometimes I get trapped in eternity and I won't merge, so I haveta hang there forever."

"Hmmm. Are drugs a problem?"

"No. They're no problem."

"Hmm. You're allergic to penicillin."

"Yeah. I'm allergic to penicillin. Also bees."

The doctor does a moment's meditation. My fate teeters on the balance. Thump, goes the rubber stamp. "Next," calls Doctor Fate.

Hailey was waiting for me in front of the induction center. Pamphleteers swarmed around him like gnats, offering him advice, telephone numbers and maps of Canada. When I stepped out the door, Hailey said, "They gave me 1-A. I tole em about my back an my foot an my sinuses, but they gave me 1-A anyhow. Whattid you get?"

"God, I didn't look. It musta been 1-A."

"That's all they give," said one of the pamphleteers, pressing a picture of a napalm-burned baby into my hand.

"Get back in there an find out what you got," demanded Hailey.

It was a hassle, but I found out that I'd been given a 1-Y and would be called again in a year's time.

"How come?" Hailey was bewildered. He figured he'd been had—figured I knew some secret-out that I wasn't letting him in on. "Whattid you tell em? How come you got a 1-Y?

"I don't know, man. I didn't tell em anything. I don't know. Maybe it's because I'm allergic to bees."

"Well how come?" persisted Hailey. "I got back trouble, foot trouble an clogged sinuses, an I still got a 1-A. All you've got is bees, an you got a 1-Y. How come?"

"I don't know. I really don't know."

And I really *didn't* know, which put my head in a rather befuddled and suspicious place, causing me to suspect that I was being saved for a much grimmer reckoning, priming me for the confused paranoia that descended like ocean fog a week later when Beau and Clyne got busted along with Bob Levin who had such a powerful vision of cold gray walls and confinement that he smashed through a window and, barefoot and handcuffed, escaped into the forest. Then more fear swept the tribe when word got around that the laws had found Bob's phone-book with everyone's name and address in it; and an article appeared in the paper mentioning "operation clean-sweep" which was going to take care of the drug problem once and for all; and several people in San Jose found strange ominous messages in their mailboxes—a printed picture of a gun sight over a bearded figure with *Traitor* written across the top; and Curt Webber and a chick named Sue Ann got beat up in front of *The Wail* by three sailors; and, on top of all that, overshadowing everything else, Preston, indestructible Preston committed himself to a mental hospital.

I heard about Preston from Zad:

"He flipped-out completely. Evidently a bad, very bad thing—running through the streets, jumping over fences, climbing across people's roofs, going right into strangers' houses to telephone people he didn't even know—just dialed numbers at random and asked who ever answered to help him."

"Acid?"

"Mmm. Don'know. I got the story from Sharon. She said he mighta been. He'd taken some the week before. Those big orange Owsleys."

"Phew."

"Yeah. Anyway, he thought Sharon had tipped-off the cops—about something—weed, I guess, or un-American activities, something—so he flushed his whole stash down the toilet and ran all the way to the Avenue, stopping people and telling them that dozens of cops were after him—thinking that everyone he knew was actually a cop and in on this big plot to get him. He ripped a battery out of a car for some unknown reason . . . oh no wait . . . he ripped it out because it was full of acid and he didn't want the cops to find it anywhere near him. Then he came back to the cottage and told Sharon that he wanted to go to the hospital and give himself up, and I don't know what all happened then, but the next morning he went to some institution in Berkeley and I guess he was pretty muddled by this time, and, oh yeah, he didn't have any underwear on and the doctors thought this was odd and they put him away. Now he can't see anyone—won't talk to anyone, I guess . . . except Sharon."

Still unable to take it very seriously, "Where's his head at now?"

"Still fairly freaked-out. He doesn't know who he is."

"Preston? Come on, man. Don't you see? It's some prank he's pulling on us."

"All I know is what I heard. Sharon didn't make it sound like Prankster-work."

"But *Preston?*" waiting for Zad to admit that he doesn't believe a word of it. "He wouldn't let those shrinks get ahold of his head. Would he, Zad?"

With a shrug, "It happened, man. He surrendered."

On the street, all the cops give me nasty smiles that say, "We got to Preston. Preston cracked. We got to ungettable Preston." But I know it's a trick. There's an O. Henry twist yet to come. They can't get to Preston. Not faster-than-light Preston. Not the mighty, bullshit-defying Preston. Not always-on-top-of-it, first to drop acid, first to eat Peyote, laugh in the dead face of stark madness *Preston.* They can't get to Preston. He's the most basic of reference points!

"He's out of his head," said Beau, out on bail, waiting for his trial, sitting behind the wheel of a pickup truck he'd borrowed from one of his partners, cruising through black morning San Jose with me next to him on the horse-blanket covered seat, on our way to Mount Hamilton. "I talked to a cat who saw him just before he went into the smile factory. Preston really blew it this time. He's out of his head."

"It's not a prank?"

"It's no prank, man," handing me a joint which I only pretend to smoke.

"Well goddamit, this really makes for shaky ground. No matter what happened, no matter how many souls went down, no matter how thin and stretched out the reality-thread got, I could always look to Preston and say, he's makin it—old Preston's gettin by—if anyone knows the right path, it's Preston—he's hanging onto the clear-light express, and if he can do it . . . so can I. You know what I mean?"

"Yeah. He was one of the originals. Preston the rock."

"Right. I saw Preston as a beacon—a lighthouse—the one never-changing norm. Now he's crazy and in the madhouse by his own hand. How could he do it to us? How could he betray the tribe by going insane?"

On the outskirts of nowhere, we were stopped by a traffic-light. A long traffic-light. No cars on the road—not a soul for miles—just us and the mechanical signal. We waited for it to agree to let us continue on.

"Remember how Preston used to laugh at the thought of traffic-lights controlling thousands of minds? He used to fantasize doomsday wars wiping out everyone but three people, who would then start treks across the burned-out nation, stopping for red lights as they went."

Beau reached into the glove-compartment and pulled out a pistol. Two deafening thunder-blasts against the quiet night, and red-stop and yellow-wait are skull-eyed gone, leaving only green-go. Beau shifted gears and drove on, saying, "Jesse James couldn't have done better. Whatta shot."

"Holy Christ, man!" when my heart slows down enough to let me speak, "Why'd you do *that?* That was the stupidest stunt you ever pulled! They'd put us in prison for a million years for doin that!"

"Have you no eye for symbolism, Abel?" eighty miles an hour up the mountain, "Have you no appreciation for significant gestures?"

Baxtor. Baxtor ought to know.

Baxtor already knew—had been told the whole story by Mercury messenger Zad. He was drinking an almost summer beer on the front step when he said, "That seems to be the pattern. It appears to be one of the steps." Glug from the beer-can; the first I'd seen in his hand since I met him. "As our Psychedelic Saint, Doctor Tim, says, we 'turn on, tune in, and drop out.' But it goes on. Oh yes, it does go on, Abel. It's actually 'turn on, tune in, drop out, freak out, fuck up, and crawl back.' Preston has evidently reached, or perhaps recently passed 'fuck up.' Now I would imagine he's working on 'crawl back.'" Glug from the beer-can. "That's the pattern. That is the pattern."

"I hope you're drunk, Baxtor. I surely do hope that's your excuse. Are you saying that *you're* crawling *back* now?"

"I am," he said seriously. "I'm trying to anyway. You see, due to the fact that having 'fucked up' you must—you are *forced* to crawl, the road *back* is infinitely more difficult to transverse than the road *out,* along which you ran . . . or, more correctly, were blown."

"Then you're crawling back to *bullshit*!"

"Exactly. Back to nice safe finite easily recognized and simply navigated bullshit. Why fight it, Abel? Bullshit is what we are given to work with, and bullshit is what we must be content with. Would you like a cold beer?"

I left Baxtor as he opened the last can in a handy-take-home six-pack, and I rode toward San Jose on my poor, nearly dead now, falling apart motorcycle. Even wrapped in the familiar thunder of the pipes, I couldn't stop wondering which way to go—which road to take. Gotta decide. Gotta decide and get at it. Back to safe, well-validated television conformity? Back to bullshit? Or should I keep hanging on—keep holding out for the something more I'd seen—thought I'd seen?

On the freeway: This whole thing—this entire section of the film—Adriel, Baxtor, Larry, Carl, Preston and all the rest, could be a test of my faith. It could be a reminder that, in the end, in the final reckoning, at the show-down, you have to do it yourself. There's nobody else there. Just you and IT.

"You got to make it on your own," I said to myself.

Myself agreed, and added, "Buddhas are made by themselves and the Truth . . . not by their friends. You got to go the final stretch on your own."

With a little help from an ergot fungus that infests rye?

Why not? It's here. It exists. It's within reach. Any boundaries you impose are totally arbitrary. You'd be a fool to ignore it.

At my apartment, I took three tabs of acid from the refrigerator (where I still kept LSD . . . a carry-over from the long-gone sugar-cube days) and dropped them into my mind, casting my fate to the infallible winds of karma. Done. Check and checkmate. I lay on my bed, convinced that this would be the time—the last move—relief is just a swallow away—no chickening-out—no compromising—no deals with the void—this is the time.

An hour passed. The clock said, tick-tick-tick, and nothing

happened. I felt drowsy. No reason for me to stick around, so I closed my eyes and drifted, waiting for the acid to come on. I went to sleep.

Eyes snapped open and focused on the clock. Take time to figure it out. The big hand's on the . . . three hours had passed. Three hours, and nothing was happening. Nothing happening because this is really it all along and here you are bumble-hunting all around it, unable, Abel, to pick-up on the glass-smooth diggable waves of the honest reallies that bounce off nearly every available equally diggable surface and perhaps something is happening because the air just snaked its way around the door-jamb, sweeping with a distinct whoosh into the kitchen, and everything my eyes touch has that barely perceptible unless you're familiar with it in which case it's a glaring something weird about it that you can't quite put your finger on and that's all the weirder because it's only just one tiny teeny micro-weenie cog-click away from yesterday's cold potatoes or maybe one entire revolution away from the same minus one tiny cog-click and with an infinite number of possible clicks how will you find your way back to the one that holds the important step of the beginning?

Dawn slowly. I let it come and regretted it too late. I saw it, understood it, remembered it, and I—capital I—panicked, slipped, freaked.

I stood up and died as a sheet of white flame seared the earth. FOOSH . . . and there's nothing but ashes. Dust to dust. One speck of dust discontent and greedy, crawling through worm-holes, searching. I got back inside, found myself looking through eyes, and the world had been drastically altered in my absence.

Thigh-bone trumpets and molasses music groaning and howling and wailing into Eternity.

Instructions that would have saved me did no good because I heard them recited by wax puppets controlled by a master who had nothing better to do with his time and didn't really dig puppets much anyway.

Terror cavorted on fire-blackened rooftops, starting and stopping the film, running it backwards, forwards, backwards, forwards, speeding it up, slowing it down. He tired of the game and became All Thought. All Thought turned to Stark Fear, the world began to wilt and die for the seventeenth consecutive time, I began to realize that it all got down to . . . and then I saw my still hung Self waving to me from the exact-same place I'd seen him last.

"You're back, man," he said. "You see? All that running around out there in the dream, and you're right back to here. There's a lesson, man. Right back to here. We still got the task. Let's do it. We got a long way to go."

Right back to micro-second zero. Waiting for me all that time—all that no-time. Right back to the point zero that I never really left. And you never do . . . not until you work it all out.

Check identification papers. Outside, and pray for survival. Work it out. Work it all out.

CHAPTERS TWENTY SEVEN AND TWENTY EIGHT— CONDENSED FROM THE ORIGINAL SIX VOLUMES.

I cut through dark alleys, emoting false innocence, dodging sniper fire and occasionally stopping to check bodies for guns, ammunition or snapshots. High on dragon's blood, even the moon blinded my cave-eyes with ultra sunpower twice reflected. I stuck to elusive pools of murk, watching for cop-helmets or the tell-tale flash of brain-burners. All around the hospital it was death and quiet because of the gas and fire beetles. A zombie screamed on Second Street, screwing the red-white-an-blue corpse of a crushed nurse—dead eyes rolled back in the gray skull, black tongue draped over broken teeth and bloodless lips, right arm gone, only an electric heart, plastic lungs and unknown germs driving it up and down, up and down on someone's one-time lover turned carrion and crumpled by a full-power mind-thrust at close range.

I ducked down Third Street in search of another quick-fix transfusion to keep me going through the six-week night. On all sides the cops were burning houses and running the distortion machines in and out of unshielded citizen heads.

After creeping into the sewer-catacombs to avoid the coming dawn, I caught a red-eyed rat and broke its neck and melted it down and geezed it full strength, fur, fangs and tail. The dragon's blood was fading and the come-down made my bones brittle, so I sat without moving for a day and a night, drawing scalding breaths through clenched and splintered teeth. At first-light it began to rain. The sewers rose and washed the hard crust of rat-juice from my maggot-white body, and I left the underground passageways in hopes of finding the Chanel Seven studios which were broadcasting confusion to comrades lost in The City.

For a twelve-year midnight I searched First Street and Second Street, first and second, First and Second, following scum footprints and slime trails, riding busses disguised as a beaten Negro, pretending to be a transistor-radio-controlled teenager, captured once by the authorities who let me go when I convinced them that I'd lost my mind fighting in Asia.

Alone on the street, I laid my face against rough stone and cried, "How much longer? When will I be given the final statement and the script? When will I know if all this is part of The Plan?" And I added my wail to the countless others that howled endlessly for an end to it all.

Friends lost, defected to the state. Friends disbanded to wander and wait. Some to The City, some to distant islands, many to the hills—all in hiding. Friendship in fact merely a long lost delusion. Now there's only dragon's blood, so out comes the kit and hit up quick and it's nova between the eyes and float free and drift like twilight ocean mist and live for a year and a half with the forest-people in their green damp huts, and then reenter slow . . . level out . . . a memory flits by and I reach out to grab it . . . miss . . . another crawls into view and I wait for it quietly . . . mind darts out fast and snags it by one of the thread-like tentacles and I examine it and it tells me who I am. The flash is over and, in newer-older body, I shudder into the realization of a task—a task left unfinished. No memory of goal or purpose. Only the hard truth of a task undone and important.

An October-April and the sky's afire.

A series of endless scenes later, in the San Jose still bowing to time, I'm downtown dying in an alley—gone mad. While my brain burns itself out, I have a peaceful vision of an early rebirth.

"Tell them it's all perfect and beautiful."

"It's been said."

"Well, we have to *teach* them."

"It's been tried."

"Well, why won't they *learn?*"

"People forget fast. People are busy. People forget."

"I won't forget."

"We'll see. In a couple of years . . ."

"I'll never forget. It's all perfect and beautiful."

CHAPTER TWENTY NINE – FASTER, TIGHTER, SMALLER AND LOWER

Peaceful vision fades under the wail of police sirens and I find myself once again forgetting. A drunk staggers and falls on the sidewalk in front of my alley sanctuary.

"Assassination!" he moans. "The nation's gone mad! Mad! Assassination! Ass, ass, a nation of asses! It's only just begun! In-san-ah-teeeeeeeeh! Mad! Gone maaaad!"

I watch drool form a dark puddle on the pavement beneath his bubbling mouth. The sirens are louder now, controlling the set. Web-like cracks jump up the walls of the city as the sound comes closer and intensity builds. Streetlights shatter and my teeth begin to chip. I try to lie still, to remain hidden, to merge with the alley and its secure garbage, but I feel a scream growing in my stomach, feeding itself on siren-sound, fighting its way out. The control-sound is everything. Red lights and yellow flashes bathe the world in hell-visions. Doors of steel slam and jackboots go wak-wak-wak on the cement. I can see the cops and I know it's the end of freedom and I try to get up and run, but my body has already died of fright and won't respond to terrified mind. Die, mind, die. Die fast and now and there won't be cops or sirens or anything to face. Die, mind, and they'll find only a ruined, bearded body where you used to be. But die-hard ego is hanging on to the cliff of life with bloody finger-nails. Mind won't die.

Red flash—yellow flash—red-yellow-red-yellow—and the cops are beating the wasted old drunk with their riot sticks, pulling-shoving him into the leering, panting, expectant car-cage to be siren-howled off into the night. I'm alone again . . . caught between dimensions . . . struggling brain in rotting carcass.

"Shadow-Gypsy! Emote joy and save me!" But the Gypsy is gone. Waiting in shadows.

The background hum drops an octave, a cigarette-butt materializes out of the jagged patterns, and I instantly slide into the reality of cigarette-butts and dirt and realize with a shudder and then a sigh that I'm crumpled in a back alley and coming down.

"Made it again," I whisper prematurely, and tumble into eternity from the very beginning once more, repenting my rash and rank foolishness in free-fall where it doesn't help at all. I'm quiet for a long time after emerging—waiting for it to be safe to think—then I look at my hands and they're hands and move my fingers and they're fingers and I sigh and sigh again and I'm in a strange, but fairly safe, dimension. I decide to settle for it rather than take the chance of holding-out for the one I had hoped for, missing it somehow and being forced to finally accept a much less desirable state.

Walk to the apartment. Walk, and it's difficult, because I'm in a place where things almost work, but not quite. Just enough not quite to confuse and bug hell out of you and then right back into you, making every moment of the day and night an incredible drag, an incredibly difficult drag, because nothing really works . . . just almost works.

Apartment found concealed among bee-hive complexes of multiple-image identical buildings. Inside, spend time wondering how. A day utilized contemplating the art of hatching porcelain eggs. Hard to talk to people, because there's really nothing to say and you can never be sure that there are actually people. Smoke a thousand cigarettes, plugging them into mouth with shaking fingers, without feeling the smoke. No color. All sounds grate on raw eardrums. No taste. All food made from sawdust seasoned with just a trace of ozone. Hot, cold—no difference. All poets are fools. All religions a sham. All music is discord. Dumb—numb—hum—it's bum, but not bum enough to be interesting.

Acid in hopes of a change . . . any change.

No change. There's nowhere to go from here.

-stuck-
-fuck-

More acid. "Take two. They're small."

Nothing. Nowhere to go. No such thing as high or low. No fast or slow. Walk out of the show.

-now-
-how?-

Suggestion E-38: Curl up into a fetal position and shrink. You could hide among your structure's illusory molecules with nobody and practically no body and no recognizable material *things* to disturb an untroubled and endless contemplation of *What Is Happening*, while you floated in the cool space between. All that no-time to work it out.

You'd go crazy.

"Damn right," says Saint Anthony, opening the door of his desert cell to evict a legion of obscene female devils. "You sure's hell would."

And that is, of course, exactly where you *have* to go (in one reality or another) before you finally get to where it's all at. You have to go out of your head. Trapped inside, you can never take an objective look around. You have to go out of your head. Insane.

And oh man and oh Lord, that is *too* scary. Why can't it just be soft and simple? Why can't we all break through effortlessly as soon as we see it and want it?

Deep in the blue flame of the central spark of all of us is the memory of the original beginning which is also the final end, and it frightens us. It's so huge and so far out and unbelievably-absolutely-believable that, when confronted with it, any ME mind-existence flashes out like a piece of lint falling into a blast furnace. Ph . . . in tiny, tiny letters.

Wise men. Seek out the wise men. Tell em you're hopelessly hung and need a hand. Wise men. Look up one in the Yellow Pages. Look under *enlightenment*.

Holy of Holies Kakamir Bagahdah reclined on a couch in his

air-conditioned penthouse where he was presently holding audience with the select few who could afford the sum necessary to enlist him enlightened aid. A beautiful servant girl peeled grapes for the famous holy man and placed them carefully upon his blessed tongue. Kakamir Bagahdah's advice and council was sought the world over by kings and queens, movie-stars and millionaires, the very rich and the unbelievably rich. In His selfless crusade to bring peace and enlightenment to the troubled people of the world, Kakamir Bagahdah refused no one access to his wisdom. Often laboring as much as three hours a week, listening to problems, offering priceless advice, dispensing truth like aspirin to the needy, He asked in return nothing more than a few foolish dollars which He, being totally enlightened, naturally had no real use for, and only accepted as a symbolic token of faith—as a joke, really, He would sometimes say, laughing and winking to His disciples.

I first learned of this Holy wise man from a reputable magazine. I read that He was acclaimed by countless educated men. I read statements by people whose names appear constantly in the news. Holy of Holies Kakamir Bagahdah, the answer to our prayers. I made an appointment to see Him at His convenience. The time had come.

Having purchased only sixty seconds of His valuable time, I got directly to the point. "I am in need of assistance," I began, after praising His existence as I had been instructed to do by his outer-office secretary. "I am troubled and afraid. I am lost and unsure. Can you help me?"

The Enlightened Kakamir Bagahdah spit a grape seed into a silver receptacle and waved the servant girl away. "How long you pay for?" He asked.

"Sixty seconds," I replied. I now had forty-three seconds remaining. Kakamir Bagahdah's grape seed spit had been on my time.

"Pah," he snorted. "Tell you what. I'm gonna give you a powerful charm. Howzat sound?"

"Wonderful!"

"You better believe it. Okay, a charm. Now don't go messin aroun an usin it lightly cuz it's really mystical an deep. You can't just fool with it an, uh, like that." He paused to stifle a belch. "You ready?"

"I'm ready, Sir."

He glanced around to see if spies had crept into the room. Satisfied that all was secure, he leaned forward slightly and whispered, "Count backwards from thirteen, thirteen times."

"Your time is up," said the intercom on His desk.

I left feeling much enlightened, clutching one of the Holy Sage's business cards in my hand. The card said:

-SHEMAIAH-
-by appointment only-

Grear ran the point over the whetstone a final time, held it up to the light to check for burrs, hooked up the pacifier and ran a little alcohol through the works before placing it carefully in its case. In three years of heavy crink, Grear'd never had an abscess. He attributed this good fortune to his fit-cleaning ritual.

Bleckmen was capping acid in the kitchen. Five hundred caps—over a thousand dollars worth of acid. He watched Grear put the fit into its leather case and said, "Okay, so he put you down. You *did* have it comin, man. An anyhow, that ain't reason enough to burn the guy. Whatta you wanna burn him for?" Grear snapped his fingers and flipped his lucky silver dollar in the air. "For thirty of these, baby. That's not too deep now is it man?"

"Shit, you make that much in ten minutes a weed deals. It's only thirty bucks."

"Thirty bucks is thirty bucks." Grear put the lucky piece in his pocket and patted his Levi's. "What's it to you, man?"

Bleckmen scooped white powder into a cap and pushed the two halves together. "I just don't like the idea of sellin out one of our own people. If we wanna make it, we oughta hang tight." He held up the finished cap as a visual aid. "Know what I mean? Divided we fall." The cap dropped from his fingers into a box of its brothers and sisters.

"It's already divided," said Grear. "It's gonna fall, and I'm lookin out for this dude right here. The Fam'ly's movin back in. I'm makin points while I can."

Bleckmen put together another cap. "I don't know, Grear. I don't think you oughta burn the guy. He did a lot for the cause, man."

"The cause is nowhere," said Grear, counting out tens from the cash-box. "It's about time we all hipped up to that fact, baby."

The comic was halfway through his act and I was halfway through a pack of cigarettes when Triggerman Chaz kicked the swinging doors from their hinges and strode into the room with a nickel-plated thirty-eight snug in the palm of his right hand. His quick, dark, ferret eyes swept the bar, appraised Betty Lou, touched and discarded Nevada Fred, then came to rest on the man behind the check-desk. Twenty seconds of glacial stare. Then, "They tell me your name's Crail."

Four tons of silence. Piano silent. Dean Martin silent. Comic silent and hiding behind the trained seal. All eyes on the newcomer.

Crail sat cool. Only his lips moved. "They tell you right, my friend. Pahtooh!" and a glob of brown plug juice arced its way into the brass cuspidor held by Willy the Midget. "They tell me your name's Yellow-bellied Mangy Pieyoot"

One clock-tick—two pistols vomited lead—one sound—two pistols—two shots—two death wishes—one sound.

Down the street, next to McLean's Feed Store, Sheriff Wako tossed a shotgun to Deputy Clemet. "A buncha the boys are whoopin it up," he said. Clem wrote it all down in his notebook.

Crail, still cool, still motionless, a thin trail of gray gunsmoke from his automatic, a thin trail of red blood from his lips. Still cool. Very dead.

Triggerman Chaz, tight-lipped and defiant, crouched like a stone gargoyle. Emotionless stone. Stone cold. Stone dead. A single grunt of grudging consent to the dark angel, and he toppled to the sawdust floor. From stone dead to rag-doll dead.

Brian sunk the eight ball and collected three-hundred dollars from Jim the Twitch who was more interested in the polished cue.

"Can you dig it?" said Bart the Fox, on his hands and knees beneath the piano. "Can you *dig* it?"

Lysa took my arm and steered me to a table behind the rattan screen. "It's midnight," I told her, "It's gonna be at midnight."

She nodded and bit her full lower lip till the white teeth drew crimson blood. "I know. I talked to Gary the Grape."

My mouth curled up at the corners and I snarled, "When'd you see the Grape? He's a prop-up cardboard, low-budget, scene filling extra. I don't want you hangin around him, Lysa! Any man who has to be *told* his own secret doesn't deserve to hear it."

"Don't talk now," she whispered, digging her fingernails into the backs of my hands, making little half-moon scratches, "Come up to my room."

I followed her swaying tail up the stairs and into the red-room. I locked the heavy oaken door behind us, asking, "What time is it, Lysa?"

"Ten minutes to."

"Time enough?"

"More than time enough."

"Take it off."

The velvet sheath fell like heavy fog around her ankles. She stood with her eyes closed, a smudge of mascara on the lower left lid, her lips slightly parted, her body trembling and swaying in the rhythmic flash of neon through the dust mosaic on the yellow-glass window. I pulled the musty leather-bound volume from the wall-safe and opened it to page eight. The serpent's hypodermic fangs sunk into my wrist as I raised a withered arm to the crystal chandelier.

Across town, Brandy June was peeling an apple with an ivory-handled paring knife. A mechanical bird sang in its gold cage. The wind was rising, screaming like lost souls in and out of the old house's corridors and alcoves, banging shutters and hurling swamp-water rain against the naked windows. The grandfather clock in the parlor struck midnight and imploded with a death rattle. Brandy June ate the apple and counted stars from the balcony. "One . . ." she counted, and went inside, away from the tempest, to read the novel that Kevin had brought her from Spain.

"What time is it?" I asked, closing the book.

Lysa rose from the floor and covered herself with a robe. "Five minutes past," she smiled. "Listen . . . you can hear the storm."

I walked down the carpeted stairs with Lysa's high-pitched laughter echoing through the empty halls of my skull. An unspoken question to Brian as I paused at the door.

"It goes on," he said, and broke for another game. Information Al watched the colored balls fly and pretended not to.

I stepped over the Triggerman's body and rolled up the sidewalk to the Fillmore. The City. "This is the City. I wasn't in the City."

"You maybe *wasn't,*" from a Shadow-Gypsy who isn't, "but you surely are now, man. That's the fast paced modern world for you, dad. Everything's instant zoom."

"What's happening?"

A finger-point to a building near the Edge. "Big dance, man. Three bands. The Airplane, The Dead, and Quicksilver."

"How'd I get here?"

"Wow, man, you're *really* spaced."

"I am. I know I am. I'm really spaced. What's happening?"

"A dance, man! You know . . . music, lights . . ."

"No, I mean what *happened?* How'd I get to the City?"

"We came up with them two chicks in their daddy's supercar, remember? The mescaline and zoom-oh down the freeway?"

"Yes." I don't remember, but it's an easier out to say yes. Thunderous sound from the building. Too much sound. "I don't wanna go in there."

"Okay, man. That's cool. I'm gonna make it inside. Stay groovie, man."

"Wait! Maybe I'll go in."

"Whatever's right, man."

"I don't know. See? That's the *thing.* What *is* right?"

"Whatever's happening, man. It's up to you. I mean . . . I'm not tryin to push nothin."

"I know, I know. That's not what I meant. I meant . . . uh, you know, I meant . . .

"Well, look, I'll be inside, so . . . so, just do whatever moves you, man. Groovie?"

"What do you mean?" But he's already gone. I'm alone on the

street. Alone with moving strangers who eye me knowingly as they dodge past on acceptable programmed missions. I'm sick to my stomach—afraid to barf. The sound-building is tempting, too tempting. I feel sure it's only a device designed to distract me—a trap of some kind. I want to move. I want to move badly, but where? I probably shouldn't move. In situations such as this, it's best to "Do Nothing." That is the teaching. That is the rule. That is bullshit when you get right down to it. People are staring. Because I alone have no mission? Likely. And then, I could be freaking more obviously than I realize. A poor thought. A nasty thought. Hide it fast.

And then a Ted puppet dropped in front of me with clay feet clatter-striking the stage. It read the lines, "Wow farout Abel I didn't know you were doing this thing."

"Yes," in visible widening sonic circles like the television bad breath commercial.

"Too much!" All big smile and glass eyes and watercolor face. "You stoned?"

"I'm . . . hey, am I reading the script wrong?"

"Huh?" clockwork brain calculating with boings and clicks. "No no I just dropped some acid myself so let's get inside," picking up cues from the blackboard out of camera range, "I wanna be in there when it comes on."

Pulled along by the Ted puppet's magnets to face a grim uniform that can be bought-off for only two phony dollars and won't even accept the rest of the paper in my wallet.

"Man, you're not maintaining so good," from the Ted.

"Listen. I wanna know . . ."

"What?"

"Is . . ." Machinery slowing down, grinding metal against metal to a frozen white-hot dead halt.

"What is it, man?"

"Should I go in there?" The universe machine picks up speed. It knows I'm back in line again.

"Sure. Why not?" Everything flickers into an acceptable silent movie continuum—only with sound—probably faked by a pipe organ. "Why not, Abel? You paid, didn't you?"

Oh yes indeed. So I creep into the building afraid to ask the question I'd intended to ask.

Sound, light, and minds plastered on the walls and the high, high ceiling. Something happening, but too fast to see. Only a color smear—a light smear—a mind smear. Blinding spotlight trained on me. Nowhere to hide. My clothes are dirty, my hair is greasy and sick-limp, my eyes are black-rimmed and bleeding down my cheeks, my fly is open, I've wet my pants, I smell bad, my breath is foul, my nose is running, and a spotlight illuminates the disgusting spectacle for all to see. *Witness the Geek, ladies and gentlemen. Careful! Don't let the kiddies get too close.* I prepare to go into convulsions for the crowd. A grand mal seizure. Give em their money's worth.

The life-beat of the sound-building is intricate on the surface, but deep inside it's a familiar thud . . . thud . . . thud. A heart beat. A big heart beat reminding me of a little one. Having forgotten to look in on it for some very long time, my heart is giving out. That's at the very core of what's happening. My heart is squeezing itself to a stop. I'm dying . . . and it's cool, it's right, it always gets back to that, so it must be the answer. Let it go.

I crawl off into a comer so as not to embarrass anyone, and start to die. Up through the fantastic galaxies, bodiless, drifting, moving toward The Light. Cool. Quiet. Peace. A glimpse of the Truth. Hide it! Jump up and cram it all back in the body wrapper and grab hold and all the way across the floor shoving through whirling bodies without feeling a step or ordering one. "AAAAAAGGGHHHH!" Just *dance,* man! Do it do it do it. Everyone's dancing, so do it do it do it. Wham! Now get up off the floor and do it do it do it. Dance—move—run—pump blood—work muscles—prove to yourself that you're alive—move!

"Come on, man. We better get you home."

Don't resist. Go with the flow. Follow the Ted. "You gotta *move*!"

"That's what we're doing, Abel. Hang on."

"No! You gotta let go an *move*!"

Out the door—mean look from a uniform—worried look from the Ted—into a chipped blue egg—through circus scenes and dancing lights, "See? You gotta *move*!" and droning moans, "Hey lemme outta this thing man."—"Cumon, be smart, Abel! Wait'll we get off the freeway," and flop on a bed.

"Do you want someone to stay with you?"

"No. I'm dead, man."

"No you're not. Can you sleep?"

"Oh sure."

"I'll come by tomorrow."

"Ted, Buddha was right about love being just another hang-up."

"Do you feel like talking?"

"No."

"I'll come by in the morning."

"Hear this. I have to say it fast. Disregard everything I've ever said and ever will say, and accept this as the truth. There is only one path to follow. Only one. Following any other is settling for much less. It's a cop-out and we all know it. And I've seen the One Path and I will be forever unhappy until I follow it to the end. And at this, the first and only true cross-road of any actual consequence, I'm afraid, man. I'm really afraid, cuz, man, it's the most frightening path of all, being the only one, the one we all gotta eventually follow, the one that means giving up everything in order to *get* everything. Do you understand?"

"Sure, man. It's beautiful. It's all cool."

"You don't understand. But you will. Honestly, my friend, you *will* understand. We all will."

"Right, man. You want me to stick around for a while?"

"No."

"In the morning then. Peace, Abel."

"Yeah. You know, I couldn't really hold it. I just got a glimpse of it. That's always the way it is—just a glimpse before you freak. But there really is only one path. And I'll never be able to forget that, man. I never will. There's just one road to take."

"It's the one we're all on, Abel."

"No it isn't. We're all just at the cross-roads."

"Equally cool."

"This is degenerating into standard bullshit."

—a very long pause . . . . it should be uncomfortable—

"Well, Abel . . . I'm gonna make it on home. Uh . . . you wanna come or stay here?"

"Here."

"Okay. See you in the morning."

"Mh."

"Unless you wanna talk some more."

"Nh."

"Okay?"

"Mh."

Day came and went like blasts of gunpowder. Nights settled like heavy smoke and I watched them turn to dawn. Sleep—magic, illusory sleep—I'd again forgotten how to do it. Sleep is just a state of mind-trick. How does one "sleep?" Somnus, you rotten bastard, why are you pissed off at me? I've prayed to you for so long now, and *still* you ignore me.

A form in the kitchen doorway. Plastic masked, but something alive behind it. "Who?"

"Don't you recognize me, Abel?"

"Adriel."

"Only the mask. Look through the eye-holes."

"Julia?"

Oriental wind-chime laughter. "Ah . . ."

"How has this come about?"

In slow-motion Tibetan dance steps, telling the story with finger-symbols and eye movement. "You've fallen through the trapdoor of madness. Now there is nothing that you can't do, and nothing really that you *can* do. Best accept it. Float free. Follow the figure-eight eternity. Follow the stream."

"Where does it lead?"

"To oblivion."

"But it doesn't!"

Tiger laughter. "Ah . . . Abel is so hungup on the Abel-game. So sad. So sad. Poor little Abel."

"Who are you? Can I know you? Should I wonder?"

Seven quick steps forward. "Do you want to make love to me?"

"Yes," and it's almost reflex.

Summer rain-fall laughter.

"Is it wrong?"

"Not if you want to, Abel. Come and make love to me."

Drift over slow and couple. The first stroke is ecstasy—ecstasy that terminates in a precise metallic clink. A noose of cold steel thread holding me inside the warm phantom. "I don't understand."

Shattered winter ice laughter. "Don't you, Abel? Between my legs, inside my love, is a transistor-powered guillotine. The choice is now yours."

"Who *are* you?"

"I am Cybele."

"Is it truly the only way?"

"How can I tell you?"

"You can't. I'm not ready. Go away, Cybele. Leave me. I'm not ready, and I'm not sure."

The pressure was increasing. I'd let it go too long. Now I knew that the release would rip many circuits loose if it didn't completely short the entire system.

The phantoms and less-than-phantom people came and went, talking to me in various voices. I answered them without hesitation, using the pre-recorded stock phrases that I kept in readiness on the top of my brain. They never suspected.

No exits. No rest periods. Never. Forever. Kill yourself, and you'll come back as nothing more, and probably less than a dead body. Even now you may be working out suicide karma. Plod through twilight.

I sat on the toilet, watching my distorted reflection in the doorknob while the bathroom window went from morning white to afternoon yellow to evening blue to midnight black. This can't go on. This is where I could be hung forever. This is where I *have* been hung forever; almost somewhere, but never quite. Break out. How can I break out?

You got to vomit it all up-

-You got to hit bottom, let yourself slide all the way down, before you can reach for the top-

-There is no bottom, and no top. This is it-

-Drop out. Drop out of everything, baby. It's all a game. Quit playing it. Quit playing it and you win because you no longer have to think about winning . . . or losing-

-What's the difference between being totally enlightened and being totally insane? The only difference is who has possession of the body you leave behind-

-All you need is love-

-There is only the Now-

-Give me a fulcrum and a place to stand and I will construct a lever to move the universe-

-Just give me a place to stand-

-You got into this with acid. You can get out of this with acid. Take more acid. Take more acid-

CHAPTER THIRTY – THE INSIDIOUSLY CLEVER PLAN

"You got to step-step out of your head," was the appropriate song that the radio was singing as Brian Kelly and I drove in his old Packard up to Carl's cabin which was now being rented by another friend of ours, Peter Cromley. The sun was getting ready to hide when we slammed car doors and greeted Peter in the yard. I had a plan. I had devised an insidiously clever plan for my final cop-out drop-out. I was going to burn my way through—sneak around to the Clear Light by way of the Black Light.

"Is it okay if Brian and I eat some acid here tonight?" I asked Peter, feigning sanity all the while so he wouldn't get wise and refuse. I needed people around to take care of the body in case I left one behind when I cut out. Take care of all possible hangs. Leave nothing to pull you back.

"Sure," he said. "The place is yours," and we smiled nice and Brian and I put the little blue tabs of wonder drug in our mouths and swallowed.

Watch thirty minutes fall into the void . . . gone. A gradual climb, then a sharp three-thousand gee whiplash that hits the very middle of the mind, and *you gotta step-step outta your head.* And I can hear this as all very true, but how does one go about it? Remember the plan. Hold on to the plan and don't chicken out. It's gonna be tough, but no compromises, no backing down, no settling for less. Falter, and you slip right back to politics, plastic, washer-dryers, spray-on deodorant, neon lies, hair dyes, smoggy skies, bow ties, hard guys, apple pies, machine guns, favorite sons, loan sharks, sneaky narks, profit wars, closed doors, sad whores, sex laws, pimps, bigots, riots . . .

Turn it off, man. You're what's making it all happen. *You gotta step-step outta your head.* There's only the void. The rest is just a cover-up. It isn't real. Don't try to figure any of it out.

Row, row, row your boat
Gently down the stream.
Merrily, merrily, merrily, merrily.
Life is but a dream.

But my *plan*—my plan is to wade through all the oceans of bullshit, follow the game out to the last possible decimal point, see it and smell it and feel it and taste it and live it all before chucking it all. I want to *know* what I'm giving up.

"You don't expect to fool anyone with that sad excuse, do you? Ego won't die, eh? Well, give er a lil jolt a *this,* baby."

-minutes-days-hours-seconds-years-centuries—one life time gone—one spent trying to find the answer to the life time before it—one as a rich fat man interested only in food and power—one as a poor idiot interested in the same—life time—death time—die-rot-flash-live-suffer-strive-die-rot-flash-live-

A low comedy skit with actors in baggy pants and clown hats. "Hmmm, what have we here? A bad case of life? Sorry, boy. No known cure. Ne-ext patient!" Comic boot in the comic seat of the baggy comic pants. Pow! Deeper into Hell. More horrible because it's still a long way from Tartarus, and Phlegethon is yet to be crossed, and crossed it surely must be. Unless . . . a diversion.

Stars, stars, fat suns all. The end a million novas, then the peaceful void. Let go.

"Aha! Almost had it there, son, but you flinched just before we could grab your arm an pull you on over. Better luck next time . . ."

-live-die-rot-flash-live-"What say we try a little of this new LSD stuff?"

"Now that just might be a kick in the old ass." And, man, you *know* the acid-game is total bullshit, but it got you *here.*

Turn up the juice. This one don't know when he's bein burned. LaMer's power-mad titan generator whining and sparking as it sucks in cosmic power for the ultimate all-time unimaginable capital-lettered KA-ZAPPPP!

And yes indeed, this is very bad. If I stop spinning long enough to spot *down* or anything close enough for jazz I will instantly bail out of the whole scene and get a job as an accountant. "I wish it were that easy."

"Baxtor! How'd you get here?"

"Same way you did, Abel."

"Well, how do you get *out?*"

"I've often wondered that myself, Abel. I've often wondered." -NZZAT—flash-live-die—up again—live—do something—do something—no time—there's no time-

"Ah! Back again for another go at it? You ain't never gettin offa this here ride, friend. This here's the one that lasts forever."

"Forever?"

"Oh yes. An you *know* just how long forever can be. An to make it a tad bit more innerestin, we decided to drop you into Hell for the duration a that there forever-forever-forever-for . . ."

"Brian, man, I'm scared. This is too big!"

Brian-voice humming, "Can't talk . . . too stoned . . . let it go, man . . . just let it go."

"I can't! You don't know where I'm *at*! If I let go here, I'll *stay* here. And here is *nowhere*! I'm totally confused. I been here too long!"

"Let it go . . . it'll pass," says Brian, and I suddenly realize that he's the one behind it all. It's the traitorous dog Brian who's responsible for the confusion.

-ZZZZZT . . . ah, back again for another go at it? You ain't never gettin offa this here ride, friend. This here's the one that lasts forever.

You gotta step-step outta your head. You gotta step-step outta your head.

Brian preening before a mirror—lipstick and green eye-shadow—he's got me where he wants me now. "Well, Abel . . . it's just you and me." Seductive wink—steps out of his Levi's and stands before me in black lace underwear. "It's just you and me, Abel."

"Anything, man. Just get me outta this."

Dissolve into fungus forest where wrathful deities sing, "It's not that easy, baby. There ain't no simple out," pounding skull-drums and plucking rib-cage harps while carrion crows and vultures gyrate to the high sounds.

"I've changed my mind! I wanna get back! I gotta *tell* people what I've learned. I gotta *tell* people!"

Blob of glup with Louie Armstrong's voice says, "Aw cumon, man. Don'you think we've *heard* that one before? You know it's bullshit. You ain't learned nothin. Nothin you can say that hasn't been said so many tired times, man. Sayin it agin ain't gon'prove nothin."

Minor devil with a mustache and 666 tattooed on his lower lip chimes in, "If you need that kind of low-level validation, read the Bible, read Revelations, read about the fall of Babylon. It's all down in black and white. No one will listen. Even after the trumpets have sounded, no one will believe."

Emaciated old long-dead leper drags himself to my feet, leaving a glistening trail of cast-off skin behind him. He clutches my ankles and gasps, "There's no copping out now. Break through or be damned trying."

It's time, past time to put on the brakes. Apply the skids—grab hold of the first scene that flits by, and I find Brian lying face down and dead in the fireplace with scorched hair and burnt flesh smell all through the bent cabin. And it's real. This is the one that's real. A frozen instant—forever—caught between tick and tock—forever. Unless you *break out.* Only there's no way, because this is the bad I always dreaded. This is the end-all-bad. This is the Hell of hells.

"This is worse, bright boy. This is insanity. This isn't playing around the outskirts of Crazy City, this is IT. This is what they warned you about. This is stark raving, frothing, screaming, crawling, twitching, freezing, burning insanity. *Now* do you know what it's all about? Now do you know why insane people are insane?"

As anyone will tell you, you gotta be cool. Don't let it take over. Don't let it get hold. Let go and float. It's all part of the dream. Let it slide. The whole life-illusion, just a dream. Now you can wake up. Wake up and it's all over and everything's cool. All just one of many dreams. All part of the same dream. Now you can wake up. Wake up.

Unfortunately, I also realize that I was part of that dream. If I wake up—if I admit that it was only an illusion, only a dream, then . . . no more me . . . and me's all I've got.

Do it. It's an end to the suffering. It's the end of all confusion. It's the realization of All Truth. Turn it off. Turn off your mind. Turn off the you.

in time to the waves of energy turn off the you
in tune with the flash of infinity turn off the you
forget the dream of humanity off off off
forget all your fears of insanity off off off off off no no
off off off no no no no no uuuuuuuummmm mmmmmmm . . .
bless all life bless the cool night air that i can feel touching body
bless the crickets and their magic conversation of tone-talk holy
the godlight of the skyeye moon bless all life tiny i thank all powers and the power for this new start for this
second miraculous chance

"Ah, back to the old game of existence, eh? You almost made it, kid. You almost made it, but you wouldn't completely let go."

"I did!"

"Nope! You kept one rubber-band finger anchored in the land of the you-game. When it got too tight, you snapped right back. Now . . . one more time. Turn it all off. Let go."

"It was too hard! I'd never make it through that again."

"Right! Now you're starting to *see*! You may understand yet!"

"Ridiculous! It's all some sort of mind-trap. I'm not gonna sit here caught in some bullshit mind-trap while everyone else is having a good time. I'm bailing out. I'm getting down." Try pleasant thoughts—

—watch the perfect flowers cut a rainbow path across the bleeding sunrise that the mist has opened up to form a view—hear the silent music that the organ of the universe is howling right in tune to all but you—

You can't fake it. Cut the crap. You'll be babbling it when they come to take you away. There *is* no out. This is it. You stay here until there's no more you. And you—any you—die hard.

eight faster than light scene shifts, all of which must be lived and dealt with before getting back to take number

> three-fifty-three which has to do with a friend burned up in a smoldering fireplace in a deserted cabin where you've taken acid and lost hold and are now incapable of summoning help

And I run into the woods screaming, with the smell of burned-up Brian in my nostrils, to be stopped by a moan from the pit of my being because I know that I can't run away from it. Back to the cabin where Brian is sitting up watching me with mad owl eyes and I understand that it's all a joke or a trick to drive me into truth or perhaps I've blundered into the wrong reality and this one has a live Brian but a dead Abel unless there's some way I can straighten it all out, like by shooting Brian between the eyes. As the thought flares in my mind, so does eternal damnation and a great truth and I fall down dead and tearfully grateful, only to rise again and see both Brian and Peter laughing at me because once again my miserable self has failed to understand. And it's been so long . . . so long and hard, and I'm still so unworthy, so hopeless and repentant that I rip out my useless brain and toss it into the fire where it bums and squirms and writhes in the flames, adding its stench to all the other stenches, and my body is completely on its own with no pilot behind the wheel, no captain at the controls, running into the woods, ripping the dirty rags from its hot flesh, falling in a puddle of mud where I find it again after a long search and activate the circuits.

Somewhere, Peter is calling, "Abel! Come on, Abel. Take it easy, man! Come back inside."

"Better call somebody," says a voice, probably Brian's.

"Who?" from someone else.

"Ah . . . wow, I can't think. This is really heavy acid, Peter. Better call somebody."

I've had it. They're gonna put me away. There's no going back to the reality I left now. It's final break-through or nothing, -kill the body-link and you can find peace—it's only the useless flesh robot that's holding you back—when you left it, it was running down to the highway to get caught or run over in order to pull you back to sad scene and sirens—kill the robot—neutralize the flesh box—Run the robot, naked and moaning, into trees head first. Is it dead now? No. Still works. Bang it into another tree. Thunk—thud—bash. Ah, a broken neck. The earth is still, peaceful, beautiful. Don't move. It goes on all around you—no longer matters—you're not part of it anymore.

But what's happening back in that last port? Are those voices? I can't resist a peek.

"He went mad, Doctor. He just went mad."

End of one life. Beginning of another. End of that one. Beginning of another. All hung at the same crossroad.

And this is forever . . . until Zad arrives in his rattly bus and hurries into the cabin to find me naked and quiet, sitting in front of the cold fireplace, sleepy Peter keeping a concerned eye on me, while I wonder where and when they will get around to running the sign that says THE END. How much longer can the movie last? I know some of these art films are *long,* but this is ridiculous. Run FINI on the back of my head. No, paint it across my ass. That'd be arty. Or, better still, run it in art nouveau lettering across the pupils of my dead eyes. "You wanna get dressed, Abel?" suggests Zad.

Zad is in the movie. That's fine. That's really beautiful. Perhaps he's the director, in which case I should follow his suggestion but, "I don't know how, Zad."

"That's all right," says Zad, retrieving my shorts from the front yard, "I'll show you. Okay, put one foot through here. That's right. Great. Now put the other foot in this hole. Beautiful. You got the idea. Can you do the rest?"

I better tell him. "Zad, I'm not comin down from this one."

Zad's all joy, standing in the doorway with golden sun streaming past him. "Those are the best kind, man. We'll go for a walk in the woods. It's raining sunshine out there."

Out into the air and the sun and the world. Walk on tiny twigs that crackle underfoot. Walk easy. Don't disturb them. Zad is a god who has come to help me. Birds sing praise to the day as we wind through the forest under a canopy of green and gold branches. Zad is saying, "It must have been a very big trip," and I understand the word-symbols. It's beautiful.

"It was Zad. God . . . what . . . what . . . ?"

"Don't even try, man. Everything's cool. You're on the way down. Look at that sun over the mountain. Wow! Is that *great?* That's too *much*!"

"Yes. The sun."

Zad and I smoked a single quiet joint on the early morning hill-top overlooking the green valley and rising mist. Zad chanted his Tibetan prayers and I humbly thanked God for creating such beauty. No one deserves such beauty. No one deserves the privilege of being on the earth.

CHAPTER THIRTY ONE – REASONABLE GAMES

After my experience at Peter's Cabin, two weeks of slightly tense disorientation elapsed before I slid into the period of peace. My acid appetite was more than satisfied. I even began to doubt that I would ever take it—ever be able to take it again. The painful craving for ultimate Truth shook hands with humble ego and the two of them settled back in comfortable chairs to dig the denouement. I saw all men as soon-to-be-Buddhas, and I sincerely loved them for their brave existence on the face of the earth. The earth itself was reborn for me. I watched it dance and danced with it to the songs of birds and the purr of insects. I understood, as we all once understood, that the earth and the beautiful little lives upon it (which are actually all one and unified and harmonious in love and . . . ah, preacher talk. But how can I . . . ? Fellow freaks, you know what I mean), the beautiful forms of life upon the earth combine and swirl and couple and embrace in the most incredibly intricate, divinely magnificent spectacle conceivable. The air makes the purest of soul-reaching, high-classic, rock-concert music. It's the sound of the miraculous space between eternity—between paradise. You only have to *listen* to hear it. And beyond the music of the earth is the music of deep within *you*. It's the magic you once *knew* existed. It *does* exist. How can I tell you? I can only tell you that I can't *tell* you. No one can. But even so, we have to *keep trying*.

Love—a word so old and tired that everyone I knew (with the exception of brand-new flower children) was sick of hearing it and saying it and trying to practice it with such sad results. I was, too. But after the cabin trip, after the events which led up to the cabin trip were behind me but not far enough behind to fade into gray, I rediscovered love and found that it's the *word* that gets old and tired and twisted from misuse. I tried to tell everyone with contented silence. I floated in sun-driven white mist, high—high—singing with the wind, meditating with the ancient quiet mountains. In silence I would tell them. Their quick minds would understand. My friends would understand that there was no longer any need for words. Everything is perfect—OM—endlessly—OM—infinity is ours—peace, my friends. I love you. I am you. We are simply IT. There's nothing else to know. There's no longer reason for fear, fighting, striving for power and material gain, hating, becoming, doing, trying . . . it just is . . . it is. Do you understand?

"Yes," said all hip friends (also silently). "Of course," and they went on playing the heavy games of separate life and power and fuck thy neighbor.

"Why?" I asked myself. "They're all beautiful, brilliant, perfect people—Buddhas all. Why do they continue to play seemingly goalless games? to be separate? Why?"

When the question condensed in my soul, the sun began to set. A harmless question. I didn't call for it. It simply came. But restlessness reclaimed me and I became much more human.

"Why do you play small power-games?" I asked aloud.

"To survive," replied Beau, and it seemed a reasonable answer. I searched for a flaw and found none. Comparing my own intellect to that of others, I realized that I alone knew very little. People continued to play games, therefore, they had absolutely valid reasons for doing so. I certainly had no business standing in the perfect path of the flow.

I watched the world in silence in order to re-learn the proper, reasonable games that must be played. On television, over the radio, in newspapers, in magazines, in classrooms, great leaders and teachers told me that war is a necessary tool, that killing in certain instances and with the support of the state is justified, that a lust for power over other men is called *ambition* and is a desirable emotional state, that cheating is a fact of life. "Well, you gotta shave a little off a lid to make a good profit," confirmed Beau's partner. "Fight force with force," said the governor. And many ex-pacifists listened to him. "When the cops push, I'm pushin right back," said Eugene who, a year before, had gone soft and quiet to jail for refusing to disperse, and was described in the paper the next day as a "peace-nik demonstrator." I watched newsreels of wars and riots, saw friends and unknown good people beaten and taken to cold jails, saw guns being bought and ammunition being stored and whole families running scared for elsewhere islands and countries, and in only three weeks I remembered where I was, and who and what was in control of the set, and I lost the period of peace and found myself at the beginning—all truth forgotten or only vaguely remembered, wide open for criticism and scorn. Pressure building, preparing for the yet to come even more tremendous screaming breaking point climax explosion.

With another winter coming on, the sky blue but pale and earlier dark, papers scuttling in the company of dead leaves in the turning-cold wind, I walk down First Street, San Jose, hands crammed in pockets, hair tucked into my collar so's not to be mistaken for a hippie. There are five psychedelic shops in town now, psychedelic music on the radio, psychedelic movies at the theaters and psychedelic children bumming dimes on the street. Preston's out of the hospital now, well-fed and strangely shy, not really Preston at all. Baxter's moved in with another chick, drinks beer and talks about returning to college. Zad and his wife and daughter gone to India, Bob Levin still in hiding somewhere, Al Vaughn in jail, Brian Kelly a devout macrobiotic living in a small shack in the Santa Cruz mountains, Sarah married to a football player, Peggy gone to Hawaii, Adriel in Georgia and some say engaged to a doctor, Carl and his wife in Canada, Larry in the graveyard, Roy Cage in the infamous Big House, David doing one-nighters at local coffee houses, and LaMer still missing in action—many crazy stories and insane rumors, but no LaMer.

At the corner of First and San Carlos, a teenage cat with an early-Beatles hair-cut and a pretty little blue-eyed blonde chick carrying a singing transistor radio walk up to me, digging my beard and long hair, calling me brother, offering me cigarettes, asking, "Hey man, can you get us some acid?" The chick smiles behind her handsome young clean hippie lover, with the radio saying, "Show me the waaaaay . . . show me the waaaaay . . . the way to go home," a great song by Big Brother and The Holding Company which fits this particular scene like a well-edited sound-track, and I know that somewhere The Man is on the job. Clear-eyed energetic hopeful cat and his cute little clean blonde chick, only a week to go before they've gotta return to a high school thing, smiling with still new happy faces, asking for the strange sacrament they've been hearing about, all set to take a trip. "Show me the waaay . . . the way to go home," pleads the radio.

I shake my head, saying, "Sorry, man. I don't deal," and feel compelled to add, "There's acid around town, though." I turn to the chick, seeing beautiful pure wide blue eyes. "Show *me* the way," which is supposed to be a very hip comment, but of course it falls noticeably short and startles her, so she does a nervous uncertain giggle as her boyfriend takes her arm and mumbles, "Thanks, man" before they hurry off down the street, the radio calling back, "Blind man stood on the way and cried . . . oooohhhhh show me the way."

I watch them go, happy and fast, disappearing around the comer, and I wonder, should I have told them . . . what? What could I tell them? Why would they listen and why *should* they listen? Everybody's telling them something and nobody's telling them *anything.* Why should they listen?

A worldly old big-city bum who's migrated for some reason to San Jose, shuffles by panhandling and doesn't hit me for a dime, so I'm forced to give him one, but make him work for it by asking him, "What can we do?"

He looks at me with yellow eyeballs, trying to decide if I'm a faggot or just a nut, then pockets the coin and says, "Ged a boddlawine," and shuffles off after the two teenagers, turning the same comer, only a little slower because he has so much more time.

All these words. All these words and there are still nine handwritten pages in front of me, both sides covered with blue-ink words. A summation, I told myself when I wrote them. But with *all these words* . . . none of this really makes any difference in a genuine show-down with the void. None of this and nothing else, with the exception of The Question, makes any difference. It's already over . . . the instant it began. On the floor, there's an unbelievable pile of paper. It represents recalled and warmed-over memories of life-time that validate existences and would otherwise, like telephone poles past a speeding car window, be unreached phantoms in the unreal because unlived distance, then, for a micro-instant, a reality . . . now . . . right there in front of you, but no time to examine it or think about it because you're *right there,* in it, part of it. Then it's gone, it's past, receding in the distance, only a memory, intangible, and the only thinking you'll ever do about it is in retrospect based on the assumption of the reality of the vision.

There is only totally go . . . forever . . . or totally stop.

My fingers are tired, my eyes are tired, my mind is tired and I'm tired.

show me the way
search for the way
out
into . . . . . .

and something was dying
and something was changing
and something else was on the way

—September 7, 1967

CHAPTER THIRTY TWO – continued

Sunlight was leaking in over the window-sill when Curt finished the last page of Abel's manuscript and tossed it on the floor with the others. With no more words to play with—guide-lines suddenly gone—he drifted rapidly back into place, rubbed his eyes with cold knuckles and looked around. The walls still held tiny spider tracks of blue electricity, but the acid had peaked and faded with the moon. Curt was coming down. His eyes were tired and his head ached from following black type across white paper all night. He rolled off the bed and went to the window where he lit a cigarette standing in the pale shaft of morning sun, shivered and blew gray smoke at the ceiling. It was bad acid. It had been weak acid. But he felt strange-funny. More than just coming-off-acid-strange-funny. Every muscle in his body wanted to do something. Every brain cell, fat with Abel-thoughts, whined irately for action. There was nothing to do. Curt's last four acid trips had deposited him in the same place—exactly the same place. "Acid isn't pure anymore," he thought. "They cut it with a lotta crap now-days." There was nothing to do.

Eddie made mouse-noises in the tower. Curt ignored them. "A whole night and a whole cap of acid wasted on words," he sighed. "Worse than words. *Written* words. Typewritten words pounded out on a dumpy machine by a cat with no more answers than I've got."

Outside, a VW bus pulled into the garage and doors banged as Christy and Ted, back from the beach, walked toward the house. "Fuck," said Curt, and flipped his cigarette at the new sun.

Curt was standing at the top of the stairs when Christy stepped in the front door followed by Ted and, "Hi, Curt. How was the acid?"

"All right," said Curt, unwilling to admit that the acid had been wasted.

"We did transcendental meditation for three hours on the beach. I really feel high! It's so *groovie*! It's really where it's at. I just get higher all the time. Hey! Where's Carla?" demanded Christy from the bedroom.

Curt thought back through the hours. "She went over to Abel's."

Ted fell into a chair and lit a joint. "How's Eddie?" he asked after exhaling.

Curt shrugged and replied, "Far out."

Nodding absently, Ted opened a newspaper and handed the joint to Curt, who took it then handed it back without smoking any. On page six of the morning news there was an article on the most recent anti-war demonstrations. "Those fuckin cops," grumbled Ted, "lookit this, man."

Curt leaned over to glance at the picture of a girl getting the shit kicked out of her by two fat cops. "Yeah," he said, then walked into the kitchen.

"Want some orange juice?" asked Christy through a mouthful of whole-wheat bread.

"No. I just want some water."

Christy handed him a glass. "When did Carla say she'd be back?"

"I don't think she said," filling the glass, draining it, refilling it, "Hey, there's white stuff in this water."

"Air bubbles," said Christy.

Curt said, "Sure."

"It is."

"It's chemicals," said Curt, finishing his second glassful, "supplied by State-Control-computers."

The front door opened for Carla and Abel. "Hi, hi, hi," sang Carla, "Guess who we saw downtown last night. Andre! And his hair's all cut off and he was wearing a sportcoat and he's got a job in a cement factory or something!"

"A construction firm," corrected Abel.

Ted let the newspaper fall from his hands. "Andre? Great holy Zot! What's the world coming to? He copped out?"

Abel put his index finger on the spot where his third eye should have been and wasn't. "Many heavy troubles, man. But it's only camouflage. He's still in there. He's just workin plainclothes now."

"Dark times," Ted retrieving his newspaper. "Gandalf has yet to reappear."

Abel snapped his fingers. "Speaking of which: Beau wanted me to ask you if Sarakus'll sell his Thompson. Beau'll trade him his sawed-off and whatever bread's necessary to make up the difference."

"I'll ask him," promised Ted, his nose again hidden in the news, "but I think he wants to hang on to it. Manning offered him two-hundred bucks for it."

Abel spotted Curt in the kitchen. "How was the trip?"

"Would've been fine if I hadn't got hungup reading that bullshit you left for me."

"You read it?"

"I read it."

"And?"

"It didn't do much for me."

Abel nodded. "Well, it was over your head."

"Sure."

"Under your head?"

"Much closer."

"Not enough sex and no concrete conclusions."

"To mention only two of its minor faults."

"It would've been better if the characters had all co-operated."

Ted peered over the newspaper and asked, "What'd you give him?"

"A headache," said Curt.

"A book I wrote," said Abel.

"Oh yeah? About what?"

"Mmmmm . . . you and him and us and them and it and what's happening . . . well, has happened, you know."

Down the hall, Christy yelled, "Somebody comeer an help! The toilet's plugged-up again!" Flushing sounds, chrome handle jiggling noises, muffled curses. Ted ran to the rescue. Abel claimed the deserted chair and the forsaken news. "Hey, Ted! You met that guy from Hawaii, didn't you?"

From the bathroom, "Yeah. He was over here a couple of days

ago trying to trade weed for some acid. (Christy, don't keep flushing. It's only fuckin it up more.) Why?"

"I was wondering what his thing was. I couldn't hear it."

From the bathroom, "What?!"

"What's his thing?!"

Jiggle-jiggle-flush. "(Sonovabitch!) It's something about the Virgin Mary, man. He's got this theory about Her being where it's at, and all the rest being an after-the-fact cover story. (See if there's some Drain-o under the sink.)"

An angry Christy voice said, "That won't work on a toilet!"

An equally angry Ted voice countered, "If you chicks'd quit throwing your rags in the john this wouldn't happen!"

Extracting the tri-color Sunday supplement from the fat stack of newsprint, Abel cringed at the insipid blank-grin family on the cover, opened it up and wasn't in the least surprised to be confronted by an article headlined:

MY SON IS HOOKED ON LSD!
A MOTHER'S TERRIFYING TRUE STORY

Abel reflected that he hadn't seen a magazine or newspaper in weeks that didn't carry at least one sensational acid horror story guaranteed to send six-thousand more young hoppers out in search of a cap after imprinting a simple, easy-to-follow map of a bum trip on their nutty-putty brains.

Abel turned the pages rapidly, picking up only the heaviest print, reading, "Violence on Our College Campuses," "Draft-dodgers in Canada," "The Meditation Turn-on" and "The Kids Today Have No Sense of Humor. An article by one of America's leading funnymen."

Ted was humming to a Johnny Cash album when Christy's sixteen-year-old brother and two of his friends bopped into the house looking for dope. Beads and buttons on their psychedelic shirts, hair as long as their teachers or parents would permit them to wear it—shy, but maintaining a hard cool in the face of so many elderly heads.

"None for sale," said Curt.

"Wow. We're really stoned," said one of the boys.

Curt ignored him and walked into the kitchen.

"I mean, wow, we're really *zonked,*" repeated the boy to Abel. "We got some really stony weed from The City, man."

"It's Acapulco Gold," said Christy's brother.

Abel tried to remember when all weed had become Acapulco Gold and all acid Owsley's private stock. It must have been while he was gone, he decided.

Christy sold them a gram of hash and they left to pick up chicks and drive to Santa Cruz.

Carla came downstairs with Abel's manuscript in her hand. "Don't let Curt spoil the ending for me."

"I didn't write one," said Abel.

Settling with a thud on the couch, she held the stack of papers aloft. "Your masterpiece was strewn all over Curt's floor." She scanned the first page and put it on her lap. "It's about your old motorcycle days, huh?"

Abel nodded, then went to the kitchen, made some hot chocolate and smoked a cigarette with Curt. "Whatta you wanna do today, man?"

Curt shrugged and made wet rings on the table with his empty glass. "I don' know. Get high I guess."

Abel tapped his fingernails on the table leg. "I wonder what Zad's doing in India right now?"

That night, Carla left Abel's manuscript in mindless Eddie's room where she'd been reading it on his bed while he watched his toes in the moonlight that poured through the tower window. Eddie ate all but one chapter, and that one he hid. Abel said it was all right, and mindless Eddie said, "OM."

Made in the USA
Columbia, SC
13 May 2019